Big Hand for the Band

Tales from Belfast's Rock 'n' Roll Years

Bill Morrison

First published in November 2015
Reprinted and published with CD in December 2016

Publisher: Motelands Publishing

ISBN 978-0-9934434-0-4

Printed and bound by
CPI Group (UK) Ltd, Croydon, CR0 4YY

Acknowledgements

Thank you to Colin McClelland for the inspiration to write this book and to Gill McNeil of McNeil Media Limited for guiding me through uncharted waters of self-publishing; to John Smyth, Sez Adamson, and Ricky McCutcheon, who played in The Group and with whom I spent many happy hours when I should have been studying for my exams. Thanks also to original Dominoes Roderick Downer, Mike Shanks and Dick Pentland; to Robin Irvine and Robin Lavery; to Linda Martin, Ann Ferguson and Keith Baker. Thanks are due also to all those who kept it lit, especially Clare Steele, Raymond Donnan, and John Wilson; and to Peter Lloyd, Blair Whyte and Gerry Giffen, each of whom made good things happen and without whom the story would have been different. Finally an extra special thank you is due to my son Michael for his inspiration; to my daughter, Sara, for her encouragement and support: to my daughter-in-law Liz for her thorough proof-read and know-how; and to my wife, Lyn, for her tolerance and patience.

In memory of Fred Isdell and Chris Doran

Contents

Foreword

Foreword

I know I am not alone in this. There must be hundreds of thousands of people of my generation who played guitar in a pop group.

But I was born in the middle of WW2, just as the tide was turning towards an Allied victory and things were looking up. I was there a year or two ahead of the baby boom that occurred after hostilities ceased. In the early 1950s I would lie awake long into the night, scratching crystal and battling with atmospheric interference in my search for 208 metres medium wave. I bought my first guitar at the same time as John Lennon. I bought my first record on a Monday morning in December 1956 after hearing Barry Alldis play it the night before on Radio Luxembourg's Top Twenty Show. It was not exactly a rock classic. It was called 'The Wayward Wind,' and the singer was Cogi Grant. Ever heard of her? I expect not.

'A band boy!' my future mother-in-law is said to have exclaimed after she had been introduced to me for the first time, clearly hoping her daughter would do better than that. As it happens, I did have a day job and academic qualifications that led to a good career, but you will not find much about that in this book. Maybe one day I will write a book about town planning – but this book is all about my first love: playing in a pop group; being up there on the stage – a world apart. I don't care that I never made the big time – or even the small time. It was not just about showing off, although I won't deny that was part of it. It was the sheer joy of rocking with your mates.

This book comprises a collection of anecdotes inspired by listening to a long-forgotten tape recording from 1968 of my band, The Group, playing live in Belfast on a Saturday afternoon in The Pound and later that evening in the Astor Ballroom Marquee Club.

1968 was a memorable year. It followed the Summer of Love when everything burst out in an explosion of colour. We had the technology to put a man on the moon. Telstar had enabled us to bond with like-minded people across the world. We took inspiration from lyrics, poetry, guitars and creative chord sequences. We were the baby-boomers and we had inherited the earth. We knew love would bring an end to all war.

And Belfast, too, was full of beautiful people at this time. Dedicated followers of the fashionable Kinks, loud but never square, would walk through the city centre with a swagger in their step. There was a time when we would strut about with a lapel pin in the shape of a tiny silver-coloured arrow. At any hint of curiosity, we would swing an arm across the chest in mock salute pointing to the little arrow, and with a wink and a nod, proudly declare: "wee arra people." We were the city swingers. We had fun and we laughed a lot. We had no inkling of what lay in store.

So is this a factual account or is it fiction?

"The important thing..." said my good friend and mentor Professor Jim Dornan, deliverer of many babies and author of a highly-rated book on that topic, "...the important thing is not to let the facts get in the way of a good story."

I have taken on board that sage advice – but let me assure readers that I have worked hard to tell it the way it was. A surprising number of precise dates were established by delving deep in the course of research. Of course there has to be some embellishment to add colour, but I have tried hard not to get carried away with my own imagination. Tempting though it is.

Despite that, there is still the possibility that I get things utterly wrong. Nobody's perfect. I remember once sitting in the back of a cab heading for the airport after my wife and I had visited The Alamo in San Antonio, Texas. I was chatting to the driver about Davy Crockett.

"He was Irish, you know," I said. "Matter of fact he came from the north of Ireland where we live. Near Omagh. He was born in Castlederg."

"That so?" said the cab driver – at which point my wife Lyn entered the discussion with one of those dry remarks for which she is celebrated. Timed to perfection as always:

"I think you'll find Davy Crockett was born on a mountaintop in Tennessee..."

Chapter 1

The Resurrection Shuffle

The idea of writing a book about The Group, The Pound and the Marquee has been around for a while. It was first mooted in 2001 when I learnt that the building we knew as the Astor Ballroom was due to be demolished. It had lain derelict from July 1972 when the IRA bombing campaign intensified, targeted at Belfast's fragile city centre. The introduction of a security cordon round the commercial core left the owners with little choice but to walk away. The premises were sealed up with everything deliberately left in place ready for re-opening when the time was right. No-one imagined for a minute that the Astor would remain closed for almost 30 years.

When the architect in charge of the demolition told me his client had bought the building complete with the ballroom fittings and fixtures in place exactly as they had been all those years ago, the urge to be there when the doors were to be opening one last time was compelling.

I knew I had to call out the instigator, because there was something in the air. I had to tell Colin McClelland, the Special One about whom you will read more. With his permission I present his email response:

Email: Colin to Bill
Sent Thu 25/01/2001 00:36

Oh, Bill, I so wish I could be there. It will be like entering a time capsule. Just think – relatively untouched for 30 years. Will there still be remnants of the old marquee structure above the stage? The smell of cheap perfume in the ladies' powder room? Will wee Gerry's smelly shoes still be there in the dressing room?
What memories – what distilled essence of our youth – lies behind those boarded-up windows? The entrance hall with its little glass cash window

where one of the McMahon brothers used to glare uncomprehendingly at the androgynous and colourfully patchworked masses suddenly assembled in his front porch; the stairway leading up to the ladies' powder room, the same room where Ashtar, one Friday afternoon, plugged in our first strobe light and let it pulse in the darkness, its light fracturing and bouncing in the room's many mirrors, and, still not satisfied, finally plunged his face straight into its brilliant, flashing lens, searching for the ultimate buzz. The little stairway that descended once again into the ballroom, down which so many fights seemed to take place, like some old, bloodier, replay of an Errol Flynn film; and the floor itself, awash with coloured light, bodies heaving in a fog of patchouli oil, smoke and alcohol; giant shadows cast upon explosions of projected colour. And that sound — two groups a night, maximum volume. All under your wonderful creation — the one thing that made it so different to anywhere else in town: the canopy of the Marquee. Now that was pure magic. Don't know why. But it was.

One Saturday night my mother, you know, forgot her house keys, and had to take a taxi down to Marquee to get my set from me. She looked at my kaftan and white trousers (remember, I was one of the original kaftan doormen) with a sudden start of panic and bewilderment. I then took her to the side door in the porch which led into the main ballroom. When I opened it she was hit with dark, noise, heat, and all those flashing lights. She reeled back, as if someone had hit her with a sledgehammer.

"Get me out of this..." she said, groping for a word appropriate to the scene from hell she had just glimpsed, "...get me out of this...this cesspit!"

Ah, such memories, Bill. We were privileged to have been a part of all that, you know. And I do really believe that it was just as wonderful as we now remember. Maybe better not have that door opened after all. I think we're too old to have to deal with the emotions it would unleash. Take many pictures. I want to see the cash desk, the stairs up past the cloakroom, the descent back into the ballroom, the stage, the bar (where I once got very drunk on Brandy Alexanders with Donal Corvin at a Hairdressers' Ball) and, well, just the whole view of the floor. You are one privileged guy. It must be the 1960s Belfast equivalent of being the first man allowed on the wreck of the Titanic. And even better, someone who had actually once sailed in her.

I find it in some ways astonishing that people still recall those days, but when you think about it, it was a remarkably colourful little interlude in between the drabness of what went before and the horror of what came later.

Tiger Taylor always says those few years from 1967 to 1969 were "like a dream," and I suppose it did have a dreamlike quality to it. Would the same feeling of otherworldliness have occurred in, say, Coventry, or Nottingham? Don't think so. It was the background of Belfast – what it had been and what it was to become – that framed the picture so well, and so poignantly.

So if you're writing the book, and I think you should, by the way – that's your landscape.

Colin McClelland
Dublin

The Astor Ballroom didn't offer up its secrets without a fight. We wrestled with the lock mechanism, getting more and more impatient as each of us in turn failed to get the door unlocked. Finally the lock gave way and we turned our attention to the heavy wooden door which simply refused to budge. We put our shoulders to it and eventually our combined weight nudged it open just enough to allow us one by one to edge our way into the dark interior. Sadly it was indeed like walking into the wreck of the Titanic.

We talked about writing a book. And then we talked some more. Eventually we realised we had pressed the pause button. We had to face the fact that no-one was sufficiently motivated to write the book. Colin seemed to have said it all in his email. Nostalgia evidently just isn't what it used to be.

One day some 10 years later I heard on the car radio the Beach Boys singing 'Good Vibrations.' It evoked a hazy memory that reached back nearly half a century. I smiled to myself at the thought of the old joke so often springs to mind at a time like this – the one about how if you remember the 60s, you weren't there. I was there, damn it.

Wait a minute. I suddenly thought of the tapes, and experienced an irresistible urge to listen to them and hear what secrets might be exposed. I was reminded of Watergate, when a White House aide revealed the existence of a taping system in the Oval Office.

 The reel-to-reel audio tape recording of The Group performing in Belfast in 1968 had been languishing in a battered cardboard box for 45 years.

I lifted it out and held it up to the sunlight. Gingerly, I drew a few inches of tape away from the reel and showed it to my son, Michael, who has more than a passing interest in such things. As I did so I was alarmed to see flakes of dusty, rusty particles parting company from the tape – which in its raw state appeared to be nothing more than clear plastic film. You don't need to be an electronic engineer to know the brown flakes are bits of the magnetised coating that carries the recorded sounds. The tape was obviously degenerating and with it the recorded sound, which suddenly I felt I really wanted to hear.

We sat at the kitchen table with headphones connected to an assortment of equipment, with pride of place given over to my vintage reel-to-reel tape recorder.

The 50-year old Grundig had had a good clean and a dose of WD40. It was in fine working order. Michael had listened to the tape of The Group and thought that the tape, too, was okay. It appeared to have survived.

Michael set it up for me with a line out to a small mixing desk, which in turn fed into his laptop computer on which he had downloaded free software called Audacity. The idea was to capture what we could from the reel-to-reel and turn it from analog audio to digital format so we could make a CD.

We carefully attached the tape to the spindle.

It was all coming back to me. This is how we used to learn the songs. It fell to me to record current hits off the wireless onto reel-to-reel. I would then sit by the machine with my finger and thumb hovering over the play lever, stopping and starting until I had noted down the words and the chords. The final task was to break down the harmonies and learn them.

"Are you ready?" asked Michael. I adjusted the headphones. This was going to be good.

"Okay, go."

After about 30 seconds I took off the headphones. This was not what I imagined I would be hearing. What I heard was rough and unbalanced.

"It's crap, isn't it?"

Michael was not so dismissive. He looked pensive and rolled his hand this way, then that.

I had been so looking forward to listening to that tape.

"What did you expect?" said Michael. "All you had was a basic tape recorder with a single microphone which you stuck in front of the PA. You had no monitor speakers. No geeks at the back of the room adjusting sound levels. Just four guys playing live, singing more or less in tune and quite obviously having a good time."

This was true. All four of us shared the vocals and we were all guilty of singing too close to the microphone. You had to do that because otherwise you couldn't hear what you were singing. All you could hear from the PA speakers was what bounced back from the wall at the far end of the room.

"Listen to it all the way through," he urged. "and don't be thinking you have to be impressed with what you hear. Don't be hoping to hear a great performance. That it ain't, but think about it like this: it is still unique. Whether you like it or not, that is the way it was. Crap it may be – but you have something of genuine value here – something that captures the atmosphere of the Astor Marquee and those Saturday afternoons in The Pound that you used to tell me about. Listen to it and you'll be right back there."

I worked out that the recording was of the band playing on Saturday 6 April 1968 – the week before Easter that year. As was the case every Saturday around this time, The Group, having played all afternoon in the Pound, would go on to play in the Astor Marquee Club that night. It was a long day. To place this momentous event in the history of the world, it might help if I were to tell you this was two days after the assassination of Martin Luther King and four days after the release of the film 2001: A Space Odyssey.

The recording was captured through the pencil microphone supplied with a made-in-Belfast Grundig TK14 tape recorder. Held in place with duct tape, the mic was just left dangling in front of a speaker – a PA system that carried vocal only. There was no mixing desk. Nothing else was mic'd up. The sound generated from every other source – back line amps, drums, punter chat and the clinking of bottles – was just picked up as background.

What happened that night in the Astor Marquee Club, the night of Saturday 6 April 1968, is a matter of public record. The Marquee at this point had become the number one beat venue in Belfast. The Marquee that night was a bit different. The place was jam packed not just with punters but also with musos who either had a night off or had checked in on their way home. Billed to appear that night, sharing the stage with The Group, was that fine group from Ballymena: Gentry. For those obsessed with historical precision, this was a time when Gentry, commendably aiming high on the world stage, changed its name briefly to Nobility so there would be no clash with a band from Memphis, Tennessee – an act called The Gentrys. The following is an extract from a report that appeared in the columns of the Belfast News Letter after this particular Saturday:

THE GREAT RAVE-UP

The Marquee Club is becoming the centre of beat music in Ireland. And if you wonder why, ask anyone who was there on Saturday night. After four hours of rave from the Nobility, Platform 3 and The Group, Sam Mahood leapt on stage as The Group were finishing their act and launched into a harmonica version of "Dust My Blues" during which he was joined by other members of the Soul Foundation.

The events described in the article took place at the end of a long day – a typical Saturday in 1968. Climb into my time machine and let me take you down to strawberry fields where living is easy with eyes closed.

Chapter 2

The Pound
Saturday 6 April 1968 – 14:00

"Yoohoo!"

Carol announces her arrival, carrying items of colourful clothing over her arm. I don't usually notice these things, but this is something else. On her head is a black leather cap, set at just the right angle to look carefree and self-confident – which she is. She looks good wearing a suede mini-skirt. Clothes, she once tried to explain to me, should be designed not to alter a person's character but to exaggerate it.

Carol Clapham is one of the growing number of trend-setting fashion gurus in the city. But she has an edge on most. She is an extraordinarily talented dress designer and makes all her own clothes. What's more – she makes our stage gear as well.

I have known Carol for years – we were at the College of Art together where she came top of the class in textile design. She has been going out for years with my fellow architectural student, Niall McCutcheon to whom she will be getting married in the summer. I am to be Best Man.

Carol has decided it is important for her that The Group has all the gear.

I can remember in the early days of the Boat Club, she witnessed the first attempt by The Dominoes to don some sort of uniform. We bought matching short sleeve yellow shirts - loose-fitting and worn outside the trousers. They were cool.

"Those shirts are not cool, you idiots," she said then. "They may feel cool, but shirts like that just make you look like buffoons." Offence was taken.

We muttered. The disparaging comments were overheard by others. The only dignified way out was to appoint Carol as our Fashion Stylist. Before we knew it we had parted with good money for much smarter long sleeve black and white vertically striped shirts, tucked neatly into a pair of casual slacks with a proper belt.

When The Group came into being, Carol started to produce made-to-measure clothes for us. Sometimes, it must be said, the outfits she produces are bloody uncomfortable. Her white shirts with a high button down polo-style collar made of a polyester material were a disaster. They undoubtedly looked good under the ultra-violet light, but we wore them only once as we were baked alive. What she has over her arm looks rather different, however.

We are to change from white to multicolour, with purple flares and fancy multi-coloured quilted waistcoats. We try them on. They are fab. We look like the Lonely Hearts Club Band.

Those fortunate enough to get in to The Pound today will be in the company of fashion trend-setters such as Beverley and Carole Glover, Joy McFarland, Clover Groves, Dorothy Mullan, Sylvia Madden, Jenny Trevithick, Judy Hill, Jenny Lockhart and Jo Phelan. And I know, because she is already in the building, eyes will be drawn to the one who transcends them all – Susie Knowles, a Derry girl who in her teens was Miss Ireland and is now married to the ebullient Arnie Knowles. Arnie is in charge of just about everything to do with The Group, The Pound and The Marquee.

Peter Lloyd is here, too. We have just spent big money on a Lloyd Sound PA system and he has kindly come along to help us set it up. Sez is in charge of that department and is deeply engaged in discussion about the controls. There are a few more knobs on it, right enough. I'm guessing the new system we bought from Pete is bound to be better than anything we have had before.

Isn't this the place to be?

The Pound on a Saturday afternoon attracts a very different crowd from that drawn to evening events during the week. The music is different for a start, but dusty, dirty and smoky though it is, it has become a fashionable place for dudes – the place in fact where you can show off your latest gear. The latest ties and tops, often purchased barely an hour earlier, look magnificent on the way in, although rarely quite so splendid on the way out. At the end of the afternoon you could expect the fashion item to be decorated with beer stains and flavoured with tobacco.

A typical Saturday afternoon sees the Pound-goer travel into town on the bus, arriving in central Belfast at around noon and heading first for Wellington Street, off Donegall Square West. He or she might then look for a coffee in the Piccolo Coffee Bar – or something more substantial served up with a familiar flourish by the flamboyant Matthew in Isabeal's. On leaving, everyone seems to experience an irresistible urge to check out the John Patrick fashion boutique. The girls feel the Indian Madras shirts and exchange observations on the latest fashion trends. The lads hang around in the hope of getting a word with the hard-working owner, Patrick Quinn. Quinn has an extraordinary talent for making customers feel they have done the right thing handing over a week's wages to take possession of the most expensive item from his extensive range of hand-embroidered tawny sheepskin coats from the mountain wastes of Afghanistan.

Then somebody leads a casual walk across the town centre and down Ann Street. The herd follows and expands as more of the beautiful people emerge from Mooney's in Arthur Square. The next gathering congregates on Church

Lane, acknowledged to be Belfast's Carnaby Street. Here the herd disperses, some to join the crowd round fashion boutique Mark Antony – others to wrestle their way into the sister shop Babalu under the watchful eye of Pat Jordan.

The three boutiques are not the only ones Belfast have to offer, but they are the most popular and are all packed on a Saturday. The girls elbow their way to the rails, and from the range of mini dresses; white knitted dresses; suede dresses; dresses with matching pants or dresses with contrasting pants, they select an item to clutch tightly and intimately for others to admire. Some go for the girl-next-door look of Ready Steady Go co-host Cathy McGowan; others have eyes only for the very latest items and collections – check trousers; hippy denim jackets; faded jeans; fab crochet dresses; tops, skirts and trousers. All scramble for the paraphernalia of jewellery, bags, deep plastic belts and go-go boots described as 'accessories.'

The guys hunt out flared trousers, leather jackets; boots with raised heels; made-to-measure suits with wide lapels; moleskin, and midnight blue mohair. There are white shirts and garish kipper ties; black shirts with narrow white ties and paisley patterned shirts with matching ties.

We have a blue Bedford minibus with The Group written in white plastic cut-out lettering on each sliding door. I am quite proud of the lettering style which has become a distinctive and immediately recognisable brand for The Group.

We have also acquired thousands of triangular We Love The Group car stickers using the same style of lettering. We thrust them upon anyone and everyone we know or meet; we leave them in waiting rooms and on shop counters. We give them away from the stage as prizes. Gilmore Signs in Middlepath Street produced them for us on the cheap to see how it goes – clear plastic film which clings to glass. We have bucket loads and it is working well for them and us.

Motorists need little persuading to display them as they are easily applied and removed.

As we drive around, we get a buzz from the sound of honking horns directed at us. We automatically give a cheerful wave even when it is perfectly obvious someone wants us to get the hell out of the way. But we are heartened by the surprising number of vehicles we see with windscreen stickers proclaiming love for The Group.

Well, Fred says he saw one on his way here today.

We have managed to grab a sandwich, and it is looking like we will be ready to start on time...

Chapter 3
The Pound
Saturday 6 April 1968 – 14:30
I Can See For Miles

There are four of us in The Group.

Smick (aka John Smyth) is on drums. He took over from Ricky about nine months ago. He comes from Comber and is at Stranmillis Training College studying to become a teacher. He made his name as the drummer with the Exiles. His kit is set up in the middle of the stage and we push him as far back as possible.

Bill (that's me). I am the tall bloke on the right of the stage as the punters see us. I used to play guitar in The Dominoes. Now I play keyboards. I went to the College of Art where I studied part-time to become an architect. Last September I signed up for two year course in town planning at Queen's.

Fred stands in the middle with his sunburst Hofner Verithin Bass Guitar which he plays with a pick in his right hand and five thumbs in his left. He is my buddy. Fred and I played together in The Dominoes for the last five years or so. He is the driving force behind the band. His bass amp weighs a ton. He has a degree in law and works as a marketing manager in Cantrell and Cochrane on the Castlereagh Road.

 **Sez** stands on the far side of the stage wielding his pride and joy – a cherry Gibson Les Paul Junior guitar he bought in Crymbles where Gerry Giffen talked him into paying the big money. He practices constantly and is really pretty good. He has a degree in electrical and mechanical engineering and works for British Oxygen. Sez shares a flat with me.

"Pint, Smick?" "Fred?"

No point in asking Sez. Not his scene. Three pints of Carling Black Label are on their way.

I look round the room. There must be a couple of hundred in already. All seats are taken and there is a jovial crush round the bar to my left. The narrow corridor to the left of the bar, leading to the toilets and to the way out, is heaving like a rugby scrum. Anyone hoping to go for a pee needs to watch for a gap in the flow of people coming the other way, either returning from the toilets or having just been let in. It is a warm day outside and it is starting to heat up in here.

There are wires all over the carpeted stage. My little living room organ is connected up to a Lloyd amplifier with a home-made speaker on the floor behind me. Sez's lead is connected to his Lloyd amp through a fuzz-box. Pete Lloyd who built the amps for us is something of a local hero. Not a hair on his head, he is known to all the bands and groups. As well as running a business building top class amplifiers, he has a recording studio and it was his connections at Decca that led to THEM getting the big recording contract back in '64. Today I have brought along my Grundig tape recorder, which I use primarily to record from the radio the latest hits we know we are going to have to learn. It mainly falls to me to work out the parts because I have a piano at home. No-one bothers with the dots these days – there just isn't time. We learn by ear and sometimes just wing it first time on stage. It is all we can do as we are playing up to three, four and sometimes five nights a week as well as this Saturday afternoon gig. Tonight we are in the Astor Marquee Club with The Gentry.

We rarely get the chords wrong, but there is definitely an element of guesswork and approximation about the words and the harmonies.

We get together once a week to learn new material. Most of the practice sessions are acoustic. Normally we meet in my mother's house where we can make use of her baby grand piano. We've been doing it for years. In advance of a session – we call it a sesh – I will have recorded the song from the wireless and spent some time stop/starting the Grundig so I can work out the chord sequence and unpack the harmonies. I allocate the parts to the boys – normally just by singing the lines one at a time until they can memorise it. We do it all by ear and very rarely feel the need to write it down. Unless you are doing it all the time, writing manuscript is a pain in the butt.

We do our best to be faithful to the original arrangement as we hear it, but we really have no idea how a new song will work out until we play it live at a gig. So we just run through the harmonies enough times to memorise them. Soon or later someone will mutter something like "that'll do rightly," or "close enough for jazz" – an indication that people are getting bored and it is time to move on to the next one.

Each of the four of us must learn our singing parts while also playing an instrument. It is not that easy. The brain can only focus on one thing at a time. There are two difficult things in singing harmonies – one is hitting the precise pitch at the precise moment the harmony comes in. The other challenge is holding steady the last note of a vocal part all the way to the end of the line when your mind needs to be shifting focus onto what comes next – like a chord change or a drum break. These are the things that separate the men from the boys. While a cock-up can always be laughed off – and that happens frequently – we really do try to get it right and not to screw up.

That is really why today the Grundig TK14 is sitting on a chair at my left hand side.

We have learnt a few new numbers in the last two weeks and I'm hoping this will allow us to listen to the harmonies which might need more rehearsal or a bit of adjustment. A spindly lead extends from the top of the recorder and held in place with duct tape across the top of the brand new Lloyd PA speaker which sits on a table just in front of me to my left. At the end of the lead is a cornet-shaped microphone dangling free in front of the speaker. Crude, but it will do the job.

The Group. It is a good name, don't you think? Evidently The Who had that name in mind when they started out. They fell out with management when they were over-ruled. Not surprised.

But The Group is a name that certainly works for us. It says what we are. It is unadulterated, pure and simple. Presumptuous, maybe – yet humble. It is a name that makes clear we are definitely not a showband. We are a four-piece beat group and proud of it. We mix pop with rock and blues. That's all we really want to do.

There is a kind of hierarchy of bands that together comprise the urban beat scene in Belfast. Venues range from smoke-filled dives to sumptuous ballrooms. In the city dance studios where the Exiles used to play, we have had rhythm and blues groups like the Alleykatz, Styx and the Mad Lads – soon to become Moses K and the Prophets. On this circuit you also get blues groups that write their own material – bands like Taste and the Trixons. You get bluesy rock and pop groups like The Fugitives, The Carpetbaggers, The Few and The High Wall. We have Just Five, Aztecs, Five by Five and the Deltones with Eric Bell.

Gigging in the bigger venues such as the Astor you have the established groups such as the Misfits, Tony and the Telstars, Gentry, Interns, Wheels and High Society. Also The Tigers, Sam Mahood and the Soul Foundation and of course Heart and Soul – formerly the Dominoes; the band with whom Fred and I played for six years from inception. Further up the scale, or down the scale depending on how you look at it, you get into the full-time world of showbands who travel all over Ireland filling the ballrooms of romance. And then you get your country rock groups like Trevor Kelly's Virginians and Colonel Spike and the Kentuckians.

As an urban beat group, we view the showbands and showband followers as a breed apart. The only exception as far as we are concerned is The Freshmen. The Freshmen are from Ballymena and have been on the showband circuit since 1962. They are exceptional in every sense of the word, and with superb musicians and great vocal harmony they are the best band around. We reconcile this by regarding The Freshmen as a hybrid – a group that happens to play showband gigs. But we have no ambition to become a showband. The name of the band says it all. The Group. It is our choice to play in dimly-lit dives – places where the pounding beat rattles your bones; where the floor is awash with spilt beer and sweat drips down the walls.

And here we are on a Saturday afternoon doing just that. Isn't it great?

I see Ricky McCutcheon is in The Pound this afternoon. Ricky was the original drummer with The Group. We are still good friends despite parting company about nine months ago. It was the usual thing – his runner had laid it on the line. 'Runner' being a word he applies to any of the female gender he would regard as a candidate for his attention.

The runner: "It's me or The Group, Ricky – which is it to be?"

Never one to rush into a decision, Ricky strives to keep all his plates spinning until they crash to the floor as we all know sooner or later, inevitably, they will. We could all see it coming. Presented with an ultimatum, he dropped out of a gig. "That's it," said Fred. The decisive one. "If Smick wants the job, it's his." He did. The job was his and Ricky was out.

"Don't remember that in the script," Ricky muttered as he absorbed the news.

It was a bit of a gunk, but he was determined not to show it. Image was all-important for Ricky. Gotta be cool. The cool thing was to accept it as just one of those things. The way the cookie crumbles. All in the roll of the dice.

Ricky walks past the front of the stage, glass in hand.

"Look what we have here, folks." I speak to the microphone to announce his arrival. There is recognition – girls clap and guys jeer in a friendly sort of way.

Ricky is popular. He still lives with his folks off the Malone Road; he has a fancy car and works hard to present himself as pretty cool. He is fastidious about his appearance, and likes to wear painfully tight jeans that he lovingly and repeatedly scrubs with stone. He has a line of chat which has worked well for him in the last few months now he has time on his hands. He knows he made a mistake. The runner who cost him his place in the band is toast.

Smick gets a little edgy when Ricky appears. Ricky knows that, and has been known to make a point of standing in front of the band with his arms folded, staring intently at Smick.

Today as he walks past the stage, glass in hand, he looks up and asks "D'youse do the Who's?"

Three of us laugh out loud. It is an in-joke that Ricky well knows will mean nothing to Smick but will provoke a fond memory for the rest of us.

It goes back to when Ricky was the drummer and The Group was appearing for the very first time in Sammy Houston's Jazz Club.

We were actually quite nervous about that particular gig. We had come from the rarefied atmosphere of the Belfast Boat Club, and had no idea how we would be received in the cut and thrust of the urban beat scene. SHJC was on the upper floor of a building in Great Victoria Street opposite the Grand Opera House. In its heyday it had been a dance school. Today it is where teenyboppers get their kicks. From the point of view of the group, it is the worst place in the world to get into. You have to haul the gear up the narrow stairway, squeezing past a disorderly queue of teenage patrons chattering at full volume.

The DeeJay in SHJC is Brian "Da" Hedley. He is known as Da because he is really old – nearly 21 years of age. While we were waiting for Da to hand over to the band, a girl called out from the floor:

"Hey Mister." At least she didn't call me Grandpa. "Mister. D'youse do the Who's?"

As it happened, that very week we had learnt 'Happy Jack,' our first attempt to emulate The Who.

"Sure we do." I said. We made a fan for life.

The Pound is a dark and dusty warehouse in Townhall Street at the back of Roddy's Bar. We have been playing here every Saturday afternoon since Smick joined the band. Live pop and blues music in the heart of the city on a Saturday afternoon – it was a winner from the start and The Group has been resident here from Day One. It seems like we know everyone and everyone knows us.

The Pound is Belfast's only Saturday afternoon music venue. It is packed to the gills every week. It is the people's bar and the people like the blend of pop and blues that The Group has to offer. But of course the main attraction is the opportunity to down a few pints on a Saturday afternoon.

I'm thinking about the opening number. We normally ease ourselves in, but Ricky has put a thought in my head – why not just hit them up the face from the start with our latest tribute to The Who.

I put it to the guys. "What about starting with 'I Can See for Miles?'"

Smick is all for it. He knows this will show Ricky.

"Are you right, then?"

Clearly the guys are not ready. Smick is still tuning his snare. Sez is twiddling away in a world of his own and Fred is engaged in deep conversation with one of the punters.

What I need to do now is set the levels on the Grundig. It is tricky enough. Miles opens with a power chord which the magic eye will tell me is distorting. If I set the magic eye to cope with it, the rest of the recording will be too low. I can't adjust and play at the same time – so I just have to guess at the levels. I have to press two controls simultaneously in advance to get the recorder running and then leap to the keyboard. Stuff it – I'll settle for distortion.

I love that little Grundig. It was actually made in Belfast. The West German electronics company opened a plant in west Belfast about seven years ago to manufacture tape recorders. My TK14 must have been one of the first to come off the assembly line. It has served me well. It's a mono, and records at 3¾ inches per second.

Here we go. Smick is counting in and Sez is poised to hit that opening power chord...

Chapter 4

Moon up in the Sky

I sat back, took off the headphones and turned to Michael. We had successfully transferred to digital format the first track extracted from the decaying reel-to-reel tapes. The interesting thing now would be to see if we could somehow enhance the quality of the recording using computer software. Michael is sceptical. We talk about the original composition.

'I Can See for Miles' was written for The Who by Pete Townshend. It was released on 14 October 1967 and reached No 10 in the UK charts. Townshend evidently considers this to be the best song he ever penned. He thought it would be a huge hit and was disappointed when it wasn't.

It was rarely performed live by The Who during the Keith Moon era as the complex vocal harmonies were difficult to replicate on stage, as indeed was the percussion style found on the original recording. Townshend's guitar was overdubbed in the studio and it has been reported that the reason the band was reluctant to play this live was because it was impossible to recreate the sound with one guitar.

Whatever the truth, The Group made a good fist of it on this occasion. Surprisingly, the Grundig recording is not half bad. The harmonies are well-balanced and fairly close to being in tune, particularly the repeated line in towards the end of the song where the voices have to sustain a tricky harmonic discord. Performing 'I Can See for Miles' in The Pound is probably my fondest memory of The Group in 1967/68.

To save you the trouble of counting, I can tell you the word 'miles' occurs 57 times in the song.

Fred and I always loved The Who. Twenty months earlier, before The Group was formed, we found ourselves with a big decision to take. It was Friday 6 May 1966.

I answered the phone. It was Fred. "You know who's on in the ABC Cinema tonight, don't you?"

"Gina Lollobrigida?"

"No, you eejit – it's Bob Dylan. Have to go."

He'll have to go. Put your sweet lips a little closer to the phone.

"Hang on a minute, is this not the night The Who play the Top Hat in Lisburn?"

Now here we have the classic dilemma. Imagine being spoiled for choice here in this neat little town they call Belfast. But that is the way it was. And it just got better and better. On Friday 2 June 1967, for example, Manfred Mann, the Turtles, the Kinks, Del Shannon, The Who and the Tremeloes were all advertised to appear at separate venues in Belfast over the weekend. And imagine Jimi Hendrix, The Move, The Nice, Pink Floyd and Amen Corner due to appear on stage, one after the other, in a single Queens Festival event in the Whitla Hall. It happened on Friday 27 November 1967. I know. I was there. You had to keep your eye on the fly posters as often chart-topping acts would appear at very short notice. What seemed to happen fairly frequently was that late in the day tours would, as an afterthought, be extended to take in a trip to the Emerald Isle.

What is more, a ticket to get in and see these chart-topping acts usually cost no more than double the normal cover charge. We thought at the time that it was dear enough.

Fred and I faced a stark choice on that Friday night in May 1966. As usual we had failed to procure tickets for either event, despite the fact that both Bob Dylan and The Who were 'must see' acts. There was nothing particularly odd about that. In those days you could usually rely on being able to get tickets at the door – except for the Beatles and the Stones of course.

The rumour was that Dylan was deserting his folk fans and making history by going electric. We liked the idea. Most people hated it so we expected to see plenty of vacant seats at that concert.

The Who on the other hand was on the verge of breaking up. The band had played without their frontman for the previous two gigs on the tour and Daltrey wasn't expected to show up at the Top Hat.

That tipped the balance for us. The Who couldn't possibly be any good without Daltrey. So we opted for the comfort of cinema seats to hear Dylan who was down to play two shows that night. We reckoned he would get stuck into the electric stuff – Maggie's Farm and Like a Rolling Stone etc.

Fred picked me up in his Dad's Ford Zephyr and we found a tight space right in front of the cinema. We were unusually early. We joined an unexpected queue for tickets and were horrified to find we were not going to be allowed in. Both Dylan shows were sold out. How the hell? All seats taken.

Numb from the shock, we climbed back in the Zephyr and drove to Lisburn. We arrived at the Top Hat minutes before The Who were due on stage, again finding a space right in front of the hall. We needn't have worried. The ballroom, Lisburn's top entertainment venue, was still open for business and we just paid our money and walked in. We worked our way to the front. We got talking to an excited kid who looked about 13 and had squirmed his way between us. He said he played the guitar and when I asked where he came from, he told me he lived in east Belfast. We offered him a lift. He was destined to become a guitar legend. I learnt much later it was Gary Moore.

The show began with a sensational burst of sound, the like of which I had never heard before in my life. The three of us were blown away. And, yes, when the curtain pulled back, there was the unmistakable figure of Roger Daltrey.

Whether Daltrey was contractually obliged to take part the Irish tour, or had simply changed his mind about leaving, I don't know. But there was certainly an uneasy truce in the band when he arrived in Ireland. Daltrey met up with Bob Dylan in the International Hotel in Belfast that afternoon and accompanied him to the ABC Cinema where they drank tea backstage during the first show interval – between Dylan's acoustic first half and the controversial electric set with a backing band, The Hawks.

Ten days later at the now infamous gig in Manchester Free Trade Hall, Dylan stood his ground when he was called 'Judas!' by angry fans because he chose to sup with the devil and play with a loud electric backing band. At the same time Roger Daltrey decided to re-join The Who.

The 1966 visit to Belfast of Roger Daltrey and Bob Dylan was memorable for me as I am sure it was for young Gary Moore. I would like to think that it was an encounter that sealed the respective destinies of all three of these great performers in the Hall of Fame.

The Group never played in the Top Hat Ballroom, Lisburn. It was destroyed by a terrorist bomb on Saturday 17 June 1972.

I once met Keith Moon.

No, I didn't meet him at some wild London party, wrenching down a jug of his champagne and brandy with my arm round his shoulders. I didn't meet him trashing a hotel room, tossing a TV out the window or flushing powerful explosives down a toilet. It was just a handshake.

It was Thursday 26 January 1978, just a few months before he died. We were 31,000 feet above the Atlantic Ocean.

The pilot of the scheduled flight from London to St Lucia apologised for the delay in getting under way – it was due to the late arrival of a small number of remaining passengers. I could see no vacant seats other than the one beside me. Eventually a bloke carrying two large duffle bags shuffled down the aisle, apologising loudly to passengers whose heads he managed to duff with the duffles along the way.

"Sorry about this, mate" he said breathlessly as he settled into the seat, obviously well aware of passenger irritation with latecomers. He was the archetypal cockney – looking and sounding like Private Joe Walker, the black market spiv in Dad's Army. He threw his head up, laughing. "You wouldn't believe it."

Peter Butler, as he explained to me, was 'personal assistant' to the wonderfully eccentric Keith Moon – drummer with The Who. Moon, he added before embarking on the story of his life, was up ahead in First Class.

"You can call me Dougal" he said intimately, drawing me into his confidence. He lowered his voice.

"Mention his name and anything is possible. We are headed for Antigua. We hear our plane is delayed, so he talks his way onto this flight to St Lucia. Man's amazing. Sorry for keeping you waiting."

I nodded. I can believe that. He is, after all, Keith Moon.

"Only two seats available. So I'm back here – and he gets to sit in the lie-back-and-go-to-sleep seats. But he'll get bored. He'll be down any minute and I'll introduce you."

I liked the idea of being able to tell my grandchildren I once met the one and only Moon the Loon. I'm a good listener and Dougal seemed to warm to me because of that. He proceeded to tell me his life story which, in fairness, I found very entertaining.

He told me how he had worked as a crooked croupier in Mafia-run casino; how he had been a mercenary in Africa before becoming a fixer – or as he described it, a "James

Bond meets Mission Impossible" trouble shooter. I learnt a lot about this character and enjoyed his stories, but I was looking forward to meeting the man himself. We were now half way over the Atlantic and there was no sign of him. Maybe Dougal was just making it up.

"He'll be down in a minute. He'll be bored up there. Want to meet him? I'll introduce you."

He repeated this promise every time he paused to light up. Dougal went on to describe how he had then found himself in the company of show business celebrities. He had been hired to look after Neil Diamond, with whom he toured the world, before becoming Moon's 'personal assistant.'

"Look – I tell you what, me old china. I'm going to leave you here for a moment while I check he's all right." He winks at me and gives me a nudge. "More a matter of checking if the other passengers are all right, eh?"

I was glad of the respite.

It was some time before Dougal arrived back.

"Gordon Bennett," he exclaimed, slumping into his seat.

Moon was not all right, apparently. He had learnt that the plane is scheduled to stop overnight in St Lucia before flying on to Antigua, and had demanded loudly that Dougal instruct the Captain to change the flight plan so the plane would land in Antigua first, so he could get off. He had had enough. Certainly enough fawning from the toffs in their whistlers.

Dougal had managed to get into the cockpit where he had apparently persuaded the Captain to radio ahead to find out what was possible. I had a mental image at this point of Dougal with his hands clasped firmly round the Captain's throat.

In a while a man with a peaked cap came down to have a word with Dougal. He spoke softly and the only words I picked up were "not possible."

"Well, will you tell that to Moon on the way back up there?" asked Dougal.

A few minutes later the curtain was yanked back. It was Moon. People turned to one another and pointed as the instantly recognisable drummer with The Who moved unsteadily down the aisle, eyes wide and scanning the passengers in a hunt for Dougal. He didn't look pleased.

He reached our row and leant down over his personal assistant, thankfully speaking in hushed tones that only Dougal and I could hear: "So here you are, you wanker. I told you I wanted to get off – now we're on this fucking plane for another eight fucking hours. Fucky-nell. Fucky-NELL. You're fired."

Dougal shrugged, and said "By the way, this is Bill."

Keith Moon reached over and shook my hand warmly. He drew me into the discussion. "Am I just going to have to sort this out by myself?"

"I guess so," I said.

Sometime later the Captain announced the plane would be making an unscheduled stop in Antigua.

Chapter 5

The Final Countdown

It is 1:00am on Sunday 28 August 2011 and it's all over. At least it is for me. I've had enough.

The father of the bride is a wealthy Fermanagh solicitor. He's the one who booked the Dominoes to play at the wedding. The wedding is in a vast marquee on his land on the shores of Lough Erne where he hopes to build a major hotel complex. His wife has fond memories of The Dominoes. He also knows me as a planning consultant who has so far failed to persuade the planners to grant planning permission for his ambitious project.

We are drenched in sweat, winding up the leads and heaving the gear out to Raymond's van. We find this a bit undignified. We grumble, as we always do, about how different things were in the days when we had roadies. Time was when we would be left to chat up the girls while someone else clears the stage.

The DeeJay has set up his gear. It appears to amount to little more than a laptop computer loaded with mp3s and a set of compact PA speakers. He has the job done in a flash. His girlfriend stands next to him, glued to her mobile phone – there in person, yet immersed in conversation with her friends elsewhere.

Suddenly the room is filled with recorded sound, played full blast. Recorded sound at high volume makes our contribution to the evening's entertainment seem limp. But then we were live. We were the genuine article. They hired us because we are good at what we do. We gave them what they want to hear. Who wants this electronic rubbish?

Punters are surging onto the dance floor. They are jumping for joy.

The boss comes over to me, mellow from his day of largess. He'll not be so cheerful in the morning, I'm thinking.

"I didn't realise when I booked the music for Julie's wedding that I had hired the oldest musicians in Ireland." He chuckles.

Words fail me.

I trouser his cheque and force myself to smile. This had been a good night but it is perfectly clear that the punters prefer the disco.

And I'm thinking: stuff this oven-ready entertainment. These buggers have it made. They can drive to a gig on a motor bike. All they need is a T-shirt, a laptop computer, a sound activated lighting pod and a microphone. They weigh in at the last minute asking "where do I plug in?"

I hate these guys. I'm knackered and have just been told I am past it. It is 1:30am and now we face a frigging 100 mile drive home.

At this precise moment I decide this is my last gig.

The Dominoes were never in the mainstream, but they did have an impact on a segment of Belfast society in the early 1960s. The band, formed by schoolmates from Campbell College, became the resident Saturday night band in the Boat Club at Stranmillis. It was actually a tennis club. The Dominoes became part of the furniture, playing on the floor because they wanted to be there - at the party.

The guys in the band knew everyone - and everyone knew the guys in the band. To this day Saturday night at the Boat Club in sixties Belfast is remembered fondly by those who found someone to love. It is remembered a little less fondly by those who blame "The Twist" for an arthritic knee condition.

The Dominoes surfaced again in 1981, after the persuasive Dr Jim Dornan became possessed of an idea that the original Dominoes should get together again and provide the music for a nostalgic fund-raising event. A one-time gig and then we could all go back to our day jobs. The idea of a Dominoes Tribute Band had a certain appeal.

And of course there was always something in it for Jim Dornan – he who is to blame for starting it up again in 1981. He would rarely miss an opportunity to be Elvis or Freddie Mercury. He was not alone. Another local personality about whom you will read more later, Eric Cairns, could always be relied upon to step up on call to the stage and produce his inimitable version of 'The Birdie Song.'

The Dominoes played over 1000 gigs in those 30 years. Not bad for a second wind. We played in living rooms, humble village halls, fancy houses and in hotels. We played in city halls at glittering gala balls. We appeared before First Ministers, Lord Mayors and Secretaries of State. We witnessed the immaculately dressed Peter Mandelson fox-trotting Betty Boothroyd, former Tiller Girl and at the time Speaker of the House of Commons, around the dance floor as we played Elvis. We played in Parliament Buildings, Stormont, where the Speaker of the Assembly, John Alderdice, eagerly grasped the microphone to deliver, to rapturous applause, a fine rendition of "Bobby Magee." We played weddings and retirement celebrations, and even on one occasion were summoned by a grieving widow to the City of London to raise the rafters at a Guildhall celebration of the life of a distinguished Secretary-General. It followed a moving Service of Remembrance at St Paul's Cathedral in London. "He liked The Dominoes," she said.

The line-up that played the Fermanagh gig – the final squad – had five good years together. We had a lot of fun. I was by then playing a Rickenbacker 12-string guitar. My son Michael was on guitar, with Robin Lavery on drums and Keith Baker on bass. The real star of that last line-up was Ray Donnan who used to be in the Freshmen. If you happen to know anything about Irish showbands you will appreciate the significance of that bloodline.

It is now three years since that Fermanagh gig. I imagine you're thinking that the band carried on without me, or alternatively that the Dominoes let people down by cancelling a whole string of gigs in the diary.

We didn't have to cancel any bookings. It's as if everybody knew we weren't going to play any more gigs after this one. There were no more bookings in the diary for the first time we started up again. No more gigs to keep us coming back for more.

You see, here's the thing. We had fun. We didn't do this for the benefit of others. We played and sang because we loved it. As soon as you hear that first smattering of applause, you cheer up. And when it sounds good, you feel good.

....

On the drive home from Fermanagh that night I finally faced up to it – I'd had enough. I did wonder why I seemed to be playing more than my usual share of bum chords and why I had to ask Robin to lift the volume on my mic because I couldn't hear myself sing. It was as if something wasn't right in my head.

There was indeed something happening inside my head as I found out later. But that wasn't the reason I decided to pack it in. I just didn't want to do this anymore.

Chapter 6

The Pound
Saturday 6 April 1968 – 14:45
Even the Bad Times are Good

Ah, the Tremeloes.

Every time we play this, I think of my first week at Cabin Hill. I can still see music master Goofy Guyll, brandishing a conductor's baton, instructing the first form class of 1950 to sing the first five notes of a major scale.

"Like this." He reached out for the keys on the piano and played the scale with his left hand without looking.

"Up – la la, la la, laaa (pause), and down – la la, la la, laaa." He lingered on the last note and swiped it to a halt with the baton. "Now altogether..."

Mumbled sounds. He beat the baton on the desk top until the mumbling stops.

"Again."

More of the same. More beating of baton on desk.

"And again, please."

"God Almighty." He sighed and looked out the window for a long time.

Having realised what he was dealing with, Goofy decided on a different tack. He called each of us in the class to come forward in turn and sing the major scale. Each time he led off by reaching over to the piano without looking. I remember wondering how he was able to do that.

"Back there..." he told us at the outset, pointing the quivering baton at the back of the room.

"...back there will be seated the non-singers. The non-singers will not sing." It was scarcely necessary to explain that, but to put everyone beyond any doubt, he added: "Those at the front will be the singers."

First up was 8-year old Gibson, C M H.

Gibson was not as green as he was cabbage looking. He worked hard to sing just a little bit flat. You have to be a good singer to do that. He was promptly despatched to the back of the class.

The rows at the back quickly filled up with cheerful youngsters: the ones sharp enough to follow Gibson's lead: the smart ones who at that tender age could right away figure out on which side the bread was buttered.

I ended up at the front.

I suppose you could say I was brought up in a musical household. There were no drawing-room recitals or anything like that but Mum was always quick to remind me she possessed a diploma from the Royal Academy of Music. She read the dots – the birdies on the telegraph wires.

Dad, on the other hand, was something of a busker, reputed to play virtually any instrument by ear. So I suppose you could say I didn't get into music – I got the music in me. After Dad died when I was 10, Mum sent me to piano classes at Cabin Hill. But like every other normal kid I felt there was more to life than learning to play Schubert. Vamping was much more rewarding. "Just like your Dad," Mum would sigh in resignation. I felt vindicated.

My earliest memory of wanting to learn to play a musical instrument was after I heard Malcolm Gooding, a few years ahead of me at Campbell College, play boogie woogie at the Shandon Park home of Hoey, D P W in the summer of 1954. I'd love to say this was a point of enlightenment. The truth is that all this made me do was defy my mother by giving up piano lessons – something I regret to this day. It was my first act of rebellion.

I knew from way back that there were some curious musical instruments stuffed away behind a load of material on a high shelf in the workshop – a room accessed from the back yard of my home at 1 Ormiston Gardens. For a youngster not yet in his teens, the workshop was an exciting place where you could find lots of things to horse around with. I remember for example finding a huge bundle of Union Jacks which I proceeded to tie to broom handles and hang out of every window in the house.

To my dismay the flags were hurriedly downed with some muttering I did not understand about people in this world who kicked with the other foot. Nobody had ever explained to me anything about micks, prods or star-belly sneetches. I just wanted to fly my flags. Talk of which foot you kicked with was bewildering. I was not aware there was a flag protocol. Certainly the subtlety of closet loyalism among middle class Protestants was way beyond my comprehension.

Actually the reproach caused me to become a little obsessed with the flags – especially with the fact that I was not permitted to hang them out of windows. I even remember wrapping myself in them to champion the return to power of Winston Churchill in the 1951 General Election. I was rewarded with cheers from bystanders on one side of the road as I rode my bike repeatedly past the Polling Station at Knock Road Methodist Church. Why would I do that? I don't know, but I was having a good time and was utterly mystified when I arrived home and was hustled into the house in case any odd-footed people saw me and took exception. As I reached my teens I became determined to establish with certainty exactly who suffered from other-foot syndrome. It seemed entire families suffered from this condition. I hoped it wasn't the family with the three rather nice daughters that I admired with growing affection from my bedroom window. I studied their legs carefully, but I could see no difference except that they were girls.

Then came the day I reached to the very back of the top shelf in the workshop and pulled out the old musical instruments. Among them was a trumpet, a broken banjo and a one-string fiddle complete with a large brass horn, a horse hair bow and a wee packet of resin. I held it between my knees like a cello. When I scraped the bow across the string it produced an awesome sound amplified through the horn.

But right at the back, behind the flags, there was something that felt like it might be a guitar. I eventually prised out an instrument that I later learned was a baritone ukulele. It had four gut strings and it looked like a guitar to me. I took it into Chas Rollins Music shop in Donegall Street to find out how to tune it. "Easy," he said, helpfully singing a sequence of notes he said I would remember as "My Dog Has Fleas." To keep the 'tune' in my head, I sang "My Dog Has Fleas" over and over again on the bus home to the consternation of other passengers.

Once I started to play my 'guitar' I felt here at last was something I could do that would put me at the top of the class. Nobody else that I knew had a guitar at this point in time. I was ahead of the posse. Within days I could make a good fist of most three-chord skiffle songs that were dominating the airwaves. I moved on to four chords with Paul Anca and 'Diana.' I would spend hours in empty attic room in a house at Ballyholme, playing the 'guitar' and listening with growing satisfaction at my adolescent voice echoing round the walls. I mastered the basic chords of all the pop songs of the day – I could be Elvis; Pat Boone; Tab Hunter; Guy Mitchell and Charlie Gracey. I transferred my new found skill of chord composition onto the piano in order to emulate Jerry Lee Lewis and Fats Domino. I reckoned I was the bee's knees.

Soon there were followers. My schoolmate Roderick Downer and I assembled a skiffle group for the end of year House Party and we were up and running.

The words 'Campbell College Belfast' are firmly imprinted in gold in the centre of the black laminated card cover. The script within – fountain pen, black ink – records the birth of our skiffle group. It was Saturday 13 July 1957. I was 14 years of age. The black Exercise Book has words long forgotten that were written with a fountain pen when I was still at school. I abandoned the venture after writing the first chapter but when I started I must have thought there was a book in it. Weird.

It represents a contemporaneous account of the build-up to that first skiffle stage performance. It describes how I played my four-string guitar/ukulele; Roderick Downer strummed a tiny banjo; Sturge Hamilton scraped his metal thimble capped fingers deafeningly across a washboard, while Mike Shanks plucked a tea-chest equipped with a string and a broom handle. The book explains how we expanded the group to five for the 1957 Dobbin's House Party when we discovered Terry Croskery had a two piece drum kit. It records that we were announced as Roderick Downer's band, and that we sang 'A White Sport Coat,' 'Worried Man Blues,' 'I saw Esau' and '10,000 years ago.'

It goes on to describe our first public performance on Saturday 7 September 1957, when we were booked to play at Belmont Tennis Club. We practised the whole day before. We played 10 tunes altogether, and, according to the book, the girls in the audience screamed at the end of every number. 'Diana' was the big hit, despite the fact that Roderick had to bow out of this difficult four chord tune.

The next quote from the black Exercise Book explains a lot for those who might wonder why anyone would ever want to play in a pop group.

We all had to sing into a single microphone that was suspended from the ceiling. Someone gave it a nudge. We had to sway from side to side to sing into the mic. The girls kept on screaming.'

It worked for me.

A few weeks later, while waiting in the wings to play our skiffle set during the interval at a dance in the Brookeborough Hall, it struck me that we were a long way short of the talent displayed by the guys at school who could play traditional jazz. How do you possibly teach yourself to improvise and beat out the syncopated rhythms? And here I was – watching those guys doing just that. I was in awe.

Stepping aside for a welcome break was the Belmont Swing College – a jazz combo formed at Campbell College in 1954 with a line-up that included original members David Smith on bass, his brother Duggie on drums and Malcolm Gooding on trumpet. On the liquorice stick was a talented Annadale schoolboy called Trevor Foster.

And we were about to step onto that stage and sing with a tea-chest, a washboard, a ukulele and a banjo. Sturge had a proper guitar – and he was nowhere to be seen.

"Where the hell is Sturge?"

"Don't worry, he's coming." I could see him pushing his way to the front, holding a bloodied handkerchief to his nose.

"What happened to you?"

Sturge was tougher than most, but I noticed his eyes had watered. Whatever had happened, it was obviously sore. I followed the nod of his head and spotted an ugly Teddy Boy sporting a quiff and a duck's arse. He was standing, arms folded, in front of a framed picture of Winston Churchill.

"All I said was that your man over there had a face like a bull-dog..."

"Who?"

"Churchill," he mumbled. "And thon Ted with the duck's arse thought I was talking about him."

"You mean that Ted there? The one with a face like a bulldog?"

"It's not funny. I have to stop this nosebleed before we go on."

By Christmas 1957 we were performing regularly as The Sugarfoot Skifflers at church halls, community halls and tennis clubs across east Belfast – and it was going down well. We dropped pop songs into the skiffle set and the reaction was more than just rewarding. It was the girls. Stuff the skiffle. This was the way to go. Rock 'n' Roll is here to stay.

On Tuesday 28 January 1958 I bought a black arch-top acoustic Tuxedo jazz guitar. I bought it from a bloke who lived in a kitchen parlour house at the bottom of the Woodstock Road. I emptied my piggy bank and was well short of the £9.5s I needed to pay for it. I borrowed the rest. I didn't tell my Ma until a week later.

I smiled as I took off the headphones and explained to Michael how this particular song provoked fond memories. The Tremeloes liked background party noises and this recording of The Group playing it in The Pound captured that naturally. We always wanted to be at the parties we were playing at – preferring to play on the floor and mingling rather than be on a stage.

The Tremeloes hit 'Even the Bad Times Are Good' was released on 2 August 1967, reaching No 4 in the Charts. It was written by Peter Callander and Mitch Murray, a song writing team that penned many hits for British performers in the mid-sixties including the enduring Tony Christie number, 'Is This The Way To Amarillo.'

'Even the Bad Times Are Good' was the follow-up to The Tremeloes No 1 hit 'Silence is Golden.' The band had chalked up its first No 1 in 1963 as Brian Poole and The Tremeloes with a cover of the Motown dance record, 'Do You Love Me.' In 1966, when Brian Poole announced he was intent on pursuing a solo career, it was assumed by the music press that this was the end of the road for backing group.

The Tremeloes had other ideas. When asked at a press interview what made them think they could do without the charismatic frontman, the cheery riposte of drummer and vocalist Dave Munder was: "Well, we're bound to be able to find someone else to play a tambourine." He was right. In the event, Poole disappeared into obscurity while the backing group went on to enjoy three solid years of international hits.

Chapter 7

The Pound
Saturday 6 April 1968 – 14:55
Everybody Knows

The crowd is getting lively and I'm thinking we should move on fairly promptly.

"Here's one of Smick's favourites."

Smick knows right away what is coming – when we were learning it off last week Smick made it clear he thought it was cheese. He feigns a collapse over his kit and gives me the fingers. He sits up and calling upon a wide range of assorted hand and face gestures he makes it clear to the audience that he hates whatever is coming up.

I tell the punters: "Fred's going to sing it – big hand for Fred."

A girl at the front claps loudly. Does your heart good.

"What?" asks Fred, looking at me.

"The one you sing. You know. The new one. Dave Clark. Hurry up."

"How does it go again?"

"For fuck's sake, Fred."

Sez turns to Fred: "Key of E, Fred. Dead simple." Sez knows these things.

"OK, I got it."

Smick is getting a good laugh at this. Those seated at the front are also enjoying every minute of it. I have a fixed smile on my face.

"Just get on with it – Sez you lead." I hit the tape deck. The reels are revolving. "Three, four..."

"Wish," Fred sings gently, "I hadn't seen you walk away..."

1958 was the year of the Gilnahirk Sessions. Fred had by now joined the Sugarfoot Skifflers and we were making the transition from skiffle to pop. Our repertoire expanded as a result of regular sessions at Linden Lea, the Gilnahirk home of Brian Davison (Davison B R F; aka Onionhead).

Onionhead's first love was motor machines. He shared Roderick's passion for Royal Enfield motorbikes and spent most of his spare time in his brown overalls working at a bench taking things apart and putting them together again. He tore himself away for one thing only – to play the guitar in the comfort of his Mum's living room with a few friends. Onion had no interest in performing on stage – in fact he would run a mile to keep well out of range of anything equating to a spotlight.

It was at Gilnahirk that we taught ourselves to play Buddy Holly and the Everlys – not just their hits but more obscure stuff from the LPs. We dissected songs that involved relatively difficult chord play like 'Wake Up Little Susie' and 'Claudette' and made great progress.

We left every session on a high. On one celebrated occasion we became the talk of the school after Mike Shanks was lifted by the police for hands-free-wheeling down Gilnahirk Hill playing his Hofner guitar. He was taken to court and fined for riding a bicycle without due care and attention. The Magistrate's comments about a circus act, headlined in the County Down Spectator, were priceless.

Soon we realised the path to stardom, down which we must travel, meant amplification.

We spent time in Smithfield looking at spare parts and second hand components that could be assembled (by Onionhead in his workshop) into amplifiers, pick-ups etc. We never once entertained the thought of hire purchase.

In Joe Kavanagh's I Buy Anything shop, we bought a job lot of ex-RAF throat microphones. We tried using them for singing but they proved cumbersome and would tend to cause choking as well as a vocal sound like Alvin and the

Chipmunks crooning through a megaphone. We then experimented with the throat mics to see if they would work as pick-ups on the guitar. They did work, but not very well.

Another hare-brained scheme was that we could use the throat mics to build ourselves an electronic organ.

This wheeze involved strapping a throat mic to the underside of a brightly-coloured blow-organ – an early Melodica. It had a mouthpiece and one octave keyboard on top. You held it to your mouth, blew hard and it produced a passable organ sound.

Our idea was to lay it flat so it could be played as a keyboard instrument. We needed a constant supply of air of course, so we created a device that connected the mouthpiece of the child's toy to a hair dryer. It was an interesting experiment. The outcome was somewhat disappointing.

We invited Fred Isdell and his Michigan guitar to join the Sugarfoot Skifflers in 1958, just as it was becoming evident that the demand for skiffle was on the wane. He had views.

"We need a horn section," Fred announced. "That's the key. We have to be versatile. We have to be able to play all kinds of stuff. We need to be able to play saxophones and..." He searched the ceiling for inspiration. "...things." Fred proposed that Mike Shanks should get a clarinet, and he, Fred, would play the trombone.

I refused to get a trumpet.

"In that case we'll just have to headhunt guys from other bands to play with us. Who plays trumpet with Dave Glover?"

"Dave Glover, you eejit."

Roderick had acquired by now a respectable drum kit from Chas Rollins, and was taking lessons from Glover's highly experienced drummer, Ernie Hicks – acknowledged to be the best in the business at the time. Hicks helped put the word about that anyone interested in forming a new band would be welcome to come to the sessions in

Roderick's bedroom. We got a surprisingly positive response. We found there were plenty of musicians in the marching bands of east Belfast who were eager to give pop a blow.

George Galway, brother of international flute star Sir James Galway was among the first to weigh in. Here was a man who was set to become one of the best reed-men ever to have emerged from Belfast, playing with top showbands Clipper Carlton, the Melotones and the Witnesses.

He must have winced inwardly at our bum notes, and wondered what he was doing here with these 4-chord wonders; but he stayed until the end. We were in a different league altogether. George Galway was awesome – and tolerant.

Then there was a fine jazz guitar player called Brian McGarvey. Too good for us, and anyway it wasn't a guitar player we were looking for.

I remember one character who appeared unwilling or unable to sing or play any musical instrument; despite telling us he could do both. It transpired he was what he described as a 'showband taxi driver.' In that capacity he would be happy to spend the evening on the stage with the band, pretending to be playing the piano. He would be cheaper than a real musician, he explained, reminding us that Musicians' Union rules meant that bands in those days had to have a certain number of instrumentalists on the stage if they hoped to get paid.

And then there was a free-thinker called Ricky Hughes whose mission in life was to put on a Big Noise show in the Strand Cinema with a band comprising 1000 guitars. We figured one way it just might work would be to let the band use the auditorium and have the audience to stand in orderly ranks on the stage. One day it will happen in the West End.

But this recruitment programme wasn't working for us.

The Sugarfoot Skifflers, like all skiffle groups, had a short life. We soon evolved into a four piece pop group playing the hits of the day on a Saturday night in the tennis club. The Saturday Night Hop became the place to be. We expanded our repertoire of pop, augmented with a few standards. We needed a name and we needed to go electric.

Mike had some success building valve amplifiers in large wooden cases with massively heavy loudspeakers, and with Onionhead's help we soon all had hand-crafted solid electric guitars. We could now tackle guitar instrumentals such as 'Raunchy' (Bill Justis); Bert Weedon's 'Guitar Boogie Shuffle' and the Ventures 'Walk Don't Run.'

And what's more: we could play them standing up.

The first pop star I ever met in person was Emile Ford. It was in 1960. He was from Castries, St Lucia. While his music owes nothing to either Motown or the Mississippi Delta, it was good stuff in its day. He is mainly remembered in UK for his first big hit in 1959 – 'What Do You Want to Make Those Eyes at Me For?' It was an old song, dating from the middle of the First World War. My mother used to sing it to me when I was a kid. The dawn of the sixties saw Emile Ford take it to the top of the charts. It stayed there for six weeks. It was a smash hit.

With his record at No 1, he topped the bill of a pop concert in the ABC Cinema in downtown Belfast. It was the first pop concert I ever remember attending. The band in the first half actually interested me more – Rory Blackwell and the Blackjacks who had earned the accolade of being the first British rock and roll band.

Their act was pure slap-bass Rock 'n' Roll. These guys had been around a while. They knew how to how to put on a show with a performance that was utterly over the top. The double bass player climbed up and somehow managed to perch on top of his instrument while he continued to play it. Others in the line-up rolled about the stage like acrobats; all the while wielding guitars and blowing saxophones. The high point came when there was an unrehearsed clash of heads. It brought a gasp from the audience and left two blokes with blood running down their faces; down their shiny suits, and on to the stage. The band played on, finishing the set. They got a massive cheer from the audience as they limped off.

But it was Emile Ford and the Checkmates we came to see and they were the ones who got the screams. We were in the circle knowing we had been invited to meet Emile at a party in Kincora Avenue after the show.

Roderick's neighbour across the street was Dr Domingo Emmanuel. Dr Emmanuel at the time had the largest medical practice in the north, operating from a surgery in Ravenscroft Avenue where he – catholic and black – served the entire protestant shipyard community of inner east Belfast.

Dr Emmanuel was a well-known and much respected doctor. He was possibly the only black man in Ulster in 1960. If you were black and had a gig in Belfast, the first contact you would make on arrival on these shores was Dr Domingo Emmanuel. He entertained Paul Robeson at his home in east Belfast – and that great exponent of honky-tonk and ragtime, Winifred Atwell, played boogie on his piano by the window in the living room.

Emile and the Checkmates arrived and there were handshakes all round. The party swung into action and I got chatting to the star himself, who was relaxed and smiling until someone asked him to play the piano.

Emile Ford had talent. He had taught himself to play a number of musical instruments. But like all emerging stars of his day, he was just a pop singer, and I had a hunch he played the piano about as well as I did. He certainly wasn't Winifred Atwell. This was an awkward situation. I knew exactly the problem he faced. In a crowded living room with loud chat and drink-fuelled frivolity, he needed a microphone.

"Come on, man – let's have "That Lucky Old Sun." Everyone at the party had been in the theatre when his freshly-released follow-up single had gone down a storm. I could feel his discomfort. Of all songs, please not that one. He wasn't Paul Robeson either.

The clamour for him to perform increased as someone wrenched off the front panel of the upright piano to expose the mechanism and make it louder for the benefit of everyone in the crowded living room. Emile was manhandled onto the stool despite his protest. Like it or not he was going to have to sing for his supper. He placed his hands with hesitation on the keyboard and, clearly wishing he had never agreed to weigh in to this party, vamped out the chord of C. The piano jangled loud but the room fell silent as everyone strained to hear the great man sing.

His lips moved.

It gave the appearance that he might have commenced a song. But nobody could be sure. Was he singing his chart-topping hit? Or was it the new one? Over the raw sound from the exposed hammer action of a metal-framed bar-room piano, the voice of the star guest was completely inaudible. Soon the room once again filled with loud conversation and laughter.

I learnt something from that. Never let anyone persuade you to sing without a mic.

We thought long and hard about the transition from skiffle to pop, and agonised over a name for our proposed group.

I mentioned this to my school friend John McGuffin. We were at a crucial point in a game of table soccer at the time and I hoped a question like this would distract him.

"We're thinking of 'The Dominoes' as the name for the band. What do you think?"

If we weren't in class or playing football, McGuffin and I would while away many happy hours playing Newfooty on a green baize cloth 'pitch' freshly ironed on smooth surface table. We were on the top floor of his impressive family home in Sandown Road. We regarded Newfooty as superior to Subbuteo.

McGuffin's fingers were resting gently on the flat-ironed baize, lining up for a flick that he seemed confident will put Manchester United ahead.

He snorted. "The Dominoes? That's passé, man." I had no idea what that word meant.

"What are you saying?"

"It's played out. Old hat. The world has moved on. You have to get ahead of the game."

I was sorry I asked. I should have known it would elicit some smart-assed retort. What would he know about it anyway, I thought as I leant down to make sure Jack Kelsey didn't let this one past.

McGuffin was an enigmatic character with what I reckoned had to be deep intellect. He had a general air of contempt for everyone and everything – except Manchester United. He had no interest whatever in the fortunes of the Dominoes. We were poles apart in many ways, but somehow we put up with one another. We kicked ball together. Neither of us were any use at the actual kicking bit, but we were passionate about First Division football.

I have been an Arsenal fan since I was nine when Arsenal topped the League in 1952/53. As a teenager I was an active member of the Arsenal Football Supporters' Club. I appointed myself as the Arsenal scout for Northern Ireland. I had surprisingly candid and quite lengthy correspondence with manager George Swindin who appeared to value my opinion about local talent – presumably not realising I was just a kid.

McGuffin and I were members of an activist group of day boys at Campbell College who preferred soccer to rugby. Oscar Wilde is credited with the remark that rugby football is a hooligans' game played by gentlemen, while association football is a gentleman's game played by hooligans. We decided we had the right to be hooligans and aligned with an expanding bunch of soccer rebels. The ring-leader was Gordon Burns, who went on to become a celebrated journalist and broadcaster, best known as the host of Granada Television's long-running game show The Krypton Factor.

We were not encouraged to play on the Campbell rugby fields which left us all a bit peeved. We were cheered, however, when Burns somehow secured permission to use the hockey pitches belonging to the local girls' school – Strathearn. We initially had just two 'clubs' – the Belmont Rovers and Knock Albion. Other clubs were formed and soon we were playing in our very own league and travelling to play matches throughout Belfast and North Down.

There was always difficulty making up numbers for a full team so McGuffin and I would usually compete for the left wing position where we could do little harm by keeping out of the way. I retired from the game after I scored three goals in one match at the Boneyard to win the league for the Belmont Rovers. I was the hero of the hour, celebrated especially because each goal was the result of an embarrassing miscue where the ball unexpectedly ended up the net.

Flick!

McGuffin grunts with satisfaction. Manchester United 1: Arsenal 0.

"Well OK, what would you suggest? For the name of the band?"

"Spendlove Murphy," said McGuffin, glancing briefly at the ceiling. "Yes, that's it: Spendlove Murphy."

I took this back the guys. "Spendlove Murphy?" They laughed it off as ridiculous. I joined in. We all agreed that was just typical McGuffin. Load of nonsense.

But thinking about it now...

Michael puts down the cans and asks me if I really want to keep this one.

"It is really just because Fred sang it," I explain.

"OK," says Michael. "That's good enough for me."

'Everybody Knows' was written by Les Reid and Barry Mason and recorded by the Dave Clark Five. It entered the UK charts on 1 November 1967 and remained there for 14 weeks, peaking at No 2. The interesting fact here is that the Dave Clark Five hold the rare distinction of having chart success with two entirely different songs that have the same title. 'Everybody Knows' from 1965 has no connection whatsoever to this pleasant, if cheesy, 'Everybody Knows,' written and recorded in 1967. Good pub quiz question that.

It was also unusual in that that the singer was lead guitar player Lenny Davidson who rarely took on a vocal role. In The Group, bass-player Fred also rarely took lead vocal, which is a great pity. His character comes through in his singing voice.

Chapter 8

The Pound
Saturday 6 April 1968 – 15:05
God Only Knows

"'God Only Knows,' guys."

The guys aren't interested. Fred is tuning up. Sez is adjusting his fuzzbox. A girl in a short, tight white miniskirt has come round to have a word with Smick. He appears to be having some success in the chat-up stakes. She giggles and turns away.

"Who was that?"

"Don't know," he says, "but she bought me a drink."

"She seemed to like your technique – what did you say to her?"

"Thighs very much."

We all laugh – it is one of Smick's favourite lines. Never fails.

The Dominoes emerged in the summer of 1959. Roderick and I decided to leave school and seek employment, while Mike and Fred stayed at Campbell College for a further year to do A-Levels with university in mind. We had all just turned seventeen.

We continued to have sessions in Roderick's draughty bedroom in his semi-detached Victorian family home in Kincora Avenue.

As the only child of a widowed mother who had made many sacrifices in order to fund my college education, it was time to consider a career. I had displayed little academic prowess at school and was considered to be interested only in drawing. I was pointed in the direction of architectural apprenticeship at the age of sixteen.

Roderick, who had skill and aptitude for technical engineering, was at the same time encouraged to take up an opportunity to gain work experience in the shipyard, where the fit-out of the Canberra was at an advanced stage. He started the day after the Twelfth fortnight and was shown round the drawing office by a man in a bowler hat who introduced him to each of the workers using the same phrase: "This is Roderick. He drums."

None of them looked up. Nobody spoke. Only when he was finally shown to an empty seat at a drawing board did anyone acknowledge his presence. A burly man occupying the adjacent chair was clearly going to have something to say. Waiting until the man in the bowler hat had walked away, he spoke without raising his head:

"Drums eh? Were you walkin'?"

"No, I came here on my bike."

The lengthy silence that followed Roderick's response was eventually broken with another question: "How old is your granny?"

Roderick was bewildered: "Er, my granny?" A further silence eventually broken by a voice from the other side of the workshop:

"Not one of us, then."

Roderick later learnt the 'granny' question was shipyard code to establish that he was in an Orange Lodge and thus protestant. The man in the bowler told him not to worry. Flute bands were always on the hunt for drummers. He will be walking on the Twelfth next year.

It was inevitable that we would face competition from younger guys, and sure enough, word got out that another Campbell College band had been formed. And they were pretty good. Dickson, A M played a mighty impressive flamenco tune on a Spanish Guitar in a school concert. I thought to myself I hope he sticks to flamenco. My hopes were dashed when I saw his band perform at a dance in Shandon Park Golf Club. They lined up like the Shadows.

Andy Dickson was playing lead just as I feared. He was good. I recognised McHugh, J E on bass, Who was on drums I am not sure, but it may have been Victor Catling (later to play with Brian Rossi and Wheels). Playing rhythm guitar was Adamson M S, the younger brother of my classmate Rusty. They had good gear; Dickson had a Watkins amplifier which produced a great tone. I wanted that amp. He also had a Watkins Copicat Echo Chamber that made his guitar-picking sound like Hank Marvin. I wanted that as well.

Esmonde McHugh's bass guitar produced a very distinctive bass thump as a result of using an electromagnetic device that had likely seen parade ground service in the Second World War. The speaker itself had to be plugged directly into the mains in order that current would flow through a coil to induce the magnetism that would make it work.

Michael Adamson, the one we would soon be calling Sez, was playing a red Futurama guitar. I detected he was just a tad discontented with the second fiddle role of rhythm guitar. But they were very polished. They played the Shadows flawlessly and they could do the walk.

It was around this time that Sez Adamson got the handle which will stay with him for ever. If you were at all familiar with the Campbell College urinals, you might know they carry the trade mark of one of Britain's oldest designers and manufacturers of bathroom products: "Adamsez." It was great publicity for the budding guitarist. Every time you went for a pee you would emerge thinking of Sez the guitar player.

But it was clear that the Shadows were the way forward. And it was not just a case of standing up and playing 'FBI' – we had to do steps and the guitar gestures. Most of all, however, we had to be at least as good as Dickson and his upstarts.

By 1960, The Dominoes had made their mark in the tennis clubs, church socials and the unionist halls of east Belfast. It was time to move into the big time. It could have happened on Saturday 5 March 1960.

We had come to a decision. We would make our mark by representing Belfast in BBC TV's Top Town – a knock-out talent competition that guaranteed fame and fortune for the town team that made it to the grand final in the autumn.

'TOP TOWN' B.B.C. T.V.
March 1960

DEAR SIR/MADAM
REFERENCE *No 46*
ON BEHALF OF THE COMMITTEE I THANK YOU FOR YOUR APPLICATION FOR A PRELIMINARY AUDITION.
PLEASE ATTEND THE EMPIRE THEATRE ON *Saturday 5th March, 10:30am*

If required bring your own props. And Music (Piano Copy)
Singers, Musical Groups, Bands, Solo Instrumentalists, Choirs etc. are invited to present **ONE NUMBER ONLY** *(of their own choice)*
The task of the Committee is to select a balanced programme of 16/18 minute duration.
Should you not be selected to go forward it does not reflect on your talent, but is dictated by the limited requirement of the Programme. Selected entries will be invited **BY POST** *to attend B.B.C. later this month.*

Yours sincerely,
GAYE WATTERS,
(Secretary "TOP TOWN" Committee)
GRAND OPERA HOUSE

"You mean we have to audition for this?" The letter had come as a bit of a surprise.

There were just four of us in the band at this time. We didn't have much in the way of equipment, but we had certainly moved beyond pure acoustic skiffle. And we did have our own secret weapon – an electronic genius called Charlie Fay who had been giving us the benefit of his personal sound system. He said that, provided he could come along, he would lend us his makeshift PA – complete with microphone and stand. Charlie loved nothing more than wiring things together and finding spare parts for army surplus amplifiers.

We had decided our version of Marty Wilde's current hit 'Bad Boy' was pretty damn good and should do the trick.

It was past 10:30 and things were running late. We were told that television presenter Peter West was in the theatre. Could we go on at 11:30 after the Irish dancing troupe and the prancing dog? It shouldn't be long we were assured – although the hula-hoop girls might have to go on ahead of us. They had to get back to school. But Peter West had said he definitely wants to hear us.

We observed the acts from the wings. Well, everything on the stage that is. We witnessed the dog depart from its script by lifting its leg at a critical moment, an act of spontaneity that was warmly applauded by an appreciative audience – presumably made up of mums and dads belonging to the hula-hoopers.

We explained to an anxious bloke with glasses and a clipboard, who was constantly referring to his wrist watch, that we would need a moment or two to get set up. Could we have the curtain pulled? Yes – and yes, Peter West was still in the building.

The hula-hoop girls each had five hoops going at one time and didn't seem to know how to stop. I glanced at my own watch. It was now 12:30pm. Suddenly it was our turn.

We help Roderick bring his drums one at a time onto a small podium at the back of the stage. A cymbal falls over with a crash. He erects the kit – bass drum, tom-tom, hi-hat. The cymbal falls over a second time. And a third. It's looking like this is going to take more than a moment or two.

We put the amps on the floor and searched for a power socket which is eventually found half way up a wall way beyond the wings.

The mains power cable did not reach far enough. Nowhere near far enough. Charlie was breaking out into a sweat.

Fred, Mike and I decided we had no option but to herd ourselves close together at the edge of the stage within reach of the mains cable, leaving Roderick and his drums perched on the podium, remote from the rest of us, in the centre of the vast stage. We also concluded that one of us at least might be unseen behind the curtain when it is drawn back.

We considered various alternatives including standing one behind the other. Roderick was no help whatsoever. Eventually we settled for Plan A. Mike volunteers to play outside left. Left outside would be a more accurate description. Not ideal.

Charlie had a theory that to in order avoid the unprofessional electronic clunk of jack plugs being inserted, we should wait until everything is wired up before we switch on the mains. Made sense. I stood by the wall socket and, on cue from Charlie, switched it on.

An electronic buzz filled the air, lasting until Charlie had wrenched out every last jack plug.

He put them back in one at a time – clunk; clunk; clunk; looking good; BUZZZZ. That's the one. Out with the soldering iron.

Meantime Mike and I have discovered that our guitars are seriously out of tune. While we are tuning up, Fred was recklessly pounding his fist down on his cornflake packet trying in vain to get rid of an unhelpful intermittent hum. "Charlie – can you do anything about this?"

Charlie didn't want to know. He had repaired the jack plug and was now crouched over his PA amp. He had the casing removed and orange-glowing valves are exposed. Wires seem to be extending to every corner of the stage. He was on the verge of a nervous breakdown.

Finally we decided we were ready to go. We looked around for someone in charge.

The man with clipboard had disappeared so we figured it was up to us to pull back the curtains. Charlie was confident he could handle it, as well as turning out the lights in the auditorium.

The lights dimmed and Charlie drew the curtain back as we played the familiar guitar intro. And I launched in with the vocal in my by now perfected Marty Wilde singing voice.

It was the first time we had performed in a theatre. Despite the distraction of a PA speaker falling off the stage into the orchestra pit in the middle of the second verse, it sounded bloody good.

We even executed a flawless fade-out ending. Charlie brought up the main theatre lights. We could now see that there was in fact an audience in the theatre – the fully uniformed Templemore Avenue Silver Band. They were due on at 2:00pm. It was now a quarter past two. They were the only folk in the theatre. Peter West had gone back to London. Someone decided before lunch that we wouldn't make the cut.

I had started work as an architectural apprentice with T T Houston and Partners a few months before, and it was there that I met Elmer Gray. The office was in College Gardens not far from where Elmer lived with his folks in Malone Avenue. He was a loveable character with the appearance of a well-dressed, slightly portly teddy boy. He had a penchant for studio photography and portraits of young ladies sitting on couches. He lightened every conversation with Goon Show inspired one-liners, followed promptly by a farting noise or a throat clearance that was pure Secombe. Elmer worshipped anything that was born in the USA. He was devoted to the architecture of Frank Lloyd Wright and the music of Elvis Presley – and he was a big fan of Eddie Cochran. He was proud to show people a photograph showing him wielding his white semi-acoustic electric guitar, and looking chubby in a black cowboy hat, pale blue jeans, a check shirt and boots.

After the Top Town debacle, I had an idea. I decided I would introduce Elmer to the boys in the band. They instantly warmed to him. We invited him along for a session in Roderick's bedroom. He couldn't play the guitar very well but he had good taste in music and could sing. With his guitar swinging loose around his neck; his legs apart and his right hand clutching a knuckle microphone on an upright stand pulled to one side, Elmer could do a fair vocal impression of both Elvis and Eddie at the same time.

We were able to call upon abundant material from the early rock and roll LPs featuring Elvis, Eddie and Gene Vincent.

We decide to launch ourselves as Elmer and the Dominoes. Well, in truth it began with the idea that we should call ourselves Fats and the Dominoes. The germ of that particular brainwave is fairly obvious and none too creative. Elmer was a little rotund.

Elmer quickly rose to the role of front man and got us a few gigs in church halls in south Belfast. It didn't take long to realise that to give the name Fats to a guy whose real name was as cool as Elmer, was plain stupid.

I have preserved an early bedroom tape recording of Elmer singing Elvis's 'Baby Let's Play House.' We loved that sort of stuff. But I also have a recording of Elmer singing 'Wild in the Country.' Only Elmer liked Elvis doing this kind of romantic movie-theme guff.

We had our differences, and in the first of what I am beginning to realise was a pattern of repeated back-stabbing, we decided after about a year that Elmer had to go. We hatched a plan to pack it in and go our separate ways. Within a few months we had resurrected the Dominoes comprising Roderick Downer on drums, Fred Isdell on bass, Mike Shanks on rhythm guitar – and me in the role of a would-be Hank Marvin. We learnt the Shadows walk. We got a lot of gigs. Without Elmer.

'God Only Knows' was a 1966 song by the Beach Boys, with Carl Wilson on lead vocal. It was written by Brian Wilson and Tony Asher and first heard on the classic Pet Sounds album. When released as a single, it was in the British charts for fourteen weeks, reaching No 2. George Martin cites 'God Only Knows' as one of his favourite songs of all time – technically brilliant in its arrangements, use of instruments and production. Mojo Magazine ranks 'God Only Knows' the 13th greatest song of all time.

It was one of the first commercial songs to use the word 'God' in its title, a decision that Wilson and Asher agonized over, fearing it would not get airplay as a result. Wilson also worried about Asher's opening line: "I may not always love you." It was certainly an unusual way to start a love song.

The Group chose to include 'God Only Knows' in its first ever set list. I remember rehearsing it in Fred's home at Seapark in Holywood and being knocked out not only by the way the harmonies came together, but also because we really didn't have a lot of difficulty with it.

Chapter 9

Anyone for Tennis?

On Saturday 9 April 1960, a few days after the Top Town audition, I was on the terraces at Highbury in London watching my team, Arsenal, getting destroyed 4-1 by Chelsea. I was with my friend John McGuffin. We travelled across by the Liverpool ferry and bus to London to stay a week with my Aunt Dorrie who lived in Chelsea. McGuffin was a passionate Manchester United fan. He was delighted with the outcome. I was distraught.

There was much rejoicing and associated banter (he always came out on top), but it lasted only until the following Friday when we watched West Ham defy the bookies' odds by defeating the mighty Manchester United at Upton Park by two goals to one. I cheered until I was hoarse.

It was actually the better match. We stood to one side of the goal at the very front of a packed terrace so close to the netting it was almost within reach. To this day I remember a moment of horror as a 90 mph rocket from Bobby Charlton, from some distance out, missed the upright and then my head by inches. I can still see the heavy leather ball in slow motion getting larger and larger until it filled my field of vision.

But the highlight for me on this visit to London was the consequence of spotting a fly poster as I left Highbury. It was a yellow notice advertising that Eddie Cochran, Gene Vincent and Billy Fury were due to appear in the Empire in nearby Finsbury Park the following Monday. These were guys who appeared on ITV – on Jack Good's Boy Meets Girl – an early evening Saturday night pop show that I watched avidly every week.

"We can't miss that," I said.

"You can go to it on your own, mate" said McGuffin who had no interest in popular music. "I'm off to a strip club."

He missed a great show – not that he cared a toss. He seemed very cheery the next morning.

We were back on the bus two days after the West Ham game, heading for home, when McGuffin picked up a late news item that an American musician had been killed in a car crash. It was Easter Sunday. By the time we got to the next stop I was able to acquire a later edition that carried the full story. At 10:30pm the previous night, the stars of the show I had seen just seven days before had climbed into a taxi which sped off in the direction of London. At 11:00pm on Saturday 16 April 1960 – at a notorious accident black-spot in Wiltshire – the car hit a lamppost. Gene Vincent survived with injuries. Eddie Cochran lay dying by the roadside. He was 22.

I was devastated at the death of Eddie Cochran. It was, after all, quite by chance that a week before his death I found myself, all on my own, at the Finsbury Park Empire that night at Easter 1960. I felt that somehow it was meant to be.

After his death, I looked out for every news item about the accident and tuned in to a repeat of his last performance on Boy Meets Girl, which featured not only Eddie but my other rock hero, the mean leather-clad rocker Gene Vincent. I studied the shimmering black and white images on the small screen absorbing every detail my teenage brain could take in. Billy Fury was also on the show, along with a tall, awkward-looking cockney bloke with crew cut fair hair. I took note of his name because he seemed to be pretty hot on the guitar. It was Joe Brown.

Cochran had arrived in Britain in January that year to join the Gene Vincent tour that Larry Parnes already had on the road. The impresario, known affectionately in the business as 'parnes, shillins and pence,' had called upon his full stable of UK Rock 'n' Rollers – Billy Fury, Georgie Fame, Vince Eager, Johnny Gentle etc, to rotate support for the American stars. Joe Brown featured regularly on the tour – not just as a backing musician but also as a support act in his own right. He was the only one in the stable to retain his own name.

I read all I could about Joe Brown in Melody Maker and the New Musical Express (NME) to discover how he had developed his playing style. It seemed it was based on what he picked up from Eddie Cochran on this tour. He would evidently sit with Cochran at every opportunity to learn his guitar licks. In words later immortalised by Heinz, Joe taught himself to play "just like Eddie."

I got into this big time.

I have to confess I was never much good at lead guitar. I struggled to figure out note for note exactly what Hank Marvin would play in the Shadows hits. I could do that, but the pure echo-laden sound produced by the Stratocaster/Vox was always a bit too wholesome for me. The clean cut image and the synchronised steps soon became an embarrassment. I yearned for a sound that was cool and would mask the occasional bum note. I had a hunch Joe Brown was into this too and that this was where I would find what I was looking for.

I bought Billy Fury's debut LP 'The Sound of Fury.' I played it over and over again. Fury wrote all the songs and Joe Brown played (just like Eddie) on every track. I loved it.

Of course I could never play guitar like Joe Brown, but I did learn a few licks that were worth knowing – and I was happy to think they all stemmed from Cochran.

One Saturday night in the summer of 1960 a small group of tennis players were sitting in an empty clubhouse bar wrestling with the question of how to raise the funds necessary for the club to survive a financial crisis. They concluded the answer was girls, a bar, and dancing to live music. It may seem an obvious solution, but at the time, for a variety of reasons, there were very few places the in-crowd could go in Belfast on a Saturday night that offered entertainment with a bar that remained open after the pubs closed at 10:00pm.

The Belfast Boat Club Saturday night hop would run for the full decade. The original Victorian wooden clubhouse was unaltered from the 1880s. It started life as a rowing club. The was an element of adventure about the Boat Club which was attractive to the new Saturday night crowd – to get to the clubhouse and grounds it was necessary to be ferried across the old Lagan Canal from the Lockview Road.

The idea of a regular Saturday night dance was driven forward by a young man called Adrian Jennions. His rules were simple: no girl gets turned away, drunk or sober; drunk males were not allowed in (it was OK to get drunk at the club bar, of course); entrance had to be through the front door and not the Ladies' toilet window – which despite the rule remained a reliable means of avoiding having to queue to get in. Or indeed having to pay. Jennions and his cohorts hired Elmer and The Dominoes and heroically paid the band out of their own pockets for the first few weeks.

Before long, the Boat Club became the favoured watering hole for students at nearby Queen's University and Stranmillis Teacher Training College. On a Saturday night, queues would build up outside the door of the clubhouse and down the wooden steps; while across the canal in Lockview Road another orderly queue would form waiting to clamber aboard the punt that would take them across the canal.

The canal had been out of commission since 1958, but it remained ponded for many years after. The only way to get to the club in the early days was to queue up and wait to climb aboard an unstable flat-bottomed punt that would cross the canal. The first aboard would be thrown precariously from side to side as those following leapt on board behind them. The task of manhandling the punt across the canal involved tugging and heaving a wet, slippery rope that was connected to the bank on the far side. A good yank on the rope was all it took to increase the hazard for latecomers clambering aboard.

On a moonlit summer night this was romantic. On a rainy night it was horrible. On a windy night it was downright dangerous. But it was warm that night in late summer 1961 when we played in the open air beneath the balcony and staircase on the concrete slip in front of the clubhouse facing the canal. It had been one hell of a party. We laughed as beer splashed down on the band from the balcony above. Trays, awash from teetering pints, had all night been carried recklessly down the steps. We cheered every time a pint was snatched off a tray by a thirsty individual heading up the stairs to the bar. Cookstown sausages sizzled on the barbecue throughout the night and strategically positioned lights cast shadows on the way of the crowd jiving on the slipway.

To add to the fun, we had been told by Adrian Jennions to look out for a punt bringing surprise guests to join the party. Word quickly spread that The Temperance Seven would be guests at the party. The highly entertaining 1920s-style jazz band was at the time at the height of its popularity with 'You're Driving Me Crazy' and 'Pasadena.' They had been performing in the Ulster Hall.

"That's them, isn't it?" guessed Mike, peering into the dark and pointing.

There was no doubt about it. Here were the eagerly awaited guests. The arrival of an ordered formation of smartly dressed gents, standing bolt upright in the punt, was theatrical. It smacked of show business.

Roderick launched into the roll on the drums that was normally reserved for the National Anthem. Attention focused on the gents as they step off the punt. The dancers gravitate to the landing stage. I'm at the mic: "Ladies and gentlemen, will you give a big hand for... The Temperance Seven!"

It wasn't them at all.

A while later we were informed that two of the Temperance Seven were already up in the bar, having arrived unannounced. The man with the megaphone, Whispering Paul McDowell, was there with another member of the band. There was nothing remotely temperance about either of them. Adrian came up to me and told me that he had found a megaphone in the boat store.

"Let's get them up," he said "Do you do any of their stuff?"

The answer was obvious – we are not a bloody jazz band. But we decide to fire up a 1920s song my mother used to sing – one that I thought crooner 'Whispering' Paul McDowell would probably know. In fact it really ought to have been his signature tune – it is called 'Whispering.'

Whispering Paul, clearly relieved we were not going to murder their No 1 hit, accepted the megaphone from Adrian and strode towards us, dragging his chum who immediately headed for the drum kit.

Roderick leapt to his feet and handed his sticks to the percussionist, Brian Innes. By the end of the first instrumental verse the Temperance Two won over hearts and minds by hamming it up with the Boat Club's resident duffers – The Dominoes. We were chuffed. The crowd was delighted.

Crooning Paul McDowell and Innes, the Goon-loving comic drummer who was also known as Professor Emeritus, were founding members of the nine-piece Temperance Seven. 'You're Driving Me Crazy,' composed by Walter Donaldson in 1930, was a standard recorded by over 100 artists including Billie Holiday and Frank Sinatra. The Temperance Seven recording was produced by George Martin and became the best-selling No 1 hit of 1961, entering the charts in March 1961 and remaining there for 16 weeks. The follow-up record, 'Pasadena' entered the charts in June 1961. The Temperance Seven were at the top of their game when they made this cameo appearance at the Belfast Boat Club with the Dominoes in August that year.

....

What the hell is wrong with me?

Something isn't right. It is hard to describe exactly, but I feel – well – I feel awkward. Not stiff or weak: just awkward. I am a tall guy and I tend to stoop, but now I feel even more gawky than usual. Compared to everyone else I see walking down the street, my movements seem to have lost rhythm and flow.

Is this the consequence of swine flu? Did I have swine flu? No-one seems to know for sure.

People think I am speaking quietly and conspiratorially when the truth is I am struggling to project my voice. It sounds okay to me, but from the other side of a table people look blankly at me and then look away. It is as if they are uncertain whether I am speaking at all.

I have had speech therapy but I don't really think that is the answer.

Chapter 10

The Pound
Saturday 6 April 1968 – 15:20
I Can't Make It

That could have been worse, I am thinking as I flick off the tape recorder, noting the enthusiastic applause for 'God Only Knows' from a bloke at the front. Next up is a song by the Small Faces.

I sit back, overcome by the smattering of applause. It doesn't take much. All it needs is a little endorsement and everybody feels good. I reach out for my pint and then remember to stop the reel-to-reel.

No point in rushing this. I spin round my stool and chat with Smick. Fred is on what to the rest of us often seems like a fruitless mission to get his bass in tune. Sez is restive and twiddling again.

Our management team, Peter Dalton and Ronnie Field, is here today. They have been looking after The Group since we made the big break from the Dominoes in 1966. Fair play to Peter, all the same. He was the one who brought rock and roll to The Pound.

But he is not celebrated for that. Peter earned respect and a degree of notoriety by winning outright the challenging 'Yard of Ale' competition in The Pound a few months ago. I point at him as he takes his seat, pint of Guinness in hand. He lifts it high. The crowd roars.

As I swivel round in my stool to operate the controls of the Grundig, I am remembering the occasion when I partied with Steve Marriott and his cockney mates. It was last year; in the Elsinore Hotel – that intimate gin palace on the Antrim Road favoured by the promoters, presumably because it is cheap. I love it when I get the chance to talk to rock heroes. I sidled over when I thought the moment was right and stooped for a chat with the man of the hour. Marriott looked up and opened the conversation.

"Goad o-migh'y, you're a big geezer."

I glanced across and smiled at a group of girls I thought would be impressed at me having a one-to-one conversation with the bloke who wrote and sang 'Itchycoo Park.'

"So how was the Floral Hall?" I asked the man of the hour as I tore my eyes away from the girls.

I was talking to myself. Marriott was no longer standing beside me. He had scarpered. Just like that. Eventually I spotted him sitting at a table in the safe company of the other members of his group.

Actually I think they might all have been standing up.

When Dick joined the band, The Dominoes once again became a five-piece group. He was a real musician with a passion for the works of American jazz saxophonist, Charlie Parker. With a saxophone in the line-up, the repertoire of The Dominoes was extended into a healthy mix of jazz and pop.

Dick was hard to stop when he had the reed between his teeth. I remember on one occasion at the Boat Club we were giving it all. It was a Cannonball Adderley instrumental called 'Sack Of Woe' as I recall. I spotted Raymond Duncan, a senior stalwart of the Boat Club, elegantly fox-trotting his way through the shaking and twisting crowd, only to stop in front of Dick, who was blowing his heart out in an extended solo. Dick rose to the special attention he was getting. At that moment he was Charlie Parker. He clearly felt the appreciation should be rewarded with a further rousing 12-bar solo.

I had a different take on it. I had had enough Charlie Parker for now. The extended sax solo in this particular number had gone on far too long. I could see the punters were ready for the Stones. I figured Raymond was standing there hoping Charlie Parker would put a sock in it.

Sometimes you can predict things with uncanny accuracy. With a flourish, Raymond produced from his jacket pocket a mud-caked rugby sock, which he waved about and then stuffed into the horn of the saxophone. It brought the house down.

We were soon playing more frequently, and reaching further afield. We secured a residency in the Willowfield Unionist Hall on the Woodstock Road, playing every Thursday from 8 to 11pm for what we reckoned was a pretty good fee of £7. 0s. 0d. We thought we were doing the job pretty well until one day we got a bit of a gunk. We were politely told the residency had been offered to another band called The Monarchs.

Word filtered through that they were good, so we decided to go see them play.

These guys had gear. Clearly hire purchase had come to town, for they were loud. I took some satisfaction from the fact that they played what I reckoned was a bum chord in 'Man of Mystery.' But there was precious little else from which to draw comfort. The Monarchs were good. The punters loved it. They were better than we were.

By 1962 we had left The Shadows behind. Happily that meant we also left behind any opportunity to be compared unfavourably with other echo chamber guitar bands.

We faced competition. Not only had The Monarchs ousted us from Willowfield; they were picking up our gigs in the Brookeborough Hall and the Belmont Tennis Club.

In fact, most bands playing in Belfast in the period from 1962-64 were showbands or groups making out to be showbands. Even The Monarchs would soon pack in the group scene and head out on the road as the Manhattan Showband, with Geordie Sproule and the young Van Morrison.

But we didn't think the showband idea was cool. That stuff just did not appeal to us at all. And anyway we reckoned we had a bit of a following on account of the stuff we did do. The Dominoes in this period didn't play in the dance halls of downtown Belfast. In fact we didn't go to dance halls as punters either. The one exception to this was that we would on occasion pay 6d to get into the Plaza to size up the talent at the lunchtime record sessions where Dino Martin was resident DJ.

We played mainly suburban clubs and halls, including the Flying Club in Newtownards and The Barn at Upper Dunmurry Lane. My architectural connections brought gigs from student bodies at the College of Art; and fund-raising events run by the Architectural Group.

In 1962, after completing three years as an apprentice and starting my post-intermediate course, the School of Architecture moved to an old school building in Durham Street just round the corner from the Seamen's Mission – also known as the Maritime.

We were all a bit dismayed to have been shifted away from the top floor of the Tech where we had previously mingled with the trendy art students. The art students were mainly female, who while often a bit eccentric, turned out to be dynamic, open and fun-loving. The best lookers were the dress designers. You could tell them a mile off – they strode along the streets with a grace that would turn heads.

We walked the length of College Square North four times a day to our favourite haunt where we would congregate – The Coffee House on the corner of Queen Street.

We didn't realise it at the time, but in 1962 College Street was becoming the 'in' part of Belfast – the streets were filling up with eye-catching people with a penchant for style, smart clothes and a yearning for an urban beat scene that would give local expression to rock, modern jazz and rhythm and blues emanating from London. If it was going to happen anywhere, it would happen, as in other cities, in and around the Art College. Belfast proved to be no exception. The Art College was where it was at. And I was privileged to be there.

It was during my first week at the Art College in September 1962 that I learned of a group who were home in Liverpool after spending two years in Hamburg. They called themselves the Beatles.

I remember the first time I heard them on the radio. It was January 1963. I was working on a drawing board in the old converted schoolhouse in Durham Street. Niall McCutcheon, perched over his board, said without looking up: "That's the Beatles. That's the sort of stuff the Dominoes should be playing."

It was 'Please Please Me.'

"A bit rough," I declared. "I can't see those guys making it big."

A few months later, on Friday 8 November 1963, I would find myself being swept along by thousands of fans surging down Wellington Place hoping to get a glimpse of the Beatles. Rumour was they had been transported secretly from the Ritz Cinema (I had failed to get a ticket) back to their hotel. The Grand Central Hotel in Royal Avenue was where we all believed (wrongly) they were staying.

By the following summer the Beatles had under their belt no less than four No 1 hits. They were the biggest stars on the planet and I was in America talking with a Liverpool accent – milking it for all it was worth – but that's another story.

On Friday 22 November 1963 I approached Chris Doran about joining the Dominoes.

They say anyone who remembers the assassination of President Kennedy will never forget what they were doing when the news was breaking. I certainly remember where I was that night.

I was at the Royal Society of Ulster Architects annual formal in Conway Hotel, Dunmurry. I had plucked up a lot of courage to invite the stunning Diane Dancklefsen to accompany me that night.

Both Chris and Diane were in the year behind me – alongside a number of other talented and entertaining people. Among them were Trevor Kelly, Plum Tyndall, Gerry Hall, Frank Hynds, Gerry O'Connor, Seamus Filor, Ken Martin and Mike Wylie. Diane was one of the few females in the School of Architecture.

Chris was at the table with his future wife Maureen. I knew Chris well, of course. Chris played piano and he also played drums. He was connected. He had been schooled at Methody along with showband legends Keith Donald and Davy McKnight, drummer with the Freshmen. McKnight became a professional musician on leaving school and has done all right.

Chris was cagey about signing up with the Dominoes. We knew he was pretty good on drums, but our thought was to bring him in as a keyboard player. He could play piano like Jerry Lee Lewis.

Chris prevaricated.

"Oh, just say 'yes' for God's sake." Diane was clearly getting impatient.

But he didn't say "yes" and we eventually voted to drop the idea. An extra mouth to feed.

Eighteen months later, Chris accepted a second offer to join the Dominoes – not as a keyboard player but as a drummer to replace Roderick who was the only one of us who had a day job at the time.

"A late night drummer?"

The boss had summoned him to his office. On his desk was a copy of the Belfast Telegraph. It was open at a picture feature on The Dominoes.

Roderick had somehow expected this would come up.

"Not quite the right image, now is it? Perhaps it explains why you appear to have difficulty staying awake at your desk?"

Roderick struggled to think of what to say. He lowered his head. He had been humming Sack of Woe as he had responded to the summons. It seemed somehow appropriate. Now here he was – and right enough. He raised his eyes and looked out the window for inspiration, but all he could hear in his head was Cannonball Adderley. Which of course was the problem.

It was no problem for me as I had finished my three years as an apprentice architect and was now studying full-time at the College of Art. It didn't seem to worry the other guys either, but Roderick was on a career path where image mattered. He took the big decision and told us we were going to have to look for someone to replace him.

Roderick had been with the band since the days of skiffle. He had been there with Elmer and there at the beginning of the decade when we churned out The Shadows and Duane Eddy.

The Dominoes could properly be described as jazz-influenced pop group. We played the current hits, but the repertoire was well populated with jazz standards – song and dance numbers from the 30s, 40s and 50s that we carried through from the early days. Songs like Hoagy Carmichael's 'Up the Lazy River' and Fats Waller's 'I'm Gonna Sit Right Down and Write Myself a Letter.'

Chris Doran and Dick Pentland were both regarded as

talented jazz musicians. They were members of the elite Queen's University Jazz Band – a six-piece group that specialised in original Count Basie arrangements, led by the omnipresent Malcolm Gooding on trumpet. Other members included Paul Gilleron on tenor and Julian Russell on piano. Chris was on drums and Dick was playing alto sax at that time.

In 1962 they entered a UK-wide contest for university jazz groups held in Birmingham. The five-piece combo that came on after them, the closing act of the evening, was the host group with whom they had spent much of the day, holding up the bar. The group featured a talented young soprano sax player called Steve, and was led by the organiser of the competition, an enterprising student named Spence. The quintet was extremely good and was warmly applauded as they left the stage and returned to the bar. Everyone agreed the host group was a worthy winner.

It was inevitable that the Queen's University Band would miss their flight back to Belfast. They stayed the night with Spence and Steve in a one-bedroom flat.

It was a year or two before the Spencer Davis Group broke into the charts with 'Keep On Running.' Only then did Chris and Dick realise that they had shared the floor that rainy night in Birmingham with Spencer Davis and Stevie Winwood.

As I pressed the key to accept the digital transfer of this recording by the Small Faces I reflected on the fact that the passage of time had eroded any memory of actually playing this number. But Michael considered it worth retaining.

All four members of the Small Faces were small – under five feet six inches. 'I Can't Make it (Without You)' was a good record but not a successful one. It was seven weeks in the charts but never rose above twenty-six. The Small Faces had reached Number One in 1966 with 'All or Nothing' and were yet to release 'Itchycoo Park' and 'Lazy Sunday.'

The East London rock group was popular in the clubs of London before being discovered by Elkie Brooks. They changed their name to The Faces in 1969 when the much taller Rod Stewart and Ronnie Wood joined the band from the Jeff Beck Group.

Steve Marriott was a former child actor who played Oliver and the Artful Dodger in the stage version of 'Oliver!' He left the band in 1968 to form Humble Pie with Peter Frampton. He died in a fire in his home in 1991. As a performer, Marriott was under-rated during his lifetime. The charming, sharply-dressed cockney Mod is now hailed internationally as the top British performer of the nineteen-sixties – the number one white soul singer who also played a mean blues guitar.

Chapter 11

Walk Don't Run

I often find myself thinking about the early days. Way back in March 1962, Fred acquired an unusual five-string double bass he called Betsy. It had seen better days. He bought it with a view to branching out a bit, and he showed enthusiasm when I suggested that he and I get together with Sez to learn off a few easy listening songs and record them on tape.

This was our first real opportunity to get to know Sez, and we were well impressed. He had a natural talent for jazz improvisation – not only had he mastered the guitar, but he could also play occasional clarinet. Sez and I were into learning jazz chords at this time and had bought Mickey Baker's amazing self-tuition book which taught us the essence of jazz guitar. I never got beyond the third page, but Sez ploughed on. I was pleased to be back doing something I knew I did well – playing my black Tuxedo guitar without a plectrum – I strummed with my thumb.

We rehearsed and recorded everything in Sez's kitchen where we reckoned the reverb would be pretty good. It was. We recorded jazz – up-tempo classics like 'Sweet Georgia Brown' and 'The Lady Is a Tramp.' We recorded Johnny Cash songs like 'Folsom Prison Blues;' 'Five Feet High and Rising' and 'Give My Love to Rose.' We only ever did one gig with this trio – before a seated audience upstairs in the Old Museum rooms in College Square North. We filled out the set with jazz standards.

Fifty-two years later, Sez, by now a highly accomplished and world-ranking pedal-steel guitar player, posted on Facebook a tribute to Mickey Baker and the influence of those kitchen sessions on the course of his musical career.

But best of all was Fred singing the Louis Armstrong jazz classic, 'St James Infirmary,' of which I have preserved a treasured recording.

In the early 1960s there was no thriving beat club scene in downtown Belfast. The skiffle craze in Belfast had been every bit as strong as everywhere else, but for a beat group there were limited opportunities to progress beyond the church halls and the tennis club circuit.

There was certainly nothing on this side of the Irish Sea to compare with Liverpool where an estimated 350 groups were playing pubs and clubs on a regular basis – the washboard and tea-chest having been cast aside the moment it was possible to make a down payment on an amplifier and electric guitar.

There were a number of factors in play, but the absence of a 'Laganbeat' to match the 'Merseybeat' can be attributed to that uniquely Irish dancehall phenomenon – the Showband.

The crowd-pulling appeal of the Irish Showband saved the glitterball dance halls in the centre of Belfast such as the Plaza, Maxim's, the Orpheus and the Astor from extinction at a time when it was evident that days were numbered for the Big Band Sound of the 1940s. The 25 piece orchestra with saxophones, trumpets, trombones, vibraphone, a rhythm section and crooners came to be seen in the brave new post-war world as belonging to another era.

The dance instructors with studios on the first floor of busy shopping streets were also concerned at this time that interest in formal instruction in strict tempo ballroom dancing seemed to be in terminal decline - despite the growing popularity of the late night BBC Television programme 'Come Dancing,'

For the dance studios of Belfast in the late nineteen-fifties, however, it was trad jazz kept the lights on. Jazz and jive worked for Cecil Clarke in Donegall Street; John

Dossor's in High Street and Betty Staff's in Ann Street. Sammy Houston in Great Victoria Street renamed his studio 'Sammy Houston's Jazz Club' – later shortened to SHJC. Miss Taylor's Dance Studio on the Lisburn Road came to be known as 'Jimmy Compton's Jazz Club.' Compton, The Rodney Foster Jazzmen, The White Eagles and The Embankment Six would stomp all night despite the strict instruction that jiving would only be permitted for the first hour of dancing in case youthful exuberance got out of hand.

But the dawn of the new decade brought with it a new generation of teenagers – the baby-boomers – who arrived on the scene wanting more than Dixieland jazz. They were looking for beat, high volume, and the raw amplified sound of electric guitars. This was a generation that had no interest in learning ballroom dancing. It was now all about self-expression and movement from the land of 1000 dances: the Shake; the Locomotion; the Watusi, and the Twist.

For those passionate devotees of traditional jazz and a cool jive, there was something distasteful about the idle drift to pop music. The jazz revival of the late 50s was a signature that would stay with them for the rest of their lives.

In December 1963, I flew to London to stay a few nights with trainee architects Plum Tyndall and Gerry Hall, who had taken a year's work experience with London County Council. I was taken to the by now famous Marquee Club, shortly before it moved from Oxford Street to the heart of Soho. My jaw dropped as I watched and listened to the music performed by the Mann-Hugg Blues Band, with Paul Jones and Tom McGuinness.

It was mind-blowing. For me it was Jones' harmonica that made it so special. But I liked the way these guys enjoyed what they were playing and exchanged jokes with the audience. They were not precious about lapsing into pop covers. I remember the biggest round of applause the whole night was for the Lennon-McCartney penned Rolling Stone hit 'I Wanna Be Your Man.'

Until this time, very few groups outside of Soho could survive, let alone make a living out of it, on authentic rhythm and blues. The urban group scene had been all about pop music, which in the first years of the decade, on both sides of the Atlantic was becoming very bland. But the fusion of jazz and blues that had flourished in Alexis Korner's Blues and Barrelhouse Club was now attracting talented musicians whose records would prove hugely influential.

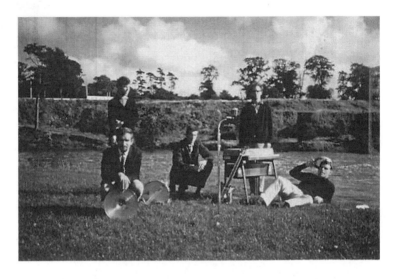

It was the popularity of the first albums by the Rolling Stones, The Spencer Davis Group, the Animals and Manfred Mann that inspired many bands across the country, including The Dominoes, to be more selective about the hits they chose to cover; to perform more obscure numbers from the popular R & B albums; to explore Mississippi Delta music and to start writing their own material.

On Friday 20 March 1964, the Dominoes were presented with an opportunity to see how their jazzy mix of pop and rhythm and blues would be received downtown. It was the time when the Beatles, having rocketed to worldwide fame, were making a well-publicised return to the nightclubs of Hamburg where they had cut their musical teeth.

The gig was being run by the art and architecture students in the Maritime; or as we knew it – the Seamen's Mission.

On this occasion we decided we could make a bob or two extra by reaching beyond the student notice boards and advertising it in the Belfast Telegraph. The wording of the press advertisement had an astonishing impact. There were queues down the street. Money boxes overflowing with cash. The Dominoes became a household name.

Well okay, not exactly. But we gave it our best shot and our jazz blues set did go down well. Maybe one or two asked "Who the hell are those guys?" But I do remember Dougie McIlwaine of the Mad Lads was reported as comparing us to the Spencer Davis Group and complaining it took the Mad Lads a year to get where we got to overnight as a result of that advertisement.

It certainly put the Maritime on the map. Two weeks later there was another press advertisement in the Belfast Telegraph – sounding out interest in starting up a rhythm and blues club. The following week, on Friday 10 April 1964, Billy Harrison's band, formerly The Gamblers, played in the Maritime with Van Morrison as lead singer. They called the band THEM.

But let the record show, M'Lud: The Dominoes were there first. And what was the key to the success of the event? What was the wording used in the advertisement that guaranteed the event would be a sell-out and put the Dominoes on the map?

Roderick, still on the scene though not playing drums anymore, was the one who came up with the three words that drew the crowds. Three words that would command the attention, and attendance, of beat groupies on the club scene who had never heard of The Dominoes. Three words that told you this band was from Belfast, and offered explanation as to why no one had heard of them. Three words that suggested these guys must be in the big league. Three words that... OK let's face it, it was a fib.

*'**THE DOMINOES** (Back from Hamburg).'*

....

The thing about speech therapists is they are all terribly nice. I'm actually on my third so far. The problem of course is motivation to do the exercises and stick with it. And deep down I have all the time been wondering if this really is the answer to my problems, whatever they are. I detect there is something more than just voice projection. I seem to be losing confidence in my ability to compose and present coherent thoughts. I don't feel ill, but I know something isn't quite right.

I have seen a throat specialist in the Ulster Clinic. He found nothing wrong. He suggested that maybe I should talk to my GP. The GP found nothing wrong.

He referred me to the Ulster Hospital for another check-up including a treadmill test. Nothing wrong here either. In fact I left the hospital with my head high and the words of a pretty nurse ringing in my ear. She said "You have the pulse of an athlete." It is a good line. I bet she says that to all the boys.

I confided in brother-in-law Peter who has worked with Chest, Heart and Stroke. Could I possibly have had some sort of mild stroke? He said he would speak to someone. "You'll have to make an appointment through your GP," said Peter, "but Dr Power thinks he might be able to help."

"Dr Power?" What a great name. I'm feeling better already. Dr Power. Power to the People. Power to All Our Friends. The Power of Love. The power to fix this.

Meantime, the Dominoes are sounding bloody good. Raymond and Robin are carrying most of the vocal burden. My voice projection is reduced but I guess that is what happens as you grow old. At 68 I am the oldest member of the group. The voice comes and goes, but up to now it has not been so bad as to cause me grief. The solution is simple – turn my mic up a tad higher than the rest.

Chapter 12

I Want to Be in America

It was Thursday 2 July 1964 when Mike Shanks and I landed in New York with a bunch of students from all over Ireland. The big attraction was that Greyhound Bus Company had a special unlimited mileage offer for students from Europe to see America: "99 days for $99." For a dollar a day you could travel coast to coast – anytime, anyplace, anywhere.

I was going to have to earn money. I landed in America with just $300 in my wallet. Of course I had the comfort of knowing that if the worst came to the worst I could sleep nights on the Dog.

We took the coach from New York, through Niagara Falls to Cleveland and on to Chicago.

We decided it was best to travel at night to save money. We travelled on through St Paul and Minneapolis to Fargo – a small city on the Red River in North Dakota close to the 49th parallel. In the first of a series of chance encounters with strangers which was to become the story of our lives in America, we met a bloke in a drug store who took us home and fed us.

The next day it was on up the Red River Valley to Winnipeg where it was still very warm but cooler. We were beginning to believe that we could charm our way anywhere into getting free meals. Everywhere we went people treated us like celebrities.

This was partly because we are Irish and partly because we had long hair – well not long exactly, but different to the standard North American US crew cut – it was regarded as a 'Beatle' haircut.

We arrived at the YMCA which we all instantly agreed we could not afford. We explained to the guy at the desk that we were penniless so the proprietor sent us to a flat nearby.

That also turned out to be too dear so he rang up several hotels he knew where he knew he could get us in cheap. We eventually checked into one (a bordello we later found out) – and were there only half an hour when we got a call from the Assistant Fire Commissioner. The Fire Commissioner? He had heard about the penniless Irish students who could not even afford to stay in the YMCA. He was wondering if we would like to see the town. It seemed odd, but there you go.

The fire chief was called Derry Newton. He took us home and fed us. Had he got in touch because he was named after the Maiden City or was it because his wife came from Belfast? Or did he think we represented some sort of fire hazard? Who knows – but he was a nice guy.

We thought we had summer jobs lined up, but nothing materialised. We were getting a bit anxious as we had no money left.

Then we had a stroke of good fortune. We were standing at a call-box looking up addresses of advertised rooms and flats when we stopped a man in the street to ask the way. He was very helpful and then asked us back to his office to phone free from there.

Then he announced that as we were "nice clean-living boys" he would put us up himself for $5 each per week (£1.13s.4d). His 15-room house (199 Elm Street) turned out to be in a highly desirable residential neighbourhood of Winnipeg. For next to nothing. We couldn't believe our luck. We had space, comfortable beds and sofas, modern kitchen with fridge, toasters and a huge cooker – plus TV, radio, record player, a pool table and even a classy acoustic guitar.

Peter Warkentin was of mid-European origin; a first generation Canadian. He had arrived in Winnipeg as a babe-in-arms in 1912. The reason he was able to offer us his house in this prestigious street had something to do with the fact that his wife had been in hospital for two years and he was temporarily living elsewhere.

The only other lodger was Jake – a shadowy figure who rarely appeared but when he did, he never spoke and never smiled. He lived out the back somewhere and shuffled in occasionally to raid the fridge.

On the Sunday before we left Winnipeg, Peter Warkentin brought his teenage family with him to Elm Street and cooked a splendid farewell turkey dinner for us. Sitting at the table already when we came in the room was silent Jake. He remained silent throughout the meal – which we expected because by this stage we had concluded that wherever he came from, he could understand what was said, but could not speak English.

The moment came for speeches. Warkentin rose to his feet and spoke in his soft central European accent of his pleasure at being able to look after his Irish friends. He began:

"I welcome you to my home for a special reason. During the War, Ireland vas neutral..."

Neither of us took on board anything else that was said. We managed to avoid looking at each other. Did we detect Jake's chair being pushed back and his heels clicking together under the table or did we imagine it? Suddenly we were both thinking the same thing – it was obvious. Peter was harbouring a Nazi War Criminal. Certainly it was not the moment to explain about the history of Ireland and its geography. We would have leapt to our feet and toasted the Third Reich had we been called upon to do so.

The Beatles began their First American Tour on 19 August 1964, just as we were leaving Winnipeg for Vancouver. The tour was carefully timed to coincide with the release of 'A Hard Day's Night' which Mike and I had seen a few days before we left Winnipeg.

The movie theatre was just across the road from the office, and I knew the fans had been queuing from 6:00am –

screaming their heads off most of the time. It was like that all day, but by the fourth show there was no longer a queue so I phoned Mike to meet me at the theatre door.

We were not really aware that the Beatles tour had begun, but it soon became obvious that something had changed the world. We knew the Beatles were popular back across the Atlantic, but we really had no idea. And we had no idea why these Americans and Canadians dug the Beatles. They didn't get the humour because they simply couldn't understand a word of Liverpudlian.

As we cruised along the plains of Saskatchewan, the first major town we came to was Regina. We got off the bus to stretch our legs and noticed that a crowd was building up nearby. They were mostly schoolgirls – about 30 of them.

"I hope they are not intending to get on this bus," said a passenger already on board. I was thinking differently.

They seemed a little excited. It soon became clear that it was on account of us. For some reason, we were generating the excitement. I was with a girl I knew from the Art College in Belfast (another chance encounter) who had got on the bus with us in Winnipeg. She laughed:

"I think you guys should be ready to make a run for it..."

It was by now obvious this was a serious case of mistaken identity. The girls began to scream, and we could hear the girls at the front say:

"Oh, my God. It is them!"

"That's John and Paul, honest!"

We thought it was a huge joke as they ran towards us. As we got on the bus I said in my now perfected John Lennon voice:

"We're not really the Beatles – we're just good friends..."

That was enough. They screamed at us and ran to the bus. They banged the side of the bus and jumped up at the windows while the ones at the front fell over one another as they clambered through the open door. All the explaining in the world couldn't stop them demanding that Mike and I, close friends of the Beatles, sign our names in lipstick on their arms. The girl from the Belfast College of Art was beside herself. The driver and the other passengers patiently waited while we dealt with the demand for autographs. When they finally did get off the bus they just stood there, crying and screaming, waiting for the bus to go.

Strange as it may seem, this story is true down to the last detail: no exaggeration. That was the way it was. There was some sort of explanation in that neither of us had had a haircut in two months and the Beatles were on tour and due to perform in Vancouver in two days' time, but this was something to relish. It was our 15 minutes of something.

While I was having fun in North America in the summer of '64, The Rolling Stones played the Ulster Hall, Belfast. It was Friday 31 July 1964, and 'It's All Over Now' was Number One in the Charts. My future bride, 16-year-old Lyn Dalton was there – right in front of the stage – alongside a school friend with whom she plays Duplicate Bridge these days: Christine Graham.

They had queued all day to be sure of getting in. It was standing room only and they worked their way to the front close to the stage, which spans the full width of the hall about shoulder height. The moment the Stones ran on there was another surge forward and they got squashed.

Christine passed out and the next thing Lyn saw was St John Ambulance men heaving her onto the stage and laying her flat before carting her off to the wings. Meanwhile fans were casually walking down on to the stage from the raked bench seating either side of the huge Mulholland Organ that forms the backdrop to this magnificent Victorian concert hall. Soon the stage was crowded with fans, mingling with the Stones as they performed.

The audience was not well pleased when the concert was abandoned after three numbers.

Christine didn't hear any of them.

....

Dr Power found no evidence of a mild stroke and has referred me to a colleague in the Movement Clinic for a second opinion. It took a few weeks before I was able to make an appointment. Another day; another specialist; another expert opinion on the record. This one wants me to go for an MRI.

Chapter 13

The Pound
Saturday 6 April 1968 – 15:35
Walk Away Renée

The Black Label is going down well.

This next song, 'Walk Away Renée' is the reason I brought the Grundig with me today. We have three of four songs by The Four Tops in the repertoire and I wanted to see if there was anything we could do to tighten them up. The Four Tops have become very popular and we are getting reports that the punters like our efforts at emulating them. We'll be performing again tonight at the Marquee. The Gentry is the guest act tonight and we don't like to be outshone.

"Renée," I tell the boys. My fingers are hovering over the keys, waiting on a cue from Sez – all primed and ready to sync with him on the opening chord.

I am pleased to see Roy Kane here today. He is the guy who played drums in the original Monarchs. I give him a grin as he wrestles with four overflowing pint glasses. A lot of beer in this place seems to end up on the floor.

I am glad he showed up. It is always good to have someone in the audience you would like to impress. Someone who knows about the journey you are on.

Good old Roy. But it reminds me of another Roy...

Unionist parliamentary candidate for East Belfast, Roy Hamilton Bradford, was sitting in my mother's living room. He looked uneasy. I was at the piano, not exactly at my ease either. I had just run through what I emphasised was no more than a first stab at the jingle he wanted. I thought it sounded rather good, actually.

"Fine, but I don't think 'Good Ole Roy' is quite what I had in mind."

"What about 'Roy's the Boy' then?"

"Roy's the Boy?" He uttered the phrase several times. "Yes, that'll do. I like it. So much better."

"Roy's the Boy – Vote for Roy?"

"That's it! Perfect."

He eased back in the armchair, now relaxed.

Roy Hamilton Bradford was on his way to becoming the Unionist Member of Parliament for Belfast, Victoria.

It was Friday 5 November 1965 when The Who released 'My Generation.' It was just three weeks ahead of the General Election. 'My Generation' was a sensational recording, and The Dominoes learnt it immediately for the Saturday night gig at the Boat Club. The power behind the opening riff brought everyone to their feet:

Dng dng dng dng,
    Dng, dng, dng, dng...

The Ox. We had played the song twice already that night when I was asked by one of the Boat Club stalwarts, Maureen Elliott, to play it one more time for Roy. "Who is Roy, then?" I asked.

"Roy Bradford – he's standing for election. That's him over there."

"Ah, We Must Not Forget The General Erection."

I chuckle inwardly at the blank looks I get from those who do not share my passion for the writings of John Lennon. I can recite lengthy passages in a Liverpool accent. Maureen knows to ignore me.

"He hopes to win over the first time voters of East Belfast and wants you to record something for him. He intends to campaign American-style and wants a catchy jingle. He likes the whoyoudo."

"The whowedo?"

"Yes. My Generation. That sort of stuff."

"Oooh-kay." I'm getting interested. "You mean a proper recording – in a studio?"

"Yes – you'd be up for it then?"

"He'll pay?"

"Yes he will. He says he wants you in a recording studio on Monday evening."

"Who writes the jingle?"

"You will. And you'll have to have it written by tomorrow."

Roy Bradford appeared at my home the next day. I wasn't the least bit interested in politics and it meant nothing when he said he was standing as a Unionist, determined to wrest this seat back from the Northern Ireland Labour Party incumbent, former shipyard worker David Bleakley. Bleakley, standing on behalf of the Northern Ireland Labour Party, was tipped to win with an increased share of the vote.

Half an hour later the jingle was written – complete with pounding intro, courtesy of The Who:

Dng dng dng dng,
  Dng, dng, dng, dng...

  "B stands for Bradford; R stands for Roy....
    ...Roy's the Boy; Vote for Roy..."

Brilliant.

"I'm thinking it would be an idea to insert a few words from me in between running the jingles – what do you think?"

"No problem," I said. "I can record them here and now if you like."

This was great. I was eager to try out my brand new Watkins Copicat tape echo chamber. The candidate took a few moments to compose appropriate messages while I erected a microphone stand. He stood up and bellowed into the mic. The echo made it sound as if he was calling from the peak of the Matterhorn. He clearly liked the sound of his voice.

On Monday evening the Dominoes met up at St Mary's Hall in Bank Street, recently converted into a recording studio by Billy McBurney, owner of the Premier Record Shop in Smithfield. Pete Lloyd and studio engineer Cel Fay were there to greet us.

Peter Lloyd is known to every muso in the country for his expertise as a recording engineer. He opened Belfast's first recording studio in Cromac Street and has recorded just about every jazz band, folk group, showband and beat group in the country. He also runs a successful business building amplifiers – which is how I got to know him. In the early days of the Dominoes we would go to him for advice on the wholesale purchase of speakers and woofers, and general guidance on the critical cabinet dimensions for the home grown equipment that Mike Shanks and Onionhead would assemble.

We have come far since then. The PA equipment we are using today in The Pound, where we are about to launch into 'Walk Away Renée,' we commissioned from Lloyd Sound at a reported cost of six hundred pounds. He is here today to oversee its first outing, having been quoted in the press saying that The Group's new microphone reproduction system 'will be of higher quality than that of any other band in Ireland.'

Pete is utterly appalled at the crude recording device I have rigged up. "Why didn't you say, and I would have brought a desk?" I didn't like to say but the truth is we have parted with enough cash to Lloyd enterprises in the last week. Cleaned us out.

Pete is a smart cookie. I imagine he writes his own press releases, too. He certainly knows a thing or two about business. While he was still at Queen's he set up a company with offices in May Street. His plan was to manufacture amplifiers to finance what he really wanted to do, which was to establish a recording studio. He did not make the amps as such – he bought the parts; handed them to The Queen's Radio Club to assemble them; and then he tested them prior to sale.

Pete is certainly is the man you need behind the glass when you want to record something properly. He has been recording since 1963, when as a student at Queen's he undertook to produce a record for Rag Week. He hired the old staff common room at QUB and recorded Phil Coulter with the Gleemen (including Cel Fay on bass). He registered an independent record label under the name UED, and launched Coulter's career with 'Foolin' Time' and 'Thunderbird.' Last year (April 1967), Phil Coulter was celebrating victory in the Eurovision Song Contest with the song he wrote, 'Puppet on a String,' sung by the delectable Sandie Shaw.

In January 1965 Peter made it possible for Irish listeners to tune in to our very own pirate radio station, modelled on Radio Caroline. Clever stuff. It was a portable device that dodged the enforcers by being broadcast from a different location every night. It kicked in after the National Anthem that marked the shut-down for the night of BBC radio.

Meantime Peter was building his reputation with sound equipment – particularly a highly regarded bass combo using his Lloyd valve amp head with a Goodman's 18 inch speaker mounted in a specially designed cabinet. It could be heard half a mile away.

This was the first of its kind and attracted requests from all over the world to supply it. Lloyd Sound flourished without help from government. The 35 Watt Bass Combo sold in 1964 at 35 guineas.

And so it was a few months later, in the build-up to the 1965 General Election, that we turned up at Pete Lloyd's new Bank Street studios to record an election jingle. Not exactly Rock 'n' Roll but we thought it might be fun.

"You have three hours, guys."

The jingle is very straightforward. We have it learnt off within 10 minutes. Half an hour later it is in the can, and the guys are talking about heading to Kelly's for a few pints. Dick Pentland is pouring on a healthy dose of cynicism as is his way, and there is a lot of laughter. Pete and Cel are amused by the whole thing. But I'm taking this seriously.

"C'mon guys, Roy's the Boy is paying for the studio."

"Yeah, but he's not paying us."

Fair point. So we used up the rest of his time laying down 'Bright Lights, Big City,' 'High-Heeled Sneakers' and other R & B stuff. We were into the Animals at that time.

On the night of the General Election, I took up the offer of a seat in one of Bradford's two campaign buses – vans essentially – that were to be driven up and down the streets of East Belfast. The vehicles were equipped with Tannoy speakers, blasting out our recording on a continuous loop. Peter Dalton was in the driving seat, peering out the windscreen to see where he was going.

Beside Peter in the front passenger seat sat Roy's the Boy, the candidate himself, visible from outside because the interior light was switched on. He mouthed the words of his short pre-recorded speeches; beaming at the voters he could see emerging from their homes to find out what the noise was all about. I sat in the back with his teenage son, Conor. From time to time the van would stop and the candidate would leap out and walk the pavements, knocking on doors.

People were actually dancing in the streets. This was going down well. The Dominoes could win the jackpot.

We stop in Pansy Street and Roy steps out of the bus to press the flesh. Quite suddenly the air is filled with the sound of an angry crowd and a disturbing chant. Round the corner a placard waving mob emerge, clearly intent on mischief.

"It's Bunting," exclaimed Conor.

Indeed it was. Major Ronald Bunting was a well-known champion of the people. He came to prominence as an election agent for socialist Gerry Fitt. He had no time for Bradford and his ilk, and had mobilised shipyard workers to deal in the traditional manner with what he regarded, correctly, as an attempt by the ruling classes to stem the tide of the Northern Ireland Labour movement.

Peter is quick to react. He fires up the engine. "Let's be like the good shepherd and get the flock outa here," he shouts, voicing one of his favourite lines. The only way out is to reverse away from the advancing mob.

"But what about Dad?" asks Conor, squinting into the darkness. There are no takers to go and get his dad, but there is no need. In seconds the passenger door handle is being rattled frantically by the startled candidate who only just manages to avoid being run over by his own campaign bus.

It turned out to be close. Roy Hamilton Bradford got 51 per cent of the vote and won the seat from David Wylie Bleakley with a majority of just 423.

I don't talk about this anymore. Too many people have made it clear to me that they think this was nothing to be proud of. But I'll let you into a secret. This was a victory for Rock 'n' Roll. Danny and the Juniors got it right. Rock 'n' Roll is here to stay. It will never die. Rock 'n' Roll will always be and it'll go down in history. Maybe I'm just a daydream believer.

Back listening to the old tapes, I take off the 'phones and sit back, feeling quite pleased with my success in salvaging 'Walk Away Renée' from the sands of time. It was one of my favourite songs at the time – and I looked to Michael for affirmation. He was non-committal as usual – but the point is that I thought it was OK.

'Walk Away Renée' was written by a 16 year old called Michael Brown. It was a great song, rated by Rolling Stone magazine in the top 250 songs of all time. The Four Tops cover version, produced by Holland-Dozier-Holland, was released in UK on 13 December 1967. It subsequently reached No 3 in the charts.

Chapter 14

The Pound
Saturday 6 April 1968 – 15:50
Heroes and Villains

"C'mon, Morr'son. Is that the best you can do? Give us something better than that. Give us some Beach Boys! Jeez, what are they paying you for?"

It's Gerry Hall. His insults are actually welcome – it provokes a bit of banter which is a lot better for us than being totally ignored. The aim of the game is to come out on top. I'll just have to let this one go. I can't think of anything funny. One nil to Gerry. But I need to come up with a gem before the afternoon is out.

A sun-tanned girl I have never seen before comes up to me. "Do you do dedications?"

"You mean play something for somebody?"

"Will you play the Beach Boys for Glenda? She's back in town. She says she knows you."

I feel a hot flush coming on, and glance across at Lyn. She is watching my every move.

Glenda. Well I never. Who would have believed it? I know her well.

The Boat Club's annual Open Tournament attracts up and coming tennis players from around the world. In the summer of '65 there was a certain amount of excitement as a young man from Holland called Tom Okker chose Belfast for grass court practice in preparation for Wimbledon. He was the Dutch Champion and a potential Wimbledon finalist. He was a big draw for other aspiring professionals from around the world who were also looking to gain experience of competing with top players on grass courts – something the Boat Club had to offer.

Glenda Swan was one such aspiring professional – a South African girl who was more than just a good tennis player. She was rather nice and a good laugh. She hung around the band and we all felt a little star struck. I took a fancy to her.

In an attempt to raise my profile in her eyes, I volunteered to be a service line judge in the Open Championships. It was a moment of madness.

Glenda looked great in her tennis gear. I had difficulty taking my eyes off her. I admired her every move during the warm-up.

The game started with Glenda on my side of the net – on the receiving end. I was not troubled by any serves which were all in court and despatched by Glenda straight back to her opponent. She was stamping her presence on the game already, moving effortlessly across the court. She looked pretty good to me. She won the first game with a forehand smash that was greeted with a well-deserved burst of applause from the large crowd who had singled this out as the match of the day.

They changed ends. It was now Glenda's turn to serve. She somehow managed to tuck her second service ball under her white skirt and performed the preparatory routine of bouncing the ball several times on the grass. She threw the ball high in the air and arched her athletic frame backwards, maintaining perfect balance. She swung the racquet in a graceful arc and, with a slight grunt, smacked the ball in my general direction. It was a joy to behold.

The umpire looked at me after Glenda's crashing serve had passed across my field of vision. There was a pause – a collective intake of breath. Then a deafening silence descended on the court.

If I had had my wits about me I would have shouted out "in!" because even if it had been out, a positive call would at least have gone down well with the new love in my life. The fact is I had no idea whether it was in or out. No idea at all. I simply didn't see it.

I stared into space. I felt the colour rising in my face and a thumping in my ears.

Eventually words came out.

"Er," I said softly, "I think it was out."

"Could you repeat that, please?" asked the stern looking lady umpire who had clearly heard every word I had said.

"Eeeh... I'm not sure."

It goes without saying Glenda never looked at me again.

And now she is back in town. "Glenda. Well I never. Who would have believed it? I know her well. Where is she sitting?" The girl in the white dress swings round and points. "She didn't think you'd remember her."

"Glenda from South Africa?"

"Huh?" she said, somewhat crestfallen. "You're thinking of someone else. Our Glenda's from North Belfast."

 It was Sez that caused the break-up. I'd known Sez from schooldays. He was a couple of years younger than me. He was never a full-time member of the Dominoes, but we would regularly session together and often invite him up to play with the band at the Boat Club. Despite appearing to be desperately shy with a propensity to hide behind the amplifiers, he really was a mean guitar-picker. He was the sub on the bench who knew the chords of everything we played and was a totally reliable stand-in. He developed licks

that established his credentials on lead guitar. Way beyond me, man.

One day Sez was round at my house. I was vamping the piano with an idea that we could resurrect the early Rock 'n' Roll material with which the Beatles made their mark in Hamburg. We were impressed with Paul McCartney's version of Little Richard's classic rock song – 'Long Tall Sally.' The bulk of the singing fell to me in those days, although I knew I was not much good. I knew I had a pretty characterless voice with a limited vocal range. I really wanted to sing like Paul McCartney but the harsh fact was that this was way beyond me. I had to drop the pitch by half an octave to get anywhere near it.

"Let me have a go." said Sez. Sez had never sung anything before as far as I knew. I certainly had never heard a peep from him, but he was welcome to give it his best shot.

His first effort in the key of C, my key, was good. Very good in fact. There was a growl in his voice. I was impressed.

"Try it up a bit," he said. We tried it in D. This was interesting.

"Try E." He was game for anything. I couldn't believe this.

"Little Richard played it in F," I said. Every keyboard player knows rock piano is best played on the white notes. I could be back in business.

"Well, let's try it then."

"What, in F?"

"What key is McCartney in?"

"G," I said.

"Well let's have a go, then."

I got on the phone to Fred. This was going to change everything.

You could have cut the atmosphere with a knife. Mike shrugged his shoulders. Dick stormed off and I thought Chris was going to cry. Their reactions were outwardly different, but underneath I knew what they were all thinking.

That last night in the Boat Club was sour. Word quickly went around that Fred and I were leaving the Dominoes to form a group with Sez.

The bonding we shared after years of playing together was lost in an instant.

Fred and I identified Ricky McCutcheon as the best man for the job of drummer with the new group. At the time he was with the Federals – a fine band with a great tenor sax sound produced by the formidable Geordie Sproule and the talented Mr Keith Donald. Ricky was a stylish drummer and showed interest when we broached the subject. But we felt we needed a frontman.

"What about Teddie?" suggested Ricky. Fred and I looked at one another. Teddie and the Exiles were the competition. This would be a bold move. The line-up of his 6-piece band included John Smyth. They were not just another band. They were good – very good in fact. And they were popular.

The Exiles had achieved something that Fred thought was the way to go. They had broken into the urban pop scene. And the significant thing, as Ricky pointed out, was that having broken in, they were now breaking up.

Teddie Palmer had got off to a good start. He and Smick met at Stranmillis Teacher Training College and formed The Spectres with Dinger Bell, later to become Mayor of Castlereagh. Palmer had written a song for Rag Week in 1965 called 'The Facts of Life' which was recorded by Bryan Somers and released on Peter Lloyd's UED label.

But it was the reaction of fans to the Exiles, and to Teddie in particular, that opened our eyes to the Belfast beat group scene that was firmly establishing itself. Teddie was a heart throb. He had the looks of a pop star and I guess he knew how to exploit it. The Exiles played the small venue first floor dance studios that attracted a teenage crowd – Sammy Houston's in Great Victoria Street; Betty Staff's in Ann Street and Clarke's in Donegall Street. As soon as Teddie came on stage, the teenyboppers would scream loudly, scramble to the front and reach out their arms in the hope of getting a touch. We all reckoned Teddie prepared his white shirt with sleeves lightly stitched at the armpits so they would rip off easily.

Teddie regularly featured in the fan letters column of CityWeek as the focus of every young girl's dream. We were pretty sure he wrote the letters himself. We heard about the lightly-stitched sleeve trick and decided to go one night to Betty Staff's to see it for ourselves. It was for real; girls screaming; shirt torn as they pulled him off the stage. Fred and I were mighty impressed with the whole scene. We heard later that Teddie Palmer went over the top that night because he assumed we were talent spotting for a record company. The punters had no doubt we were plain clothes policemen.

Did we reject Teddie – or did Teddie reject us? Hard to say, but Teddie went on to form Teddie and the Tigers with Tiger Taylor – and The Group decided to make a go of it as a four-piece.

The Dominoes were not long in finding replacements for Fred and me after the break-up. Mike Shanks changed over to bass guitar and they brought in Robin Irvine who quickly stamped his personality on the band.

They decided to become a soul band. After a time the Dominoes changed the name to Heart and Soul, with Ray Ferguson and Dick Pentland forming the brass section. Smick, the drummer from the now disbanded Exiles, was recruited to play organ. After a short time, logic dictated that Smick should take over on drums, and that Chris should revert to his first love and principal talent as a keyboard player.

The Group quickly established itself in the local pop scene. Its first publicised gig was on Thursday 10 November 1966 in Square One – a first floor club in Royal Avenue that amounted to little more than a cube with hard surfaced walls and a box stage. They had a good light show, but acoustically this place was just awful. In many ways ahead of its time, Square One quickly became a popular rave-like venue for teenagers. You didn't hear the sound; you just felt the throb and went home with earache. It had opened 12 days earlier on Friday 28 October 1966 with THEM featuring Van Morrison and a new line-up that included Misfit John Wilson.

Seven months later, in the summer of 1967, drummer Ricky McCutcheon left The Group. We offered the job to Smick, who was now playing drums with what had been The Dominoes now playing as Heart and Soul.

Dick was incandescent. I knew what he was thinking. We had done it again.

I still feel guilty about the break-up of the Dominoes. We had been together for six years without a harsh word. The five-piece line-up had changed a little, but we had evolved into a good little pop and rhythm and blues band, playing with a continuously refreshed repertoire to capacity crowds every Saturday night at the Belfast Boat Club.

As resident Saturday night band for almost all that time, we felt we belonged to the Boat Club, and that the Boat Club belonged to us. It was a bombshell for the rest of the band when Fred and I announced we were leaving to form The Group. It was the end of an era.

I take another quick slurp of my pint, having decided to give Gerry Hall and Glenda from North Belfast what they want.

"Okay," I say to the boys, turning my head away from the mic. "Heroes and Villains..."

Important we come in together on this one. We take a moment to compose ourselves before looking to Smick for a silent count in.

When I first listened with Michael to the recording of The Group playing 'Heroes and Villains,' I was astonished at how good it was for live performance and an amateur recording. I remember at the time we got a lot of credit for having a go at what was perceived to be quite a challenge for a four-piece group.

'Heroes and Villains' was written for the Beach Boys by Brian Wilson and Van Dyke Parks. It was in the UK charts for 9 weeks, first appearing on 23 August 1967 and rising to No 8.

Brian Wilson is known to have been deeply influenced by the music of George Gershwin at an early age – especially 'Rhapsody in Blue.' That struck a chord with me. I was brought up in a house with a huge radiogram and a collection of classic shellac records from the thirties, including 'Rhapsody in Blue' which I adored. The influence of this Gershwin classic on 'Heroes and Villains' is readily apparent.

The Beach Boys clocked in for at least 20 recording sessions for this song over a period of several months. Wilson became obsessed with it. Later, as a time when he struggling to recover from a nervous breakdown, he would hear a constant buzzing in his brain, and voices he referred to as his "heroes and villains."

While based on a deceptively simple three-chord pattern, it was a very difficult challenge for The Group to cover. But we had to rise to it because we had made our name by emulating the distinctive sound of the Beach Boys. 'God Only Knows' and 'Good Vibrations' were among the very first songs we learnt when we formed The Group.

I was well used to dissecting current hits for The Dominoes and working out vocal backing "oohs" and "aahs," but we knew this particular hit record would be a challenge – most pop groups wouldn't even think of trying it. There was a risk it would turn out to be too much for us – we were only a four-piece. Undaunted, we worked out harmony parts and were pretty chuffed when we first performed it live. It went down well with the punters and became our trade mark. In effect, it meant we had created something different – a pop group with four lead vocalists.

The tapes expose one fact that should have been self-evident at the time. Drinking pints of beer before a gig was a bad idea.

Chapter 15

Arnie Knowles

The Pound was the brainchild of Arnie Knowles. It began in 1967 as an Irish traditional music venue, established by Knowles with the help of fellow members of the Irish Traditional Music Society.

Knowles is a larger than life character – a maverick from east Belfast who now lives abroad. Fifty years ago he won the heart of Susan Riddell, with whom he lives happily to this day. Susan was crowned Miss Ireland in 1958.

Arnie told me how he stumbled on the legendary rock venue. He had been running a midweek music club in a derelict house in Donegall Street and was on the hunt for a second hand bottling machine. As to why he needed a bottling device we can but guess. Why he thought he might find what he was looking for in amongst the stalls of the former city animal pound off Townhall Street at the back of the Law Courts Hotel is another unanswered question.

But Arnie and Susie were knocked out when they saw the place. It was a step back in time. It was indeed the old city animal pound and for the most part the building had never been used for anything else. The pens were still there, and indeed had been in use in relatively recent time for the stabling of horses awaiting shipment abroad. It was a hidden place, lost behind the Law Courts Hotel. Neighbouring properties included the Musgrave Street Police Station and what was formerly the city morgue. And there was history. It was the scene of the murder of two members of the Royal Irish Constabulary in 1921.

Knowles outlined his proposal for a new folk/jazz venue to Ceoltas Ceol - modelled on Eamonn Doran's popular pub in Temple Bar in Dublin. Despite the fact that the roof of the near derelict building had collapsed completely at the front end, he could see immediately that with a bit of work, and a bit of cooperation from St George's Boxing Club who had a sparring ring at the far end of the building, the place could be turned into an exciting music venue.

The grandly named Law Courts Hotel was in reality a pub owned by the Roddy family. It was better known as Roddy's Bar. It was well placed to fortify those due to appear before the courts. It also served the farming community on market days and benefitted from being the first watering hole for bus travellers from the country whose journey had terminated in the nearby Oxford Street Bus Station.

Knowles worked out a deal with John Roddy over the proposed folk/jazz club and decided the new venue should be called The Pound. His vision was to have a resident folk group augmented by guest groups and performers. He enlisted the help of supportive musicians to help him re-build the roof, and The Pound opened its doors for the first time on the evening of Saturday 22 April 1967, before 200 invited guests.

Musicians appearing in those first few months included Sean Maguire, at the time rated as the leading fiddle player in Ireland. He performed with Joe Heaney and Ted Furey, and Willie Clancy dropped in a few times. Arnie's idea was that there would be three nights for folk and three nights for jazz, anchored by George Chambers and the Apex Jazz Band.

Arnie and Susie set about putting the old animal pound into good enough order to host customers. They used original materials to restore the damaged roof beams and rafters which were left exposed. Jackie Fallis, a guitar player of distinction, made the bar counter out of five book cases acquired from the United Services Club in Montgomery Street. Fallis also made the big wooden entrance door to fit the arched opening, complete with the brass knocker and peephole through which you had to pass once you were through the main gate and into the courtyard.

Inside, the general motif was traditional Irish. Knowles installed an assortment of UTA bus seats that he acquired from Eastwood Scrap Yard on the Falls Road. Susie set about stitching covers of multi-coloured Irish Tweed; they bought second hand dark mahogany refectory tables and a collection of cane-backed mahogany chairs. The walls were painted white with oil lamps and old muskets suspended close to the roof timbers, high beyond reach.

A heavy wooden purlin running the length of the shed relied on the support of black-painted cast iron columns. The mighty purlin carried the exposed rafters of a double pitched roof. Naked light bulbs dangled from the ridge beam, along which electric cables were loosely slung on their way to a master switch by the entrance door. When barmen were ready to go home, one brief flick of the switch was all that was necessary to send punters scurrying for the exit. The Pound was a scary place in the dark.

The cast iron columns set the grid for the waist-high partitioning that divided the pens. Your senses would be stimulated by the music emanating from performers gathered on a grubby carpeted stage half way down on the right. The stage was a tight fit, leaving a passageway of barely four feet across the front of the platform – along which all must pass on the way to the bar and the toilets which were to the left as you entered the building.

Knowles recalls how the club very nearly did not open as planned because at the last minute the Head Constable for the area came to tell him he would have to apply for a music licence. When the police chief learned the intention was to run Irish traditional music and to charge at the door for certain events he threw his hands up. He was horrified that this particular spot, the site of the 1921 assassination, should be used for what he described as 'Fenian music.' It was a complete shakedown with hours to go. Knowles got the situation smoothed over with the help of a close friend: unionist politician and brilliant barrister, the late Desmond Boal.

There was no advertising sign outside in the street. Nothing to tell people that behind these heavy gates was a music club open to the public. To get into the courtyard involved pushing open a little door in one of the gates at the back of the footpath, making sure not to trip painfully over the six inch sill or having a bruising encounter with the angle iron that surrounded the door opening.

Patrons would be let in one at a time by a guy with one arm. He held with his one arm a white soup bowl rattling as coins tumbled in in return for a right of entry. His large frame filled the doorway. He greeted everyone like a long-lost friend but nobody got past until the soup bowl rattled with fresh coinage. No-one needed to ask how much it cost to be let in. It was two bob.

But it was the Saturday afternoon gig with The Group as the resident band that established The Pound as a legendary rock venue.

It all started with a need to find somewhere to rehearse. John Roddy made a quick call to Arnie, who saw no problem in letting The Group have the keys of The Pound for a Saturday afternoon practice.

Saturday 29 July 1967 was a hot sunny day and the doors to Townhall Street, a well-trodden route from the Bus Station to the city centre, were left open. Passers-by, hearing live music as they walked past, stopped to listen. Some ventured to explore the dark atmospheric surroundings. Soon there was a queue of customers reaching from the courtyard into the front bar, seeking refreshment. John Roddy got on the phone to Arnie Knowles. Arnie was there in a flash and the bar in The Pound was hastily opened, for the first time, on a Saturday afternoon.

The idea of a Saturday afternoon drinking pints and listening to a beat group was something new to Belfast. Nobody was sure it would work, but the idea of making it a regular gig was tabled at a meeting in the front bar with Arnie Knowles and John Roddy two days later. Our proposal was that The Group should be the resident band. I remember suggesting that the easiest arrangement would be for the band to take the door on Saturday afternoons. Against the background crack of the wooden men on spindles of the table football game, Knowles and Roddy glanced at one another, and then smiled to let me know there was no way that was going to happen.

A deal was done. The Group would get the Saturday afternoon spot on its normal fee and not a penny more. Belfast's first Saturday afternoon rock music venue swung into action the following Saturday without any advance publicity.

It was decided there would be no advertising. The Pound would be promoted by word of mouth as a cool place where you could expect to rub shoulders with chart-topping pop stars relaxing before a Saturday night gig in Romano's, the Starlight or the Orpheus.

The Group at this stage had taken on Ronnie Field and Peter Dalton as its management team. Field and Dalton had worked their way into a select group of helpers who were trusted by local promoter Jim Aiken to look after pop stars brought across the Irish Sea. The entourage included Blair Whyte and that irrepressible impresario, Gerry Giffen. Gerry seemed to be on first name terms with all the stars.

"I will have Cat Stevens and his band at Arnie's place next Saturday afternoon," he said confidently.

Soon the word got out that Cat Stevens would be there in person at a cool new celebrity venue in Townhall Street. On the Friday afternoon Stevens and his backing group, a fine combo from Liverpool called the Hip Hooray Band, were escorted to the Elsinore Hotel on the Antrim Road. Giffen took charge. He assigned Field to look after the band and

Peter Dalton was given the task of driving a limo carrying the man himself and ensuring he got to the gigs on time. The first gigs were that night in Portstewart and the Sammy Barr's Flamingo in Ballymena. The Saturday night gigs were the Queen's Hall in Newtownards and then the Starlite in Arthur Square. The plan was that all would meet up on the Saturday afternoon in The Pound where The Group was playing.

Perfect.

But it wasn't perfect. Peter Dalton pulled up outside the hotel at the agreed time. His girlfriend gave him a peck on the cheek and moved to sit in the rear seat as they waited for Stevens to appear. When he did eventually emerge, Dalton swung open the front passenger door. Glancing at the attractive girl in the rear seat, Stevens announced he would prefer to sit in the back. Dalton was not expecting to be treated as a chauffeur, but that was clearly the role he was obliged to fulfil as he set off for the north coast. With one eye on the mirror, Dalton could only imagine what the hushed conversation was about. He became more and more annoyed at the attention his date was getting from the pop star – especially as she appeared to find it pleasing.

On the way back, words were exchanged and Stevens was left to sit in silence on his own in the back seat. They got as far as Templepatrick when the Rover ran out of petrol. Dalton had never thought to glance at the gauge. Tension mounted as they hung about the Templepatrick roundabout, with Peter insisting that they all walk half a mile together to the nearest phone box where they could call up a taxi.

The Hip Hooray Band partied in The Pound that Saturday, but Cat Stevens failed to show. He was still in a huff from the night before. He finished the tour the following night with a gig in Dublin, and without a word to anyone, returned to England.

There was a lot of good natured banter that afternoon, with the Hip Hooray Band in the thick of it. It soon became apparent that no-one cared whether the star attraction was there or not. Nevertheless Gerry Giffen felt compelled to step up on stage, grab a mic and apologise to those present as we knew he would for the non-appearance of Cat Stevens.

We knew what was coming next. Without waiting for Gerry to finish what he had to say, I powered up the opening riff of his favourite rock song, "Lucille." Gerry feigned surprise and launched in. Little Richard meets the Everly Brothers. His reward, as always, was to be cheered off the stage. The party stepped up a gear.

The Hip Hooray Band enjoyed it so much, they opted to stay in Northern Ireland and see if they could make a go of it. As far as they were concerned, it was like being back in the halcyon days of the Cavern Club, their home venue in Liverpool. They performed well, played The Pound with The Group every Saturday afternoon for that first month, and then went their separate ways.

Sez and I offered the Hip Hooray Band a bed for the night in our flat in Malone Avenue. Steve, the singer with the band, took up the offer and left the band. He stayed with us for three months. Another member of the band, sax player "Zoot" Sinclair, volunteered to be put up in Belmont Park with the Dalton family because he was interested in Peter's 19-year-old kid sister, Lyn. I was jealous of Zoot because I was interested in her too.

To my displeasure, Zoot hung around for a while as well. I really wanted him to get on the ferry and bugger off back to Liverpool.

The opening of The Pound on a Saturday afternoon broadened horizons for Arnie Knowles. Jake Chancellor had been his associate since the jazz/folk club opened little more than three months before; but now he had a team, including Ronnie Field who presented himself as the manager of The Group. Colin McClelland, initially doing art work, offered to help out on the door. He was appointed to the job full-time when it became evident that his door take was twice that collected by the guy with the white soup bowl and one arm. What was never clear was how the one-armed bandit physically managed to trouser half the takings.

The Pound initially had seating for about 100, but the number of patrons on a Saturday afternoon would double that figure. Work was carried out in 1969 to install a balcony and thereby increase capacity to around 200 in addition to those who were prepared to stand. The place was normally full on Saturday afternoons when The Group took to the stage. From a band's point of view the acoustics of this ancient raftered, brick building were good. We would set up the gear over lunchtime and the door would be open from 2:00pm. We would be on stage until about 5:30pm.

The Group was exclusively resident on Saturday afternoons for over a year. The slot was shared other popular groups such as the Tigers, the Carpetbaggers and Pennyfeather when the Mint Imperial opened in competition.

Much later, into the seventies, arriving customers would not be surprised to detect the whiff of dope, but in 1968 Belfast, such a culture was not yet out in the open to any significant extent. That is not to suggest there was no sign of it. But the vigilance of David Dunseith, the public face of the RUC Drugs Squad, made sure there was no overt dealing in drugs at the city clubs. Dunseith, of course would soon move to the dark side – he became a journalist and broadcaster with the BBC.

The attraction was simply loud music and a bar.

Swilling pints in the middle of the day may not have been exactly wholesome, and outdoor sport would of course have been a healthier way of spending Saturday afternoons, but The Pound was of its time and met the needs of a forward-thinking and fun-seeking generation. Catholic and Protestant mingled with common purpose in having a good time and with not the slightest inkling of the conflict to come. Nowhere else offered such a Mardi Gras atmosphere week in and week out. The place was unique. This was underground.

A description in The Belfast Telegraph summed it up well: *Dim lights cast eerie shadows on the walls and on the faces. The patrons call it a dive. It is not an insult.*

And then there was the Marquee...

Chapter 16

The Marquee

I'm not going to be humble about this. The idea of a Saturday night Marquee Club was mine, and it was my idea to approach the Astor. Of course it would never have happened had it not been for Arnie Knowles. Knowles was on a roll with the commercial success of The Pound. It was time to expand the business. Pop music punters had come of age, and Arnie had already earned the reputation of being the Pied Piper. He was invited to a meeting in Manchester where he was offered a management opportunity to take over the Plaza, the biggest dancehall in the city, and turn it into a nightclub.

My idea was a lot less ambitious. A Saturday night club with The Group as resident band. Sure we could do two gigs every Saturday. And why not just pinch the brand name Marquee? The London Marquee Club was still the top UK venue for progressive rock and pop music. I was there in December 1963, watching and listening to Paul Jones and the Mann Hugg Blues Band. I was impressed with the venue every bit as much as I was with rhythm and blues.

London's Marquee Club opened its doors as a fashionable jazz club in a basement ballroom beneath an Oxford Street cinema in 1958. By 1963 it had become the leading venue for showcasing the best rhythm and blues bands in the country. At the same time in city centres of England and Wales, the rough-edged beat group was growing in grass roots popularity. Liverpool's Cavern Club, forever associated with The Beatles, inspired similar venues to open all over the country in the early sixties. The Cavern opened in 1957 as a jazz venue modelled on the cellar clubs of Paris. This was the true birthplace of the British urban beat group.

Ireland missed out on the first wave of beat groups that led the way in Great Britain from the early 60s. One would have expected Belfast and Dublin to have followed hard on the heels of the popularity of the Mersey beat. Certainly until the Maritime opened its doors in 1964, there was no venue in Belfast to match the Cavern. The few urban beat groups that were in business at this time struggled to survive on meagre pickings on offer from the dance studios, tennis clubs and suburban community halls. The high capacity dance-halls continued to be the preserve of the Irish Showband. Despite repeated failure to persuade the courts to allow the sale of alcohol, dancehall promoters could see that the ballroom and the showband were still drawing the crowds.

The explanation as to why Belfast's beat groups were eclipsed by showbands in the early 60s can in part be put down to a fear on the part of the promoter as to would happen if the dancehalls were invaded by under-21s. The image of the place had to be protected. Equally important was the image of the band. Bandleaders knew that they would be wise to wear suits if they hoped to be asked back. The bandleaders also knew they had the Federation of Irish Musicians to thank for enforcing a job-protecting 'rule' that meant a dance promoter could only employ bands that put a minimum of seven musicians on stage – thus relegating the popular three- or four-piece beat group to the role of a low paid support act.

But by the mid-60s, the big dancehalls in the city were again struggling anyway to attract punters. Dancehall owners were paying the price for imposing rules on length of hair and mature appearance. The Astor was no exception.

Survival called for throwing all eggs into a one-night-a-week basket, and facing up to what until then had been unthinkable – putting a beat group on stage for the night. The Astor was among the first wave of dancehalls to promote a beat group as the main attraction. Others quickly followed, and the Federation backed down.

The Misfits, a four piece group in smart suits, were given the opportunity to play in a manner that had sprung from the Cavern Club in Liverpool. They did break the mould, and quite suddenly Belfast night life came alive. The Group was also seen to appeal to a younger crowd and found itself in the right place at the right time. We were offered Wednesday night residencies – first in the Starlite and then in the Astor ballroom.

"So you know the McMahon family who own the Astor," said Arnie. "How do you think they would react to your idea of a Saturday night club?"

I said I could only guess, but offered to arrange a meeting with Pat McMahon at the McMahon family home at No 1 Townsend Street. Pat struck me as an honourable man. He dressed like James Garner in the TV series 'Maverick' - complete with bootlace tie and silver shield.

He readily understood and agreed to the proposition. Knowles would promote and run Saturday night dances in the Astor under the name of the Marquee Club with The Group as resident band. He would be rewarded by a percentage share of what potentially could be a significant increase in anticipated door takings.

Arnie discussed it with Susie and with their close confidante, Jake Chancellor. They were all taken with the idea. It sounded like a lot more fun than overseeing the further decline of the Plaza.

Arnie called a meeting in the Duke of York. He was keen to hear the views of Colin McClelland who had become part of the management team at The Pound. Jake and Colin were quick to grasp the concept. Obviously the 'Marquee' name was a direct steal from the London club of the same name – an association we knew would have currency. There would be two groups on every Saturday, with equal billing – and there would be no showbands. The Group would be resident. There would be a DJ booth in the corner and a double stage so groups could hand over seamlessly to one another as the night progressed.

The challenge was to transform a 1940s ballroom into an intimate club. Creating the club atmosphere was not going to be easy. We suspended light material on invisible wires – a striped tent top that encouraged patrons to feel at one with the groups on the stage. We acquired the latest lighting technology – strobe lights, ultra-violet tube blue light and follow-spots. Blobs of moving colour were projected onto the wall at the back of the stage; a beam of ever-changing colour just above the heads of the dancers that quickly filled with swirling smoke that dulled the senses and transformed the dancehall into a dynamic cellar club.

But the instant success of the Marquee Club can largely be attributed to McClelland and his zany advertisements in the Belfast Newsletter. In contrast to the familiar 'Neat Dress Essential' censure, the Marquee Club advertisements conveyed a liberating message that made sense only to the cool dudes of Belfast who were tuned in and turned on.

Ground-breaking psychedelic lighting was in place from the first night of the Marquee in October 1967. Mounted on a scaffold at the back of the hall, Colin, Jake, Gerry Hall and Blair Whyte experimented with messy pigments, oil and soapy water in the hope the heat of the projector would produce constantly moving colour images on the wall behind the stage. It was a messy operation. They would descend from the scaffold looking like Red Indians ready for war. But when they progressed to using endorsing inks compressed between glass slides with the help of Ronson lighter fuel it was not just messy – it was downright hazardous.

Eventually with some mystical help from Gregory Ashtar Brown, the renowned Fanny Flickers Light Show came into being. Ashtar spoke with an English accent, but nobody knew where he came from or where he was going to. He maintained he was from Venus. It seemed plausible.

Arnie certainly thought so. He gave Ashtar slack because he felt his life could only be enriched by pyro-techniques and loud unexpected bangs. Certainly there can be no other explanation why he continued to finance his experiments.

Colin McClelland was the creative one. His ideas were inspired by something beyond rational understanding. He wrote those irreverent ads that appeared every Friday morning in the Newsletter. People bought the paper solely

because they didn't want to miss what was written. The ads were always in pole position in the top left hand corner of a left-hand page; three inches across two columns topped by the familiar Marquee logo. Always tongue-in-cheek, they featured insane eye-catching titles.

Colin would dream up absurd poems; inconsequential serialised tales and eye-catching headlines to draw you in to read the small print – often featuring members of the by now well-known and popular Marquee team – for example:

HOW TO SAVE MONEY
Don't go to The Marquee tonight. You'll save ten bob.
Of course you will miss:
that well-known string quartet **THE GROUP**
musical entertainment and *de luxe* singing from **TASTE**
the only appearance in the world of **SAM MAHOOD**
recorded musical tunes by **Mr Michael Henderson**
frightening piano music by **Geraldo Hall**
unusual electric lighting by **Mr Desmond McVeigh**
sparkling stage decoration by **Mr Marshall McMonagle**
decorative rope from **Mr Blair Whyte**
impersonations by **Miss Brown**
Treasure Island by **Robert Louis Stevenson**

We thought initially we would lure one of the established DJs, such as Dino Martin, to drive proceedings from the spot lit corner booth, but I managed to convince Arnie and Colin that I had someone lined up for the job. It was just as well I succeeded because as a result of an inebriated

conversation in the Botanic I had already offered the job to stand-up bar room comic and discontented bank clerk, Michael Henderson. DJ Hendi joined the Marquee team and never looked back.

Hendi took to his new role as Disc Jockey like a duck to water. In May 1968 he rose to a Simon Dee Oxfam charity challenge to beat a 100-hour world record for non-stop jockeying. Rival Dino Martin was quoted in the press as saying Hendi wouldn't last the night.

I buy Dino's take on this. Hendi was seen playing records in the shop window of the Marquee office in Donegall Street for five days in a row. It was claimed he had beaten the world record by 16 hours. Dino was probably right, but no-one came forward with verifiable evidence. A reliable informant, Kieran Ward, assures me Hendi was in fact credited with the record but not for long. His feat was eclipsed within 48 hours.

Among the punters who sought admission to the Marquee Club on a regular basis was a nineteen-year-old DeeJay by the name of Terri Hooley. I remember him from my apprenticeship days as "Terry." He was the photo printer who worked in C & P Douglas, a drawing office supplies company on University Road owned by a relative of mine.

I remember him well as a regular at the Marquee. I met him again a few years ago for the first time in years. We were basking in the evening sun outside the John Hewitt, pints in hand.

"They going to make a film of my life!" he exclaimed.

Yes Terri, I thought. That'll be the day. But 'Good Vibrations,' that great 2013 film by Colin Carberry and Glenn Patterson about the punk rock scene in Belfast in the 1970s, proved me wrong, of course.

....

"You have Parkinson's?" The nurse has a pen in one hand and a clipboard in the other. The papers on the clipboard obviously tell something about me. I hesitate. Probably because I'm not sure it was actually a question. She looks up, raising an eyebrow. She expects an answer.

"Parkinson's? Not at all – the purpose of this is to eliminate it from the enquiries." I am speaking to the eyebrow. "I had swine flu. The man just wants to check everything is OK. I've had this done before, you know."

"Have you?"

"What?"

"Have you had this procedure before?"

"Oh, yes. I used to get headaches that lasted three days. They ran my head through the tunnel and found nothing wrong."

"When was this?" She is now taking notes. "A while ago – they said it was migraine. I reckon now looking back that it was just hangovers."

The eyebrow lifts again. The pen is set down. Not amused. For the next few minutes I am answering questions. This is clearly a serious business. "Your scan will take place at five minutes past one." She looks at her notes. "That is in three hours' time. Right now I'm going to give you an injection of radio-active material into the back of your hand. You've taken the tablets?"

Of course I had taken the tablets. You don't mess with the Department of Nuclear Medicine. But why am I here? "Meantime you can do whatever you want – but avoid the company of children and pregnant women."

This is really exciting.

Three hours later I am ready to be guided into the tunnel. "Are you OK in a confined space? Have you ever experienced feelings of claustrophobia?" I smile. "I'll be fine – sure haven't I done this before?"

"Well, lie back and rest your head and make yourself as comfortable as you can. It will be noisy. You must keep absolutely still." "For how long?"

"About three quarters of an hour." I am having my first experience of claustrophobia.

"You're joking, aren't you? I don't remember it taking anything like that the last time."

She puts down her notes. "There are different forms of neuro-imaging. I imagine what you had before was a CT Scan – this is an MRI scan. It uses strong magnetic fields to get very detailed pictures of your brain without the use of X-rays or radioactive tracers."

I lie here thinking of Homer Simpson.

Chapter 17

Parisienne Walkways

"Oh bollocks."

I had been told the exam results would be posted on a noticeboard in the cloisters of main university building. I fought my way to the front and there it was. Or actually, there it wasn't. My name was not on the list. Bollocks, bollocks, bollocks. That meant a bloody re-sit in September – just when The Group was already signed up for a lot of gigs.

I had just failed my first year as a mature student at Queen's.

Mature. That is bit of a joke. It is not a bit of wonder I failed the exam, given the amount of time I was prepared to allocate to my studies. The subject I failed was geography. I thought the night before would be time enough to do my revision. It seems some techniques I rely upon had let me down – like theories for subconscious learning. The Morrison theory of subliminal reception of knowledge involved going to sleep wearing headphones and keeping my eyes open as I slept through a lecture.

I scanned the rest of the noticeboard just in case my name had appeared on some other list by mistake. There it was!

No, not my name – a handwritten note to say someone had pulled out of a student flight to Paris leaving from Dublin the following day and was offering a cheap ticket. I made up my mind on the spot and found the nearest call box.

A few weeks previously, I had declined an invitation to attend a wedding in Paris. My friend Jack Kerr, had fallen for Françoise – one of the au pair girls who frequented the Boat Club. I decided on the spur of the moment that I would buy this spare ticket and arrive at the wedding unannounced. Until this second Paris had seemed like a long way to go to see a knife slice through a wedding cake.

It was at the Boat Club that I first met Françoise. The fact that the Boat Club was a gathering place for French girls was one of the main reasons guys would go to the lengths of climbing in through the window of the ladies toilets. The girls liked it here. Many decided to stay.

I had known Jack from schooldays – he played the trombone and had qualified as a dentist. And now Jack and Françoise had become an item. They were going to be mighty surprised at me turning up at their wedding.

Paris was incredibly hot. I found my way to a fairly rough hostel where I spent an uncomfortable night. I had an address for Françoise who came from a respectable family who ran a one of the best food shops on the Right Bank. It was a fashionable place but it was also the naughty district. At eleven o'clock on a Monday morning I was unprepared for the sight of naked women arranged provocatively up the confined staircases of rent-by-the-hour hotels.

I made contact and immediately was treated like a star guest. None other of Jack's friends appeared to have made it, so I commanded the full attention of every mademoiselle in the room – and Françoise had a lot of mademoiselle friends. I made the most of my schoolboy French.

"Cela va sans dire." I would say when expected to offer something to the conversation. Smiles all round. It worked every time.

This phrase which was one of the few expressions I had remembered from school. I was discovering that it could win over the heart of any French girl. I don't really know why this expression stays in my mind. I had offered it up one time under pressure as an example of an idiomatic expression. Monkey Mark, the French master, was mildly impressed. He told the class it was a useful expression for idiomats like me. He was right.

Here in Paris it was proving useful. I knew the phrase meant "that goes without saying" – but until this moment I had no idea how useful it would be. The combination of a foreign accent, a shrug and a hint of a smile won over the girls every time. If there was any doubt about whether I understood what was going on, I got the benefit of it. I was getting on famously.

I staggered back to the hostel where I was kept awake for hours comforting a US student who was homesick. He was on the run after dodging the draft.

The next morning I faced up to a reality. I had no money. No means of getting home. Here the draft dodger was helpful. He told me where I might find a student rescue service. This happens a lot, apparently.

After standing in a lengthy queue for about an hour, I ended up in amongst a bedraggled bunch of students, most of whom were clearly destitute. We were bussed under what seemed to be military guard to a field we were told was somewhere near Calais. We were then marched to an Avro Anson the main use for which (in its day) was to transport parachute troops into enemy territory.

We clambered aboard the Anson. There were no safety belts; in fact there were no seats. We had to stand, holding on to the kind of hanging leather loops like you would see in the London Tube. The metal airframe was uncovered, exposing the outer skin of the fuselage which we could see and feel vibrating violently. The access door was left open and the noise inside was terrifying. It felt like we would be pushed out if we didn't jump out.

The plane took off over the cliffs, lurched down and flew across the English Channel. We could see out of tiny windows we were flying at about 100 feet above the waves, the engines revving up to clear the white cliffs of Dover before we landed in a rugby pitch in Kent. I hitched my way to my cousin's home in Surrey where I was able to borrow the cash to get home to Belfast.

But it was not the journey home that stayed with me. It was the flight out. For weeks afterwards, all I could think of was a French air hostess who sat down beside me as the plane was coming in to land in Paris.

My eyes had been drawn to her from the moment she welcomed me on board. What is it about air hostesses? Is it the glamour; the whiff of perfume as she walks by; the hour-glass figure? Maybe it is just the uniform.

And so I was struck dumb when the uniform sat down in the empty aisle seat beside me. I was sitting in the front row. I could feel my pulse racing as I sat there with my landing card on my knee. What I wanted was an ice-breaker. I needed a pen. Wasn't the word for pen? Is it 'plume?' 'La plume de ma tante' and all that?

"Avez vous une plume, s'il vous plait?"

"Voilà," she said – and with a flourish she pulled out a pen from the upper part of her tunic. Unable to divert my thoughts from what the pen had been close to, I wrote my name and address on the card. She was watching me. In fact she was staring at what I had written.

"Bill Morrison?" she gasped. "The Dominoes? The Boat Club?"

I am struck dumb again. I am just an ordinary guy. These things happen to other people – they never happen to me.

She turned to face me and carried on in perfect English with an accent I was falling in love with. "I was an au pair in Belfast and used to go to Boat Club every Saturday night. I thought I knew you from somewhere."

I wasn't falling any more. I was in love. How can it be that I didn't remember her? She was beautiful. It has to be something to do with the uniform. We talk about Jack and Françoise. I explain I am going to be a surprise guest at the wedding. Will she be there? Sadly no.

Suddenly the plane hits the runway. She has duties. I'm at the front of the queue to step off the aircraft. She gives me a hug and a kiss at the top of the steps. Other students on the flight behind me were now eagerly looking forward to the same heartfelt welcome to Paris.

I never saw her again.

Her last words to me were "I'll see you on the flight back."

 The summer of 1967 subsequently became known as The Summer of Love.

We played every August Wednesday in the Astor and the crowd numbers just grew and grew. It was a fun time and we entered into the spirit of things by collecting flower petals and scattering them over the dancers like confetti at a wedding.

I remember having a brainwave that the small, sweet pears from an Asian pear tree at the foot of our garden in could be a useful novelty item at the Astor Marquee in the spirit of flower power. Mother called them 'love apples' and they were plentiful. Having played out the flower petal idea, why not graduate to something more substantial? The idea was that we would toss them to the crowd, and those who caught them would nibble them if they felt so inclined.

What a dumb idea it was. The pears came back at us like a barrage of artillery.

It seemed like a good idea at the time.

Chapter 18

The Pound
Saturday 6 April 1968 – 16.05
Reach Out (I'll Be There)

I stop the tape recorder and rest for a moment. We are going down well this afternoon, but we must be careful not to peak too early. I'm thinking of calling another number by The Four Tops – "Reach Out." It was the first Four Tops number that we learnt when we formed The Group 18 months ago.

"Cheers, ma'hearty – aye: Black Label."

Smick gives the thumbs up to confirm his willing acceptance of the offer of a pint coming from a punter who is heading for the bar. I see Sez catch Fred's eye.

Smicker is a star performer in the band. He gives it 100 per cent and the punters love him. He has achieved celebrity status on account of a photograph in the window of Van Buren's in Wellington Place. Occupying the centrepiece of the photographer's display is a large framed photograph showing Smick in a monkey suit, sound asleep, being skilfully hoisted into the upright position for the camera by an attractive girl in an evening dress.

The attractive girl in the picture is the lovely Lyn Dalton whom I have been dating for a few months now. She is here this afternoon – right over there. It is a picture taken by professional photographer Perry Zachary at a Queen's formal in the Whitla Hall in September. I know because I was there when the picture was taken. The photograph has been on display for months and is the talk of the town. It hasn't done The Group any harm at all.

What does cause harm, of course, is that with booze on board, the concentration goes. That goes for all of us. For a band that relies on harmony singing, it is not good. Harmonies will fade out or drift off key. For the guy on the drums there is not just the risk of losing the pitch of a harmony – there is the added challenge of keeping the tempo. The tendency will be to start too fast and then run out of steam towards the end of a driving number.

Sure as eggs is eggs. It will be like that tonight.

Tonight we are in the Marquee with The Gentry. I know it is The Gentry because I saw the advertisement in the paper. The place will be bunged, because for every pop and blues fan in Belfast it is the only place to be on Saturday night.

The problem is that Saturday is hard work. This afternoon at The Pound is separated by only a few hours from our next gig tonight in the Astor Marquee. Most of those hours will be spent in the Hercules Bar.

And it won't stop there. Odds on we will go on to a party after the gig. We will head first to Concetta's chip shop, the Venice Café, on the Crumlin Road near Carlisle Circus where we expect to meet up with guys from other bands who can talk the hind leg off a donkey.

A couple of weeks ago we were in Concetta's with Sam Mahood. What a sensation he is. A brilliant soul singer – but a total spacer. We watched him put away most of a flask of vinegar as we exchanged opinions on soul music. People tell me that when Otis Redding died in a plane crash last December, Mahood marked the occasion by downing a bottle of aftershave lotion. If he survives – indeed even if he doesn't – Sam Mahood will become a legend. You mark my words.

But I am worried about Smick.

Smick has been in the band since last summer. Before that, the former Exiles drummer was the one to whom we would turn when we had to urgently find a stand-in for Ricky McCutcheon.

Smick is one of the good guys. I am thinking this as Sez steps up to the mic. Smick is funny and popular. He makes everyone laugh and sees humour wherever it lurks.

When Ricky missed a gig last June, Smick was the obvious candidate for the job. Fred put it to him that he should defect from Heart and Soul and join The Group. Ricky was a popular member of The Group and Smick knew he would be a hard act to follow.

"Why would you want me?" asked Smick, fishing for reassurance.

"Because you're a chap." said Fred.

Clearly the idea that we all thought he was not just a good guy but a chap helped to make up his mind for him. He would join the band. As it has turned out, Smick is more than just a chap – he can sing and play the drums rather well as was apparent when he began rehearsing with The Group last summer. The first gig for the new line-up was at Malone Rugby Club in Daddywinkers Lane off the Cregagh Road. It was Saturday 26 August 1967.

Daddywinkers – what a great name. It is not only the first gig for The Group with its new line-up. It is also a first for the club – the first time its doors have been opened to the youth of Cregagh and Mount Merrion. The entire Malone pack has been hired as bouncers. The cheerful and plentiful throng who have flocked to this heavily advertised opening night grew quiet as they enter the building, seeing fit to give the muscle men a wide berth.

Fred was in his element. All the rugby players knew him on account of his dad, Fred Isdell senior, a rugby personality still playing for Malone veterans at the age of 66. He is roughly twice the age of the rest of his team. Young Fred had to take a lot of stick. He and I have been helping out in preparation for this first night. I am quite proud of my Rubber Soul-inspired graphics drafted up at my desk at Queen's when I should have been revising. It was in the shape of a rugby ball, announcing that The Group would be playing at Daddywinkers.

We had a couple of practices on the premises this week to get Smick into the groove, and used the opportunity to run through some new songs. We were excited about the brand new record that everyone is talking about: 'Hole in My Shoe' recorded by Traffic, featuring Stevie Winwood who was formerly with the Spencer Davis Group.

What excites people about this record is the middle bit – the meandering psychedelic interlude that escalates the mind through a crack in the clouds into another consciousness, where a child narrates a tale of being carried to a faraway place on the wing of a giant albatross. Weird. Cool.

We have an idea that we know will knock them out. We have taken a line out to the PA amp from the trusty Grundig. Also connected is a toggle foot pedal which I activate at the appropriate moment. We all stop playing and at that point mix in the original recording. I hit the pedal again to stop the recording and we resume. We have it cracked, having rehearsed it all week. It works really well and we are pleased with ourselves. We grin to each other in anticipation as the crowd responds audibly to the opening riff of the number that is leaping up the charts. The floor fills up immediately; excited faces looking up at the stage. All credit to The Group. Nothing is beyond these guys.

It was, of course, bound to happen. I forgot to return the tape to its starting point after the last practice session.

Need I go on? I kick the pedal as planned expecting the psychedelic bit will swing into action – but of course the monologue had passed, and we are left high and dry while Traffic played out the remainder of their number. We looked bewildered. The crowd was bewildered. 'Hole in My Shoe' was promptly dumped from the repertoire.

Smick now knew what it was going to be like playing with a pack of eejits.

'Reach Out (I'll Be There)' got to Number 1 in the UK charts in 1966. It was the Four Tops biggest hit and remained in the charts for 16 weeks. It was written and produced by the brilliant song writing and production team made up of Lamont Dozier and brothers Brian and Eddie Holland.

The Four Tops recorded 'Reach Out (I'll Be There)' in just two takes. It was kept in the can for a future album – just one of many songs written exclusively for the quartet by the Holland-Dozier-Holland team. It was not seen as a potential hit and was only released as a single on the insistence of the record company.

In this rendition, Sez performs brilliantly while the rest of The Group warble ineffectually in the background. 'Reach Out (I'll Be There)' was the first Four Tops song to be covered by The Group. The Philicorda organ was well suited to the intro and the hook is in the diminished chord that swells into the chorus.

Chapter 19

The Pound
Saturday 6 April 1968 – 16:20
Good Vibrations

'Good Vibrations' was at the time of its release, October 1966, dubbed the most expensive pop song ever recorded, costing about $50,000 to make. It followed the acclaimed album, 'Pet Sounds.' Brian Wilson became obsessed with the orchestration and recording techniques. 'Good Vibrations' was recorded over a two month period using top Los Angeles session musicians - the Beach Boys didn't play any instruments on the track. About 90 hours of studio time and 70 hours of tape were used, and at least 12 musicians played on the sessions, including Glen Campbell on lead guitar and Hal Blaine on drums. Beach Boys lead singer Mike Love wrote lyrics hastily at the end of the process – inspired by what he detected as a psychedelic vibe.

It was widely held at the time to be the most complex pop song ever recorded and was a huge hit in UK, just as The Group came into existence. Undaunted, the fledgling four piece group from Belfast set about emulating the hit. The heads in the Freshmen were the only other local musicians who rose to the challenge of emulating the sound of 'Good Vibrations,' but for The Group it became a signature tune that immediately proved to be a crowd-puller on the urban beat group scene.

Meantime the Marquee empire was expanding, and The Group was part of the family. We were no longer 'managed' as such by Ronnie Field – Ronnie had thrown his hat in with Arnie and The Group was content to play along, taking the gigs as they come.

We began to detect a bit of tension between Arnie and the owner of the The Pound, John Roddy. The success of the Saturday afternoon gigs and the fact that The Group, at Ronnie's instigation, had been poached from The Pound to play the odd Saturday afternoon at the Mint Imperial may have had something to do with it. It was all a bit difficult, because the truth is we would have preferred it if things had been kept the way they were.

The Mint was another Marquee creation. A deal had been struck between Arnie and Dan Morgan who owned the Imperial Hotel on the Cliftonville Road at the corner of Cliftonpark Avenue – close to the former home of Belfast-born Chaim Herzog, the sixth President of Israel. The idea was to open a night club, and the task was delegated to Ronnie Field.

Ronnie went about it in style, making full use of the Marquee publicity machine now firmly in the hands of Colin McClelland.

A large L-shaped room on the upper floor was transformed into a trendy place. The papers all carried feature articles. CityWeek actually published in full a press release containing another outrageous fib but it certainly did the trick. "...a personal friendship between Beatle McCartney and Ronnie Field, entertainment manager, has enabled the club to have a complete wall covered with enlargements of pictures of the fabulous four."

Whatever the explanation, the opening of the Mint Imperial made an impact. It was launched a couple of months ago - on Tuesday 16 January 1968. The press had been called to a by-invitation-only pre-opening party the night before with Heart and Soul playing and television's Simon Dee present as the Guest Celebrity. Eight of the best-looking women known to the Marquee team, wearing matching white dresses designed by Susie Knowles, were lined up one at a time to be photographed with the celeb. There was much camera flashing and pictures of Simon Dee with the enlarged images of Ronnie's 'fab four' friends in the background. But there was more. Simon Dee in a short speech announced that Manchester United footballer and local hero George Best would be present at the opening the following night. The Marquee promotions team did well. The press, who turned out for what looked like a big story, now had good reason to be back with friends and work colleagues the following night.

I was there that night, gazing out the window at the crowds that had gathered in the hope of catching a glimpse of George Best on that cold, dark night in January. The Cliftonville Road was besieged – not with football fans, but with teenyboppers – jumping up and down with excitement at the prospect of seeing the football star. They were too young to be admitted to the new Night Club, but a crowd's a crowd and the Marquee team was delighted. They knew the papers would be full of it the next day.

Wearing a dark suit over a polo neck jumper, George Best fought his way through the crowds and, with his family in tow, was escorted into the building by a particularly smug-looking Ronnie Field. The Best entourage quickly tucked into the champagne. Many publicity photographs were taken of Best that night, sipping bubbly with the girls in the fashionable white dresses. And in the background once again, endorsing the whole idea, were the enlarged black and white images of Ronnie's other personal friends. It was not just the Mint that had arrived on the scene. Belfast was now cited in the national press as the trendiest place in the country.

On Saturday 3 February 1968, The Group played the Mint Imperial for the first time. It was a Saturday afternoon. We were not entirely happy about letting another band in to our cherished slot in The Pound.

Looking back on it, the success of the launch of the Mint Imperial was all thanks to George Best. The twenty-one year old is not only the most exciting player in the Football

League; he has the looks and the style of a pop star – in fact I have heard him described as "the fifth Beatle." He is also seen as a fashion icon, having opened his own boutique in Sale in 1966. He is a quiet unassuming lad and I understand there was no big appearance fee involved.

Simon Dee on the other hand – the groovy talk show host on our screens five nights a week at peak tea-time viewing – commanded a huge fee and expected star treatment.

Peter Dalton was appointed as his escort. As he was waiting at the airport Peter overheard an upset flight attendant telling her colleague that Dee had commented loudly on the plane that he was entitled to expect better service from someone that was, after all, nothing but a "flying waitress." It wasn't long before Dee's rudeness and condescension got to Peter as well.

Dee had another appearance that night – at the Student's Union at Queen's University, and Peter had been primed to alert him to rumours of a student prank, which was to kidnap him and hold him to ransom for charity.

"You better make bloody sure that doesn't happen," said Dee, humourlessly.

Peter, who happened to look rather like Dee (something he was beginning now to regard as a misfortune) decided at that point not to divulge the second part of his instruction. A plan had been worked up in detail for Peter to act as a decoy to foil any attempt at a kidnapping. He was now determined to assist the students in any way he could to give this arrogant git a hard time.

Sadly he never got the opportunity. The rumours were unfounded.

But the Marquee was at the centre of it all. The Saturday night Astor Marquee Club has been on the go for six months at this stage. Arnie had opened an office at 33 Donegall Street, just beside Commercial Court and handy to the Duke of York pub. Despite becoming a favoured hang out for long-haired hippies there was a dynamic about the place which was business-like. Colin always wore a suit. Colin, Jake and Arnie worked well together, and that was the simple reason the Marquee became so successful.

Arnie was a respected boss man who walked the talk. He was a showman himself – a familiar figure who, as he drove round the town in a striped Mini-Moke promoting the Marquee gig on a Saturday afternoon, represented all that the young people of Belfast were celebrating at that time.

The Mint Imperial lasted just 4 years. On Thursday 14 September 1972, it was destroyed when the UVF exploded a car bomb, killing three civilians.

....

I'm back at the Movement Clinic in the Ulster Hospital, sitting waiting for the medic. The room is sparsely furnished with a hospital trolley bed against the far wall, and a desk with a computer. There are three chairs, and I have been ushered in to sit on the one beside the door which is left ajar. I have been here for a while.

I hear a male voice talking outside the door.

"We will run a few physical tests and get him to walk down the corridor," says the voice. "You know what to look for. One thing you have to be very careful about is depression. His notes indicate a family history."

Bloody hell. I need to put him straight about this. He must have the wrong file.

The door is being held open to admit a young woman in a white coat, followed by a man in a suit. The man I presume was the bloke I heard outside the door. The man I had come to see.

The door opens and a young woman in a white coat enters the room, closely followed by the man I had come to see.

"You don't mind if Miss Wong sits in on this, do you?"

Not at all. I am thinking this is going to be a useful lesson for the attractive Miss Wong in recognising someone who does not have Parkinson's.

"I'm going to ask you a few questions and get you to walk down the corridor." I smile inwardly. I know what you are going to ask me to do because I overheard you brief Miss Wong outside the door.

He studies me as I answer his questions.

Yes, I do think I am slowing down. I am eating slower; thinking slower, talking slower and moving slower. Yes, I have to say I do feel pretty shattered a lot of the time. Yes, my main concern is speech. Yes, it is more than voice projection – it is about my capacity to order thoughts, articulate them and speak coherently. Yes, I do get anxious and apprehensive in crowds. Yes, I do find it difficult to focus on more than one thing at a time. No, I am not depressed.

Miss Wong is taking notes. I hope she is learning something from this. Whatever might be wrong, it doesn't sound to me like the doc is barking up the right tree.

He holds my hands, moving them about. He gets me to relax as he rotates my arms, seemingly looking for some signs of rigidity. There's none that I can detect. He asks me to slap my left palm with my right and vice versa. He asks me to tap my knee as fast as I can with each hand in turn. Finally he gets me to put my palms together as if in prayer.

You cannot be serious, I'm thinking. I'm a celebrity: get me outa here…

Chapter 20

Chips off the Old Block

Life before The Troubles was joyful and carefree, but it was not without its hazards.

"Bill, dear…" It was my mother on the phone. "I need your help to dig something up in the garden." I groaned inwardly. One of the benefits of living in the flat was I didn't get have to deal with mother and her bloody garden.

"Of course, Ma. I'll be there at around six." That should ensure I get my tea made for me.

It was the Asian pear tree from which I had harvested the love apples a few weeks before. I stared at the hole in the ground beside the trunk of the tree. She had left a neat pile of soil beside what what looked like a steel helmet scarred with marks from her spade. What the hell is it? It was metal, cylindrical, about two feet long and rounded at one end where there is something best described as a large nipple. The rusty casing is scarred where it had been attacked by the spade.

"God, it's a warhead. It's a bomb." I took two steps back.

"I thought that's what it was." Right. And I'll know how to defuse it?

"It's obviously a dud," she says with the insight of someone who can speak from personal experience. She did right enough huddle under the stairs during the Blitz in 1941. "It didn't go off. Just dig it up and carry it over to the bin."

I called the police. The police called in the TA. The TA called in the Army. The Army helicoptered in a bomb disposal expert who pronounced it to be highly dangerous unexploded ordnance which he believed to be in an unstable condition.

It was in fact a naval shell from the First World War. It made the papers and the Army expert was quoted as saying it would be hard to find anything more dangerous and unpredictable. The shell was gingerly transported to Ballyhornan beach where it was blown to bits in the sand dunes.

The fact that the previous owner of the house in Ormiston Gardens had been a Commander in the Royal Navy might give some clue as to why two live shells were buried under the pear tree sometime during or after the First World War.

Wait a minute, you say. Two shells?

Two weeks after reading in the paper about the delicate disposal, I found myself having to phone the police a second time. Mother had called me to say that she had excavated "another one of those ruddy things." She had found it on the other side of the tree, but everything was all right. I was not to worry.

She had not only dug it up. She had carried it to the other end of the garden, safely out of the way so she could get on with what she was doing.

On Wednesday 1 March 1967 my mother came to hear The Group for the first (and only) time. We were doing the warm-up for Cream and I got her a seat in the balcony. She had never heard of Clapton, Bruce or Baker. High volume psychedelic blues was something for which she was unprepared.

She had driven into town in her Austin A30 and queued up with the masses to get in. She sat through the entire show. She was getting ready to drive home alone when I found her after it was all over; after Baker's astonishing 5-minute drum solo that had the crowd on its feet cheering from start to finish. She was unable to hear a word I said. I felt guilty leaving her to find her own way home, but there was nothing I could do about it. We were booked to go on to another gig.

We had a frantic rush after the concert to get the gear in and set up in the late night Penthouse Club in the top floor of Sammy Houston's Jazz Club in Great Victoria Street. There I was introduced to the Ginger Baker who had accepted an invitation to come to SHJC after the gig. Yes, he looked a bit wild and spaced out. Yes, he spoke in riddles. No, he didn't seize the opportunity to play drums with The Group (I suspect he wouldn't have remembered how to play with only one bass drum). But he is an extraordinarily talented jazz drummer ranking with the all-time greats.

I had been going out with Lyn Dalton for almost a year. She agreed to let me take her to last year's May Ball at Queen's University.

I knew from experience that you could invite any one of the opposite sex to a formal without any serious risk of either rejection or commitment. No girl in the land is going to turn down the opportunity to exhibit a new frock. Nor is it seen as anything more than that. The main thing is to be there. You arrive with your date, spend the night in the bar with your mates, meet up again at the end and take her home. She would have had a great time with the girls and everyone goes home happy. I liked going to formals because of this. I have formed lasting platonic relationships by this route.

But for some reason on this occasion I felt the need to get some reassurance from her brother, Peter Dalton, before I took the plunge. Would she be cool about this?

More to the point, perhaps, was whether I would be able to keep my cool. Lyn Dalton had been part of the scene for a while, but things suddenly changed that night our eyes met across a crowded room just a week before the Ball for which I needed a partner. I was disturbed by the fact that after that fleeting moment my eyes seemed to be magnetically drawn to her. I ended up thinking about her all the way home.

What I think I really liked was the way she ignored me.

Peter gave me the reassurance I was looking for. "Don't worry," he said, "I'll take care of it." I'm not at all sure why I was comforted by that, but there you go. Anyway I asked her out, confident she wouldn't turn me down. We fell in love on the way to the Ball.

By July 1969 tensions were mounting on the streets of Belfast. As the 'marching season' reached its height there was serious rioting in Derry, Belfast and Dungiven. Many families in Belfast were forced to move from their homes.

The Group was history. Smick was long gone and was by now leader of the powerhouse John Smith Band, comprising Paul Lyttle from the Carpetbaggers; Alastair McKenzie and Derek Drayne from the High Wall and Keith Baker from Heart and Soul. Fred had cleared off to study in England. Ricky McCutcheon, re-called to take Smick's place, took up a better offer to play with Jim Armstrong and Kenny McDowell in Sk'boo. Confused? Well, of course you are – don't worry about it.

It was the second major re-shuffle. The Group had managed to stay in business through a merger with what was left of Heart and Soul. We had become a five-piece band. Sez and I had played on for the best part of a year in The Pound with RI (Robin Irvine) on bass; RL (Robin Lavery) on drums and DP (Dick Pentland) playing a top-rated Farfisa Professional organ. It was still billed as The Group, but the Mk 2 version produced a sound that was very different. I had traded in my Philicorda for a Hohner Pianet electric piano - a sturdy instrument that was great for power chords if I kept it simple. All I was good for, if truth were known.

Robin Irvine had effectively taken over the band. Sez, by now fondly (if inexplicably) known to the punters as Cecil

Sedgement, still carried The Group, leading on vocal as well as guitar. Young Lavery on drums made his mark as a vocalist with his version of 'Bridge Over Troubled Water,' and Irvine had a few production numbers up his sleeve that always went down well – such as 'And When I Die' by Blood, Sweat and Tears. And he sure knew how to milk 'Green, Green Grass of Home.'

But when Sez had announced he was clearing off to Edinburgh to study, and The Group was deprived of its principal asset. Colin McClelland, now firmly settled into a management role, said "Leave it to me" and organised an advertisement and audition in what today is the Black Box in Hill Street.

The intention was to find a singer/guitarist to replace Sez, but Colin thought there would be no harm in seeking expressions of interest from girl singers. None of the singer/guitar players made the cut. As for the girl singers that we didn't really want – well, the consensus was that two of them, Ann Ferguson and Linda Martin, were not too bad.

But to me, things were not looking good.

"Look here. What's the point of taking on a girl singer? I could see it might make sense if we were taking on a lead guitar player as well, but we're not. So why are we even thinking about this?" I was getting ratty. "I'll tell you why. Because we didn't think either of the only two guys that showed up were any good. And we don't want to go through this all over again. I mean one of them didn't even own a friggin' guitar!" My rant was greeted with silence.

"That's why we're here. We need a lead guitar. Name one band that doesn't have a lead guitar. Go on – name ONE. C'mon McClelland, make your mind up time. This is a management decision." I knew this would be like a red rag to a bull as far as RI was concerned. As Colin opened his mouth, RI said "Take them both."

There would be no lead guitar. The name of the band was chosen as a tribute to Concetta.

It was the summer of '69. The birth of Chips.

On Wednesday 15 October 1969 Chips opened for Fleetwood Mac in the Ulster Hall. We joked about playing our top song in the popularity stakes at the time, Irvine's over-the-top rendition of the Kenny Rogers hit "Ruby, Don't Take Your Love To Town." We reckoned blues/rock Mac fans would chase us out of the hall – but RI, forever perverse, launched into it anyway. It provoked the first jeers of the night. The jeers gradually turned to cheers. Somehow instead of the contempt I was expecting, we were being rewarded for having the audacity to play something so outrageously inappropriate on this gig. The cheers got louder at the end of every number from that point on. This was turning out to be some warm-up.

Lyn, by then my fiancée, was sitting with other band widows on the steeply rising bench seating behind the stage, when someone slipped in the bench behind her. She had already been introduced to Mac guitarist, Peter Green. He leant over and, giving a fair impression of Butch Cassidy in the big movie of the moment, breathed:

"Who are those guys?"

"That's Chips," replied Lyn.

"You'd see them better from down there," he said helpfully. "Your man's in the band, isn't he?"

"Yes," said Lyn, glancing at her sparkler.

"Nice," he said, following her gaze.

Lyn was pleased he noticed the ring on her finger.

Within weeks of Chips' first gig we were invited by Mervyn Solomon to come to his Ann Street studios where we recorded demos with Pete Lloyd at the desk. The demos were brought to the attention of Decca Records in London, and record producer Tommy Scott came across to Belfast, complete with contract documents. We laid down at his request a cover of a rockabilly song called 'Sock It To 'em Sister Nell.' Now a collectors' item I understand. We signed that off, but we drew the line at his next big idea – a cover of Nancy Whiskey's 1957 skiffle song "Freight Train."

Chips turned pro. I walked away.

One of the tapes that emerged is a recording of my last gig with Chips performing the Boat Club on Saturday 21 March 1970. In an intermission, my recorded voice announces that Dana had just won the Eurovision Song Contest for Ireland.

I never could have imagined that 22 years later our Linda Martin would also be a Eurovision winner. I watched her on TV that night in 1992 like a proud father. When I saw her take the accolade, speaking confidently with a strong Dublin accent, my mind wandered back to that day when I collected this girl in her school uniform from outside the gates of Dundonald High School in east Belfast thinking maybe I should have had a word with her dad.

Chapter 21

The Times They Are A'Changin'

In the early 70s Lyn and I, along with our close friends Mike and Liz Shanks, embarked on our own enterprise. We negotiated an arrangement with Teddie Fix, a Holywood restauranteur who bought the Glenmachan Hotel in east Belfast. The proposal was to open a disco in an old coach house in the grounds of the hotel. We called it the Coach House, but it was more commonly known as The Stables.

In many ways it was a building similar to The Pound, another nineteenth century building with brick walls, no windows and a stone floor. We approached the owner of the hotel and worked out a deal. It resembled The Pound and became a very successful venture very quickly. I felt a bit of a traitor to live music running discos, but after a time we had it open several nights a week with live rock, blues and folk bands.

In winter The Stables was, like The Pound perishing cold. The first thing that had to be done on a winter's day in both venues was to light overhead gas heaters that were wheeled into position. The heaters were mounted on a steel frame with a tall gas cylinder chained in to maintain its vertical position. You turned the knob on the cylinder to release the gas to the heater above, to which you held a flaming match. The gas fire would ignite with a "whoosh."

Bloody dangerous, those things.

Our resident DJ and all round good guy, Lewis Hall, was on the roof fixing a tarpaulin that we had figured would be a cheap solution to the challenge of keeping out the rain which was finding its way through the roof. The roof had lost a few slates. I had said to Lewis as he was climbing up the ladder: "You do that; meantime I'll light the gas heaters to warm up the place."

I had to install a new gas cylinder in one of the heaters – which were exactly the same as the ones in The Pound. It was not difficult. All you needed was a spanner and the knowledge that gas cylinder connections are designed with the safety measure of a left hand thread.

I had become well used to the task, but on this occasion I must have lost my mind.

I installed the cylinder, connected it up; lit the match and "whoosh." I was in business. As I lowered the match, a thought entered my head that it might be a good wheeze to check that the cylinder connection was good and tight. The brainwave was that I had in my hand a means of checking whether there was by any chance a gas leak.

What a good idea it was. I held the flaming match close to the connection – and with a tiny plop there it was. Aha. A little blue circle of flame around the nut. Evidence of a tiny leak of gas. I could deal with this. Clearly all that was needed was a twist to tighten the connection.

I shook out the match and reached for the spanner. I could hear Lewis on the roof over my head.

I put the spanner to the nut and gave it a yank.

When it was all over, I lurched out into the open air – breathless, my heart pounding, my shirt in tatters and not a hair left on my arm.

"That should do it," called Lewis. "Did you hear that jet engine being tested over in Shorts? Long time since I heard that." He was obviously oblivious to what was going on and totally unaware of his near-death experience.

He noticed my appearance. "What happened to you, by the way?"

You know what they say about seeing your life in a capsule when you really do believe your number is up? Believe me, it is absolutely true.

I reeled back. The roar was instantaneous and deafening. The flame was huge and I was immediately bathed in heat. The tip of the flame reached right up to the rafters above. I could see an expanding scorch mark on the timber sarking. This was it. I was done for.

My first thought was to run and get help. I reckoned I wouldn't make it to the door before the building would be alight. I was transfixed with the giant flame. It was really quite beautiful. Shaped like a candle flame – with the threatening orange tongue far above me licking the roof. But I also noticed there was a less threatening blue core rising from the cylinder where the gas was being driven upwards, sucking oxygen out of the surrounding air.

I had yanked the spanner the wrong way of course.

I am not going to suggest it was presence of mind. I'd say my mind had left the building. But I thought I just might be able to reach the spanner into the heart of the flame and turn it the right way this time. I reached in, expecting to lose my right arm.

Astonishingly it worked. The abrupt release of gas had spun the nut and loosened the connection. It needed three turns of the spanner. I rejoiced in the sight of the flame reducing step by step with each turn until it was totally extinguished.

I lost my shirt and the hairs on my right arm were reduced to cinders – but apart from that I was all right. Somebody must have been looking after me. And Lewis.

In July 1972 I was working on the 8th floor of River House in High Street. The city centre streets were open and we had all become somewhat blasé about the bombings which we felt were normally accompanied by a timely warning. This was despite the horror of Saturday 4 March 1972 when without warning a bomb ripped through the Abercorn Restaurant killing two people and injuring over 130.

It is difficult to explain, looking back on it. But life carried on. I remember one occasion when we were on a coffee break in a canteen on the top floor when the building rocked to the unmistakeable 'crack' of a nearby explosion. I lifted my eyes to look out the window over the shoulders of my two work colleagues sitting opposite, and witnessed the roof lift off a building in Waring Street 50 yards away. Rafters flying through the air. My colleagues carried on their conversation without turning round to look at the mayhem.

Then there was the time a security announcement advised that there was a security situation and the building was in lockdown. Lifts were disabled and all exit doors were sealed. Everyone should move to the back of the building or take shelter behind filing cabinets. The police were dealing with a suspect vehicle on the other side of the street.

I scooped up my paper and muttered to myself "not again." Then I heard someone say "That wouldn't be your car by any chance, Bill?"

"Oh my God."

I ran to the lifts. Not working. I sprinted down the eight flights to the front door. Locked. The back door. Locked. I could see a terrified constable edging his way across the street towards my car. I don't know what he was hoping to do, but I felt I should communicate somehow. I banged on the front door from within the building and yelled soundlessly. "It's OK; it's OK. It's my car. There's no bomb in that car!" At this point the River House doorman appeared out of nowhere.

"Thank God," I said. "Let me out."

"Can't do that, son. There is a procedure to be followed."

"Well, what is the procedure?" He started flicking through the leaves of a small booklet, patting his pockets in the hope of finding his glasses. I had had enough. I burst through the locked door of his little office, obviously locked in accordance with procedures.

I lifted the phone and dialled 999.

I returned to the 8th floor to await some sort of interview with the RUC. I hadn't done anything wrong but I expected a visit to at least confirm that it was my car. It turned out a conversation with the doorman was, according to procedures, all that was necessary. My last abiding image was looking out the window and seeing the constable sitting on the kerb with cap in hand and head bowed, being comforted by his colleagues.

If we thought it was cool to carry on regardless and make light of all that was going on, the events of Friday 21 July 1972 changed everything. They called it Bloody Friday.

Roddy's Bar, formerly The Law Courts Hotel, was a pub of long standing. It was built in 1880 and had been in the hands of the Roddy family since then. It was a fine Victorian building of three storeys that curved round the corner into Townhall Street. It was rendered in smooth stucco, with rounded pitch slate roof, moulded window surrounds and tall brick chimneys. The upper part of the building façade was painted light green with the substantial mouldings encasing the windows painted yellow.

Just across the road was the Oxford Street Bus Station – a building typical of its type with a two-storey box-like curtain walled structure at the northern end. The building stretched down Oxford Street towards a red brick pumping station, beyond which lay the urban wasteland that once housed busy markets. Rows of neatly parked blue single decker buses faced the mud flats of the tidal River Lagan.

At precisely two minutes past three that day, a car which had been driven into the rear of the Oxford Street Bus Station exploded without warning, killing 6 people and injuring nearly 40.

The IRA planted and exploded 22 bombs in the city that afternoon. On the 8th floor of River House in High Street, we heard the first four or five in fairly rapid succession. A silence fell across the open plan office. We were all thinking the same thing. Do we get out of town fast, or are we safer to stay put?

In the space of 75 minutes, the IRA killed 9 people and seriously injured approximately 130 others. Bombs were placed in locations such as banks, bus stations, railway stations and in residential streets. In addition to the bombs there were numerous hoax warnings, adding to the chaos in the streets that afternoon.

I decided it was time to get out of town. The drive home was terrifying. Movement was slow with vehicles impeding the movement of the emergency services. Every parked car looked like it contained a bomb. Horns were beeping; drivers gesturing. Minor shunts were ignored as every driver clutched their steering wheel and prayed. As I edged towards the Queen Elizabeth Bridge I could see the pall of smoke rising from the bus station in Oxford Street – opposite John Roddy's Bar. The car bomb had killed two soldiers and four civilians. Mutilated bodies were swept up and collected in black plastic bags, scenes that were broadcast that evening on the television news.

As John Roddy's son Chris put it many years later: "It broke my dad. The front bar was used like a morgue."

The Pound as a music venue lived through two epochs. The first began with the Knowles conversion in 1967 and ended at 3.02 pm on Friday 21 July 1972. The second period, the punk era, lasted from that moment in time until The Pound closed its doors for the last time in 1981. The building was demolished in 1983.

Chapter 22

Who Do I Think I Am?

My mother was born Joyce Isobel Duffin Boyd. The Boyds came from east Antrim. Grandfather James Boyd was an accountant, born in Belfast, who married Emma Sarah Duffin of Cullybackey. They were the Edwardians, raising a family at a time of peace and plenty. James Boyd made a success of his business ventures and the family was able to fulfil the aspiration to live in the Osborne Park, a fashionable suburb in south Belfast. Joyce was sent to Ashleigh House and would always consider herself to have been "well brought up."

Hanging on the dining room wall at home was a print of an eighteenth century engraving of Sir Robert Boyd KB, Governor of Gibraltar – a man who is celebrated to this day for a wheeze that put an end to Spanish efforts to capture the strategically important fortress. Gibraltar has remained under British control from that day since. The story is described in detail in the Museum of Gibraltar, and is quite interesting.

The daylight attack from the sea on 13 September 1782 was unexpected. Accurate cannon fire from the Rock had on all previous occasions succeeded in despatching the Spanish fleet to the bottom of the sea. Through a spy-glass, Boyd saw that on this day the British guns were on target as always, but somehow the enemy batteries remained afloat. He figured, correctly, that this could only be because each vessel had been constructed with a double hull, and that the cannon shot, having lost velocity breaking through the heavy wooden outer skin, could penetrate no further. It also appeared that the British cannon balls were being returned, having been captured in the gap between the hulls – an early example of re-cycling.

Boyd's wheeze was to direct that the British cannonballs be heated in a furnace so the shot that the cannons would fire would be red-hot. The Great Balls of Fire found their way to their ultimate destination – gravity causing them to roll down the gap between the inner and outer hulls to the lowest point. A bit like a pool table, I guess. Within a short time the entire flotilla, expressly designed for the capture of the fortress, was ablaze. Our man was the hero of the hour and he was rewarded with a knighthood and appointed Governor.

I inherited an engraving of Sir Robert Boyd which I pinned to the wall of my living room so I could talk proudly about how an ancestor of mine saw off the Spanish scoundrels once and for all with Great Balls of Fire – until the day I was pulled up short by a penetrating question: "How do you know your mother didn't buy that print in a Jumble Sale, simply because his name was Boyd?"

The painting doesn't hang there anymore.

My mother could play the piano rather well. Very well, in fact. She was an accomplished reader who without advance notice could play from any sheet music placed in front of her. She was proud to possess an LRAM Diploma from the Royal Academy of Music.

The one thing she could not do on the piano was improvise. She would never attempt to play "by ear." My father on the other hand had no formal training, but was capable of lifting any musical instrument and giving it a go

Charles Rutherfoord Oliphant Morrison had a comfortable upbringing. His Edinburgh family had long association with the printing and publishing firm of Morrison and Gibb, founded in 1837 by his great grandfather, a prominent city bookseller named William Oliphant. The Oliphant family name has deep ancestral roots that can be traced back to the fourteenth century struggle for Scottish Independence led by Robert the Bruce and 'Braveheart' William Wallace.

Oliphant is my middle name as it was for my father, my grandfather and my great-grandfather.

Charlie Morrison was the youngest in the family and for that reason enjoyed that bit of extra affection from his parents. He was just 14 years of age when the heart-breaking news came through that his brother Billy (after whom I would later be named), had been killed at Buissy in France in the last offensive of the Great War. The pain cannot have been eased when the announcement of the Armistice came just a few weeks later.

Charlie was sent as a day boy to a private school then known as the Edinburgh Institute, leaving at 16 to enter the family business, where he worked hard to earn the qualification of Master Printer. Life in the Scottish capital was good in the nineteen-twenties. By the age of 20 he was the centre of attention wherever he went. He was amusing – and a great mimic. He could sing and he could dance. He was a popular man about town, cutting a dash with his fashionable moustache. He charmed the socks off everyone he met. He possessed the casual air of an aristocrat with an engaging personality that was well received wherever he went. He was a gentleman in the true sense of the word.

It soon became evident that he had little appetite for a career in the printing business which was thriving under the firm managerial control of his father. His father – who died in 1926 – had in fact been following in the footsteps of his father before him. But none of that for Charlie – he had other fish to fry.

His first love was jazz – a collective word that covered not just Dixieland, but Big Band and Swing. This was 'hot' dance music – care-free foot-tapping music that had its origins in the Mississippi Delta. It was music brought to Britain in the nineteen-twenties by Jelly Roll Morton, Duke Ellington Jazz Orchestra, Paul Whiteman Orchestra, King

Oliver's Creole Jazz Band, Benny Goodman, Bix Beiderbecke and Fats Waller.

Charlie met a few of these now famous band leaders. He spent time in the company of impresarios who afforded him opportunity to chat with the popular band leaders when they were in town. On occasion he would rise to a song or accept an offer to sit in on drums. The story goes that on one occasion Paul Whiteman, appearing with his orchestra in Edinburgh, got his biggest cheer of the night when he invited Charlie to come to the stage for a few numbers in order to give drummer George Marsh a cigarette break.

In 1928 at the age of 24 he established a business to print, publish and sell sheet music. He wrote popular songs under the pseudonym of Dennis Arnold. His sights were set high – and why not? The nineteen-twenties have been described as an age of optimism – sometimes equated with the 1950s and the 1990s. The world was changing as a consequence of invention and innovation – telephones, typewriters, sewing machines, motorcars, aeroplanes, and wireless.

Charlie's interest was in new techniques for sound recording.

Until the 1920s, recording had been a purely mechanical process. He saw an opportunity to establish Edinburgh's first recording studio. He chose to invest everything he had in his own talents, inspired by his love of popular music. He quickly established his credentials as an accomplished electrical sound recording engineer.

It was at this time he met and fell in love with Joyce Boyd. Joyce was from Belfast – tall, softly spoken and with a shy personality. She was attending 'finishing school' at Atholl Crescent in Edinburgh. After a short courtship, he offered her his hand in marriage. She didn't hesitate.

It would not be the first time the Morrison family had reached across the Irish Sea. His mother's maternal grandfather was Sir Robert Boag – a Scot who married a Belfast girl and became mayor of her city in 1876. Before that, his great-grandmother, bookseller's daughter Margaret Oliphant, had forged the connection by marrying the Rev Charles Morrison, an Ulster Presbyterian minister who came from Saintfield, County Down. Not only were they great grandparents of Charlie – they were also great grandparents of one of notorious Cold War ring of spies known as 'The Cambridge Five,' Donald Duart Maclean. Well, you can't win them all.

But there was nothing to warn the young couple of the impending Wall Street Crash of 1929 and the Great Depression that was to follow abruptly. The nineteen-thirties would not be kind to those who chose to make their own way in the world.

Struggling to get clients, Charlie drew the conclusion that Edinburgh wasn't yet ready for sound recording. They decided to make a fresh start in Belfast, having tied the knot in St John's, Drumbeg on 20 December 1932. With generous financial support from Joyce's parents, they set up home at 1 Ormiston Gardens off the Upper Newtownards Road.

Charlie quickly settled in and forged new friendships. He mixed naturally and effortlessly into Ulster society. He tried his hand at yachting. He got involved in road racing, taking part in the Ards TT Circuit race. But as his business ventures struggled and failed, Charlie refused to reset his sights. He continued to aspire to a lifestyle that Joyce and her parents could see was some way beyond his means.

Despite the financial pressures, the early years of marriage were happy and colourful. They would go together to all the Big Band events in the Plaza Ballroom where Charlie would inevitably end up back stage – and frequently on stage.

Joyce maintained a degree of detachment from an ever-widening circle of fun-loving friends that welcomed Charlie into their midst and led the cheers as he stepped down from the stage after these spur-of-the-moment performances. She didn't smoke and only sipped at a glass of wine. She began to observe with concern that Charlie was rarely seen without a drink in his hand. She accepted that he didn't drink to get drunk and was not driven by alcohol, nor did he seem to be dependent on it, but she detected a problem. With increasing frequency he would arrive home from work in a condition she would describe as 'squiffy.'

Charlie inherited a number of valued domestic possessions on the death of his mother in 1933, but soon to Joyce's dismay, most of them had to be exchanged for cash at the pawn shop. The harsh truth was that there were no opportunities anywhere for paid employment at this time. By the end of the nineteen-thirties, Charlie was describing himself as a travelling salesman 'on his own account.' Life had descended to a hand-to-mouth existence and the outlook was bleak.

Joyce struggled to keep up appearances while shouldering the burden of making ends meet. Charlie was finding life difficult as well, alcohol offering a means of escape from the realities of having to borrow money and cope with mounting debt. He was deeply unhappy at the fact that he had become dependent on the generosity of his in-laws. The situation became no easier when, after her father died in April 1939, Joyce decided that her widowed mother Emma should come to live with them in Ormiston Gardens.

A few months later the nation was at war with Germany. At the age of 35, Charlie Morrison volunteered for military service. He enlisted as a private with the London Scottish Regiment (The Gordon Highlanders) and trained to be an officer with the Pioneer Corps.

Military service brought in a regular income and took the pressure off their financial problems, but as with all couples separated by war they found they missed each other terribly. Joyce kept a diary which, while containing extraordinary understatements about the horrific blitz of April and May 1941, was revealing in regard to my unplanned arrival on 16 July 1942. Many years later, Joyce's diaries were referred in lectures around the world given by my good friend, Jim Dornan. Professor Dornan, leading obstetrician and gynaecologist, the man responsible for the resurrection of the Dominoes in 1981, found that the diary record gave him what he described as profound insight into how women feel about their first labour experience.

A month before I was born, Charlie was posted overseas. His military career was short. A month after I was born, he was wounded by a landmine while training in South Africa and detained in Oribi Military Hospital for eight months with concussion and a smashed ankle. He composed songs in hospital, posting the hand-written sheet music back to Belfast. Eventually he was sent home on board a hospital ship, declared unfit for active service. On 10 April 1943 he was, to use the phrase the authorities used at the time, 'relegated to unemployment.' It meant he could go home.

When back on his feet, he completed a course to become a 'Messing Officer' with a view to working with the military catering organisation NAAFI. He was appointed warden for Londonderry District, which took him away from home for much of the week. He remained in the army and was granted an honorary rank of major.

His dependence on alcohol persisted, and at a time when the world was celebrating the end of World War II, relations between Charlie and Joyce became strained to the point where, according to her diaries, Joyce was contemplating legal separation. At the beginning of 1946, Charlie was prepared to acknowledge he needed help. He returned to civilian life firmly resolved to overcome his drinking problem.

Charlie picked up where he left off – as a commercial traveller. It was soon apparent that the post-war years were going to be a lot busier. His principal client at this time was Kiddicraft, a toy company which was now launching sets of what were described in associated literature as 'self-locking bricks.' It was the forerunner of Lego. Imagine the fun I had with that.

He joined with a small group of like-minded people to establish Ireland's first Alcoholics Anonymous, located on the Albert Bridge Road in Belfast. AA believed that the right approach to the disease required the consent of the victim to keep away from the bottle. This may seem obvious, but before the nineteen-forties standard medical practice had been to confine the alcoholic in hospital to dry out. AA encouraged victims to proclaim without shame 'I am an alcoholic,' and to recognise they faced lifelong vulnerability. AA offered the support of others who knew that repeated affirmation was the key to managing the condition. AA helped society come to see alcoholism as a total disease, not just a medical one. I had this truth drummed into me at an early age.

In the last years of his life he worked for Short Brothers and Harland which began a programme of diversification by establishing a Division in Newtownards to manufacture and sell carpet sweepers using the trade name Metoluk. He was appointed Assistant Sales Manager.

He became ill with what was diagnosed as a duodenal ulcer, and died in hospital on 22 May 1953, aged 48. I hardly got to know him. I didn't even know he was ill.

Joyce loved him to the end. I remember exactly where I was standing when she sat me down and broke the news. I remember her exasperated cry a few days later as I repeatedly sought to comfort her with a phrase drawn from the limited vocabulary of a 10-year-old: "It's no use crying over spilt milk."

"Will you stop saying that," she cried in exasperation, pushing me away.

It was the moment I grew up.

Chapter 23

Strange Brew

John McGuffin – my pal at school with whom I played Newfooty and the one who came up with the proposal to name the band Spendlove Murphy – was indeed a bit strange. For my twenty-first birthday he gave me the Complete Works of William Shakespeare. Well, I thought that was strange at the time.

McGuffin was brought up in a middle-class Presbyterian family in Sandown Road, just a few doors away from where Sez lived on the King's Road. At Campbell College, McGuffin and I spent a lot of time together and the friendship continued after I left and he stayed on to do A-levels and go to Queen's. We were an odd pair: he was short, tubby and intellectually capable; I was tall, gangly and – well let's just say I wasn't just so smart. My mother liked him, although she would not have been too thrilled if she had found out that we would spend many happy hours playing poker.

We also shared interest in wrestling, snooker, Johnny Cash and football. Not exactly mainstream at a rugby-playing college. He became accomplished at Newfooty, and for a time hardly a day would go by without a match between his Manchester United and my Arsenal. He would always win on the green baize pitch. His wee fat stubby fingers seemed to possess extra kicking power.

The only time I remember beating him at Newfooty was after the Munich Air Disaster. He was devastated by that terrible event. We prepared ourselves to play a memorial match. McGuffin selected his best substitutes for his very own deceased Busby Babes – Roger Byrne, Tommy Taylor, Billy Whelan and others.

Out of compassion this was one match I was prepared to lose, but the bastard, forever contrarian, let me win so I would feel bad.

On the day I left Campbell College, I noticed he was wearing a little red and black circular badge on his lapel. When I asked him what it was, he told me politely that it was something he wouldn't expect me to understand. When I pressed him for an answer, he said he was a communist-anarchist. He was right. I had no idea what he was talking about.

I lost touch with McGuffin while he was at Queen's taking an honours degree in Modern History. I was downtown at the College of Art pursuing a qualification in architecture. After that he taught in London and Saudi Arabia before returning to Belfast where he was employed as a lecturer.

He became associated with the People's Democracy Movement, which comprised mainly students involved in the Northern Ireland Civil Rights Association. He was among the marchers who walked from Belfast to Derry on New Year's Day 1969 and came under attack from police and loyalists at Burntollet. Eamonn McCann recalled many years later that McGuffin arrived with an impressive banner to champion the anarchist cause, but was unable to persuade anyone to carry the other pole.

When I was at Queen's as a mature student 1967-69 studying town planning, I would come across from time to time the charismatic Bernadette Devlin and others who would later become associated with political activism and the call for 'one man, one vote.' I was not particularly interested.

I had other things on my mind. I was playing in The Pound with The Group.

But the attack on the student marchers at Burntollet Bridge on 4 January 1969 was a turning point. It marked the end of peaceful co-existence and the beginning of a horror from which the only escape was to leave the country.

Leading the loyalist ambush at Burntollet that day was Major Ronald Bunting – the man who tormented Roy Bradford during his election campaign in 1965.

If Burntollet was, in the words of the distinguished academic Lord Paul Bew, 'the spark that lit the prairie fire,' it was the decision two and a half years later to suppress republican opposition by interning suspects without trial that ensured the fire would rage relentlessly for 30 years.

McGuffin was arrested in the early hours of Monday 9 August 1971. In his own words, he was kidnapped from his bed by armed men, taken away and held as a hostage for five and a half weeks. He was aged 30, a lecturer at Belfast Technical College. He had been branded as a political activist and this led to him being lifted in the first internment swoop when 342 men were arrested.

McGuffin was one of only two Protestants to be interned – the other being a worker for the Civil Rights Association who was also brought up in the middle class suburbs of Protestant East Belfast.

His name was Ronnie Bunting, the renegade son of the aforementioned Major who had rejected everything his father stood for and was now firmly aligned with the republican cause.

McGuffin in his first book, 'Internment' [1973], tells how Bunting (23) was beaten by the Special Branch for 'having disgraced his father' – the man McGuffin described in his book as the 'buffoonish' Burntollet ambusher.

In 1974, McGuffin published his second book 'The Guineapigs.' In this book he documented the consequences of brutal treatment meted out to a selected group of fourteen internees by the security forces from August to October 1971. On account of the liberal use of words such as torture and brutality, the book was banned by the government. It was re-published in 1981 when the government could no longer deny that the group were selected for a cold-blooded experiment with extremes of sensory deprivation.

McGuffin never espoused or condoned violence, nor was he in any way involved in acts of terror. He was not at all that way inclined. He spent the 1970s pursing his own brand of political activism, earning the respect of the more thoughtful activists at home and abroad.

When I returned from living abroad in 1978, I received an invitation from McGuffin to stop by a flat in Malone Avenue where he was living. Eccentric as ever, he had told me in his phone call that he was in the middle of writing a third book 'In Praise of Poteen,' "celebrating the talent and anti-authoritarian spirit" of the poteen-makers.

He had put on weight, comfortably resting in what was clearly his personal armchair. He welcomed me without getting up, gesturing that I should sit beside him in the only vacant chair in the room. I had expected him to be on his own but this appeared to be something like a party. About a dozen casually-dressed characters were sitting around in groups. Distracting post-punk sounds filled the smoke-filled double room. Not all present were speaking English. One of the groups was watching a football match on television.

McGuffin poured me a glass of poteen and we talked about our days at Campbell College – to the obvious delight of his partner who sat on the floor at his feet so she could hear every word. Behind her, a rack of wall-mounted shelves groaned under the weight of books and files. We exchanged fond memories of Newfooty, and without rising, he reached across and produced from the bookshelf the game – in its original box, complete with baize cloth.

It was sweet; it was bohemian; it was calm and seemingly innocent – and yet to an outsider, it was more than a little bit threatening. I was glad he did not want to talk about what he was up to, because I picked up from other conversations in the room several mentions of Baader and Meinhof. I didn't want to know. I decided not to stay long.

I learned later that Malone Avenue was not in fact the fountainhead of international terrorism that I was beginning to imagine. McGuffin had evidently been appointed to sit on an international committee investigating the deaths in custody of Red Army Faction members in Germany. But as I left the building that night with an armful of rebel LPs produced for NORAID, I was convinced (as I am to this day) that Special Branch were in the car across the street waiting for me to emerge so they could record my every movement with a high-definition camera.

I never saw him again.

As McGuffin was being interned, in a parallel universe Dick Pentland and I decided to form another band. Sez was back in town, and the John Smith Band, which had struggled after Paul Lyttle left to take my place in Chips, had finally broken up after Alastair McKenzie took off for London, ending up with Suzi Quatro.

Smick was back in on drums and Keith Baker played bass. A name for the band must have come to us in a blinding flash of light. Dunno. I can't imagine for one minute how we could possibly have figured 'Dunno' would be a suitable name, but we stuck to it even after we were billed on one occasion as "The Don't Know Showband." We never even considered Spendlove Murphy.

We released two records on the M&M Label. One was a number Keith Baker and I wrote together called "Sunday Girl." It sold 587 copies for which Keith and I earned joint royalty of £4.22. It got a play on Radio One. The 'B-side' was a Dick Pentland freakrock composition called 'Magic

Beat' – only DP could come up with anything as weird as a song about attempts to revive corpses by exposing them to dance rhythms.

By the mid-seventies, people were getting the hell out of Belfast if they possibly could. Many of us just left the country. Dick took a job as Port Engineer in Halifax, Nova Scotia; I took off for St Lucia.

As we waited to board our flight at Heathrow, we noticed what one could reasonably assume to be a 5-man heavy metal rock group standing in a queue for a different flight to the New World. Long-hair concealing their faces, two of whom were conversing in a familiar drawl and a dialect where the word "man" seemed to be a required ending to every sentence. Three-year old daughter Sara spotted them first. Lyn followed her eyes.

"That can't be...surely not...is it?" I homed in on what it was seemed familiar and gasped "Look who it is!"

It was my old rock buddies Robin Irvine and Robin Lavery.

I hadn't seen either of them for about five years. And they were just as astonished to see me. What would be the odds of this happening? They were on their way to America. It turned out RI and RL had separately left Chips, which under the management of Louis Walsh was now in great demand touring the dance-halls of Ireland. Irvine had decided he would put together a new band called Bananas with an ambitious plan to head for New York and take America by storm. Many man-hugs later we found ourselves at the back of our respective queues. Lyn was fit to be tied.

Robin Irvine stayed in the US after the band failed to make the Big Time and broke up. RI is still living in the States, and when he isn't pottering about with boats on the Hudson River, he is managing tours for leading performers. Big names he has worked with include The Eurythmics, The

Monkees, Celine Dion, Fleetwood Mac, Steve Winwood, Emerson Lake and Palmer, Cyndi Lauper and Foreigner.

Robin Lavery stayed for a few months in New York where he met John Lennon and worked with and for May Pang, infamous for her intense involvement with Lennon in what became known as the Lost Weekend – a period of eighteen months when the ex-Beatle left Yoko Ono to live with Pang in her New York apartment.

Chapter 24

Don't Stop the Carnival

In 1968 I could never have imagined that a few years later I would be living and working in Emile Ford's home town of Castries, St Lucia. I'd love to be able to say that I met Emile there, but I didn't.

I did, however, meet a bloke from Belfast who was taking part in a banana-eating contest.

It was odd enough to see a honkie competing with the rastas in a competition to see how many bananas could be stuffed down the throat in 10 minutes. But to find out that this guy was from Belfast was intriguing. It turned out that not only was he from Belfast – he was from east Belfast. The centre of the Universe. In fact he was brought up in Greenwood Park, 100 yards from where I used to live in Ormiston Gardens. This was spooky. A coincidence, yes – but was it more than that? Was there a guiding hand that caused me to glance at the poster outside the community hall that day and think hey, let's go in and see what this is about?

It wasn't the first time I pondered this.

Maybe I should explain how I

ended up living and working in a banana republic in the first place. It was August 1974 when my boss in Craigavon drew to my attention an advertisement for a job in St Lucia. Nixon had just quit over Watergate, Cass Elliott had died and West Germany had won the World Cup. We had a child of two and there was another one on the way.

Northern Ireland was not a happy place. We had just come through the Ulster Workers' Council strike that brought down Faulkner's five-month-old power-sharing Stormont Executive. It was impossible to get petrol for the car. Masked men prevented us from using the filling stations. I couldn't get to work and unwisely copied to the BBC a letter of protest I had penned to the Secretary of State. When I walked our dog Murphy round the block at night, the only building that had power (and it was lit up like a Christmas tree) was the HQ of the Ulster Workers' Council in Hawthornden Road.

This was not a good time. For example we had no choice but to stand by and watch armed vigilantes from the Knocknagoney UDA claim territory by marching through our disco at Glenmachan. The future did not look too bright – certainly Northern Ireland was not a place where you would want to bring up a family. James Young had died leaving the feeling that there was nothing in the future that would ever make you laugh again.

So I sent off my application form. I got a free trip to London for an interview and to my astonishment (or was it dismay?) I was offered the job. Gulp.

I remember asking a colleague, an old cynic, what would happen if it turned out I wasn't up to the job.

"How long is the contract?" he said.

"Two years."

"Sure it will take them at least two years to fire you."

I was obviously comforted by that response, but it didn't convince me to take the offer. I contacted Stormont with a request for secondment, and weeks went by. I heard nothing.

Then I got a call from a bloke called S I D McKee, the guy who was actually doing the job; the one who was leaving and thereby creating the vacancy. He was moving on from St Lucia to Fiji. He said he could meet me in Dublin if it would help me make up my mind.

Here's the thing. Was it fate or coincidence that the incumbent in the job was from Northern Ireland?

We met in Dublin as he suggested. He put our minds at rest. This would be a life-enriching experience. Despite hearing nothing to confirm the secondment we took the decision. Let's get out of here. And so it all happened. Number two child was born. Christmas came and went. We spent weeks packing all our belongings into tea-chests.

The day after the tea-chests were collected from our home by the shipping company – the very day after – I got a shock message from Stormont to say the government of Northern Ireland would not be seconding me to work overseas. I would have to resign and sever all connections to the civil service.

What the hell, we flew out from Heathrow, and it was there, of course, that by chance (fate or coincidence?) we bumped into former band mates Robin Irvine and Robin Lavery on their way to seek fame and fortune in New York with their new band, Bananas. There seems to be a lot of bananas in this story.

And there's more: on the hour-long journey from Hewanorra International Airport to Castries there were bananas to the left of us and bananas to the right of us. We seemed to be travelling through an endless succession of banana plantations.

At the airport we had been greeted by a large number of taxi drivers jockeying for pole position. The one wearing a rastacap seemed to know what he was doing. He grabbed our suitcases and with a jovial "Follow me, man" he ushered us past a long queue of vehicles in the direction of a pale blue and white car with a massive bonnet and fins like wings. Fair enough, our man's car was at the head of the queue. He loaded the suitcases into the vehicle and laughed heartily when I observed there was enough room in the boot to sleep a family. We were admitted to the ample back seat of the car which was driven off at speed, tyres squealing as our driver swung it from side to side in skilful avoidance of the deeper potholes. He kept up a running commentary throughout, laughing all the way. His uncontrolled laughter was infectious.

It was like a furnace in the car, and we were utterly shattered after the flight. And what we had here was a comedian. "This is a 1958 Mustang," he announced proudly. "Top car in St Lucia. And you know what? You think it has a boot? It has wheels – no boots. That there in the back is a trunk, man. The Mustang has a trunk. You know – like an elephant. This is an elephant, man." I had no idea what he was talking about but he was laughing – so I started laughing. I laughed until I was sore. I rolled about at his explanation as to why he had to drive at this scary speed. "Best to reach Castries before nightfall," he chortled. Someone had broken into his headlights and stolen the bulbs. Now *that* I believed.

Lyn, Sara and baby Michael were all gazing at me open mouthed. Why was I laughing hysterically at every bump and thump as this wretched heap bounced up and down and lurched from side to side? Was it the heat? Gasping for air, I wiped the sweat from my brow and the tears from my eyes in an effort to stop laughing. I groped for words to comfort Lyn.

"How did we ever think this would be a good idea?"

It was fate. It was all about destiny. S I D McKee was a few years older, but like me, he was 6 foot 4 inches tall; he looked like me; he talked like me. He became an architect and then a town planner as I did. He came from – you guessed it – east Belfast. And, like me, he had been schooled at Campbell College.

I was meant to take this job.

I soon found myself on what was described as a steep learning curve.

At the office, I had to learn how to communicate.

The difficulties emerged in the first day at the office. I was told to wait at the hotel until I was contacted by the team leader whose name was St Helene. He took me to the office and the staff line lined up as if it was a royal reception.

St Helene moved swiftly with the introductions. "This is Yarde; this is Phulchere; this is O'Shaunessy..."

O'Shaunessy? Wait a minute.

"Hold it; go easy – I would like to know your first names." There was a silence.

"Look, I'd like you all to call me Bill."

"If you wish, Mr Morrison," said one.

"Bill," I reminded him.

"Yes, Mr Morrison." This time the whole team answered in chorus.

"Look, I really would like us to use first names."

The silence was eventually broken by the team leader. "OK. I'm Leo," he said, "Leo St Helene."

He carried on with the introductions, clearly not to be deflected from his determination to use second names: "And this is Yarde..."

"Nice to meet you," I said as he shook my hand warmly. "And your first name is...?"

"Scotland," he announced with more than just a hint of colonial pride. Nobody laughed. I tried hard not to smile.

O'Shaunessy wouldn't tell me his first name. It transpired nobody knew if he actually had a first name. He was Rastafarian.

You might think that an odd name for a St Lucian, but it was not unusual. Enslaved workers from the West-African coast, brought in to work on the sugar plantations, would in many instances have been adopted or been given the surname of their former colonisers, many of whom were from Ireland originally.

O'Shaunessy's greeting always was "whasappnin?" Loosely translated "whasappnin" means "hello." What was confusing is that he would use the word "hello?" when he failed to grasp what you were saying. He wasn't good with the Ulster accent. So if he phoned me the conversation would be along these lines:

Phone rings. I lift it.

Me: "Hello?"

O'S: "Whasappenin." I take it to be a question.

Me: "Nothing much."

O'S: "Hello?"

Perhaps we have lost the connection. Well I'm hearing him – perhaps he cannot hear me. I'll try again:

Me: "Hello?"

O'S: "Hello?" Evidently he can hear me okay, but he sounds puzzled.

Me: "What's happening?" Believe me, I really want to know.

O'S: "Whasappenin."

I asked first, for Pete's sake. But never mind.

Me: "I said nothing much..."

O'S: "Hello?" Confusion all round. I'm getting cross.

Me (loudly): "For fuck's sake, O'Shaunessy – where the hell are you anyway, and what do you want?"

O'S: "I'm in the office, boss." He's just outside. "Can I come in?"

Slowly but surely, and obviously by necessity, I picked up new communication skills.

We learnt how to behave at garden parties in the residence of the British Government Representative and how to stay on our feet as an endless supply of gin and tonic, handed round on silver trays, was forced upon us.

One day, in May 1977, I received an unexpected phone call from the British Government Representative inviting my wife and me to stand alongside him at a ceremony on Morne Fortune, overlooking the capital city Castries.

I knew St Lucia had a long colonial history under both French and British rule. I had been told that, during a turbulent period of the eighteenth century, the island changed hands fourteen times.

What I did not know until that day was that the Twenty-Seventh Regiment of the Royal Inniskilling Fusiliers won the final victory, against all the odds, in one of the most distinguished battles in its regimental history. It was explained to me that as a mark of respect that was to become a prized battle honour, the command came after the French surrendered to raise the Regimental Colour over the fortress for one hour before the raising of the Union flag. I was amazed to learn that no other Regiment in the British Army has ever been awarded this honour.

The event, attended by the Governor and the police band, took place at dusk. In a deeply moving act of remembrance, Lyn and I stood there, tear in eye, as the Regimental Colour, which had been flying from the flagstaff for exactly one hour, was lowered and replaced by the Union Jack. On this occasion, 27 May 1977, I felt I was not just representing the British Government. I was representing Enniskillen, the home of the Twenty-Seventh Regiment.

But the most extraordinary thing I was told that day was that this ceremony was something that had taken place on the twenty-seventh day of May every year since 1796.

I learnt to love reggae and to worship Bob Marley. I found I could select my own goat and scoff it cheerfully that evening for dinner. I learnt how to eat a pig's ear with a knife and fork and how mix splendid rum punch – and was that ganja I smoked that night on the beach?

We learnt how to survive in the company of career ex-pats who found comfort ladling a lethal mixture of Scotch and Drambuie out of a punchbowl. Rusty Nails they were called. They took you to the end without going through the middle. We learnt how to deal with biting centipedes, stinging hornets, flying cockroaches and bird-eating spiders.

We learnt to play Bridge and how to pursue a white ball round a golf course. I embarrassed myself playing cricket on the beach with St Lucians. We learnt how to pace ourselves so we could survive a jump-up fuelled by Mount Gay rum and reggae. We did the Carnival street shuffle swaying gently to imaginary rhythms long after the steel band guys had passed out.

We created a folk club where locals, ex-pats, drop-outs, bearded mariners and Peruvians armed with stringed instruments, pipes and harmonicas would assemble in ever-growing numbers for beer and vocal self-gratification every fortnight.

And of course I learnt a thing or two about urban planning. St Lucia, an island the size of Lough Neagh, had in 1975 a population of around 130,000. It was in the process of becoming an independent nation and my job was to help in the transition. I produced a National Plan in association with the United Nations team under the direction of Richard Bigwood, and I drafted Anglo-American hybrid planning law with the help of legal gurus Desmond Heap and Roger Suddards.

For much of the time I reported directly to the Premier, John Compton – a man deserving of the greatest respect. He led the country for many years long before, and long after, my short time there. One time he called a meeting of the full Cabinet lasting the whole day so I could take them through the National Plan line by line.

The St Lucian economy relied on the export of bananas, and the National Plan looked for both consolidation of the agricultural industry and diversification. At the time I was there, the main areas of growth related to the tourist industry.

There were challenges in the job. One day I was summoned to a dinner party at the residence of the British Government Representative. The BGR had invited eleven guests in total, most of whom spoke with American accents. The Premier was there and the guest of honour was Leon Hess, who was introduced to me as the Chairman and CEO of the Amerada Petroleum Corporation, at the time the largest producer of crude oil in the United States.

The BGR had a quiet word with me before the meal. "There is a proposition on the table," he said out of earshot of the other guests. It was something of an understatement. "Mr Hess wants to build an oil storage facility on Cul-de-Sac Bay." He added royally: "We thought you might have something to say about it."

I swallowed deeply. This was awkward. The unspoken words were risk of oil spillage. I knew that my boss, Premier John Compton and his governing party would be all for it because it would generate considerable income, which could be critical for the island as it edged towards independence. On the other hand I imagined my paymaster, the British Government, would want to kick this into touch. In advance of the handover, the former colonial masters would hesitate to sanction a proposition where there was even the perception of a risk that could harm the tourist economy.

I remained silent throughout the meal which was served on plates carrying the royal insignia ERII, listening intently to enthusiastic voices explaining what was involved. As he leant back in his seat at the end of the meal, lighting his Cuban cigar, Leon Hess brought the conversation round to what was clearly in his view a dark art – planning regulation.

He told a story at the dinner table about walking the length of a train looking for a carriage where he can smoke his cigar. Every carriage carries a 'No Smoking' sign. When he reaches the final carriage it is full of people and the air is filled with smoke. He asks the conductor, "Am I right to assume that despite the 'No Smoking' sign on the window you are happy for me to smoke in this carriage?" The conductor replies firmly "Absolutely not. You cannot smoke in this carriage." "Then how come these people seem to think it's OK to smoke?" The conductor answers...

Hess paused for effect before he delivers the punchline, looking directly at me.

"...Because nobody asked me."

Hess and his associates laughed heartily. I didn't. Neither did the BGR. Nor, to be fair, did Premier John Compton.

When silence descended on the table, the BGR said quietly: "Well, I'm going to ask Bill Morrison what he thinks of the proposal."

I swallowed deeply and quickly gathered my thoughts. I had the floor. All I felt competent to offer at this juncture, and indeed the full extent of what I thought would be prudent, was a cautious observation that the impact on the environment would need to be assessed, and that perception of risk would be a factor that should be taken into account. Such a facility on the sheltered Caribbean coast on which most of the new hotels had been built would be bound to raise a few issues for tourist promotion. My lukewarm response killed the conversation and the dinner party ended soon after.

Two days later, I was boarding a four-seater Lear Jet, heading for St Croix in the US Virgin Islands, 600 miles to the north, tasked to examine and report on what at the time was the largest oil refinery in the world. I could have written the report without going near St Croix, but it was clearly thought that a little trip would put me in a better frame of mind.

The pilot welcomed me on board and immediately explained that the airstrip at Vigie in Castries was way short of what was needed for a jet to take-off and land safely. "We'll just have to push things a bit," he said casually. He started the jet with what looked like a motor vehicle ignition key and placed the jet at the end of the airstrip as close to the back boundary hedge as he possibly could. I noticed considerable numbers of locals lining the hedges on either side of the airstrip.

He gunned up the turbofan and the aircraft set off in an astonishing acceleration towards the hedge at the far end of the airstrip. The pilot waited until the last minute before yanking back the stick to lift the jet over the hedge at the end of the runway and set out on a near vertical climb. He rose to what seemed to me to be the stratosphere, levelling out at what he told me was 41,000 feet above the blue Caribbean Sea. Minutes later he was explaining to me how he proposed to dive straight down to St Croix, so I should watch out for the island which should first appear as a tiny dot dead ahead.

I inspected the immaculate oil refinery and filed my report the next day. I expanded on the factors that would need to be considered, and submitted that the principle of the proposal should be a matter for political judgement.

It was a good call. It turned out the decision had already been taken.

I learnt something about appearing on live television.

The TV studio in St Lucia was in an old Victorian ammunition store on the top of the Morne Mountain outside Castries. I was there to chair a debate about the St Lucia National Plan. I arrived 30 minutes before we were due to be on air – before any of the guests and as it turned out before anyone from St Lucia TV Inc. The door was ajar. Inside a cine projector was running. It was broadcasting 'Bonanza' to the nation by projecting an upside down image into the lens of an unmanned portable TV camera perched on a pile of books. It seemed to work surprisingly well.

My guests arrived and I moved furniture about. Then I took it upon myself to move cameras across the floor. I positioned a large camera in such a way that it would cover all four panellists sitting behind a desk. I was getting anxious. The "on air" time came and went. No sign of a cameraman or a presenter. No sign of anybody at all actually. I sat down facing another portable camera on a stand and at that point spotted a shadowy figure behind a glass panel at the back of the room. A red light came on.

Gradually it dawned on me that it was possible I might be – just might be – live on air. I looked to the shadowy figure for confirmation and posed the obvious question. It came out in the local dialect.

"Whasappenin?"

This one word was the patois equivalent of David Frost saying "Hello, good evening and welcome." The guys on the panel nodded their approval for the way I was handling this, and picked up the cue to offer opinion straight away on the content of National Plan.

But then they didn't see what was broadcast. My ex-pat friends who were watching told me afterwards they were well entertained as the camera remained on me for the first sixty seconds of air time.

They told me that if it hadn't been for the bewildered look on my face I might have got away with it.

Chapter 25

Back in the Thick of It

The original plan was to live in St Lucia for two years and then return home under what was explained to me as a scheme that provided for "reinstatement" of former employees of the Northern Ireland Civil Service.

But as the end of the two-year period approached it became clear that this was not going to be possible. Jobs, plentiful when I left in 1975, had been lost through cutsback and restructuring. There were now no vacancies. The unions responded to the cuts by withdrawing support for reinstatement on the grounds that it would block promotion paths for in-house staff. I was therefore somewhat relieved to receive the offer from the British Government of a one year extension to the contract so I could stay in St Lucia for a third year, giving time to consider our predicament.

This was a difficult time. Suddenly the island paradise lost its appeal as we became more and more anxious about the uncertain future. Then out of the blue, a letter arrived from my former Department with the unexpected announcement that an agreement had now been reached with the unions. Reinstatement was back and I was eligible to apply. I would have to fly home to be interviewed, and if accepted I would be reinstated at the point in the salary scale I was on when I left. There would be no negotiation over salary or grade; no value placed upon the three years' experience of working abroad. C'est la vie.

We expected there would be a last minute bid by the British Government to stay to see through the final stages of St Lucia becoming an independent nation – and sure enough, in came the offer when the crates were packed and the journey home had been paid for. It was a far better deal, on vastly enhanced terms and conditions, but we decided to go home. We had had enough. There were widowed mothers to look after; we had kids we did not want to have to send to boarding school; there was a yearning for fresh milk and fish suppers, we had unexplained allergies. On top of that was a well-founded anxiety – an unspoken fear we later found out we shared – that if we didn't go home, we would end up... well OK, let's personalise it: I would certainly have ended up a gin-soaked beach bum, spending my days perched on a barstool in Doolittle's in Marigot Bay, rising unsteadily to my feet and saluting every time the piped music recycled Bob Marley's "No Woman, No Cry."

I was assigned to the Belfast Planning office to head up a pro-active team called 'Design and Special Projects.' Special Projects included the major challenge of revitalising the city centre, and the planned implementation of a new neighbourhood to be built on green fields at Poleglass, beyond the much neglected Colin Glen that marked the local government boundary between Belfast and Lisburn.

Poleglass was the immediate priority. The first phase of infrastructure, roads, water, sewers and street lighting was in hand; to be followed by the building of 2,000 homes by the Northern Ireland Housing Executive, with the coordinated delivery by other agencies of planned schools, shops, community and industrial facilities, and the restoration of Colin Glen.

It many ways nothing had changed. We had left Northern Ireland to get away from the political unrest and violent acts of terrorism, and here we were – right back in the thick of it. But there were good things, too. Belfast City Council had acquired Belfast Castle; the Crown Liquor Saloon had been taken over by the National Trust; The Arts Council was defiantly restoring the bomb damaged Grand Opera House under the guiding hand of Robert McKinstry, the esteemed architect for whom I was proud to have worked in the summer of 1966; Belfast Zoo had been re-opened with a plan to house the animals in exciting new buildings and enclosures – a commission that would in due course fall to Dominoes drummer/keyboard player Chris Doran to fulfil. And, to my delight, my schoolmate David Cook had been elected Lord Mayor of Belfast.

The three year absence left gaps in our knowledge of 1970s popular music which catch us out in quizzes to this day. We left in the glam pop era and became immersed in reggae for three years, to the exclusion of almost everything else.

I wasn't playing in any groups at this time and felt I had left all that behind me. I was invited by Linda Martin to come to Dublin and sit in on the recording of a new song by my old band Chips. I felt my contribution was less than useless.

I was somewhat dismayed at the emergence of punk music. I listened to Radio One and remember John Peel on Radio One play the Undertones record 'Teenage Kicks' twice in a row, but the significance of this passed me by until Colin McClelland took me down the Damascus road to see his new protégés Stiff Little Fingers perform 'Suspect Device' and 'Alternative Ulster' in The Stables at Glenmachan.

The noise of the British Army Gazelle on the lawn in front of Parliament Buildings brought everyone to the windows. I walked down the front steps and, crouching for fear of decapitation, I ran over to the helicopter where the door has been opened for me. I looked up at the faces at the windows and found myself raising my arm in acknowledgement. The pilot pointed to the passenger seat and indicated with gestures how he would wish me to strap in before handing me the headset which clamped firmly to my head, shutting out the sound of the rotor.

"How's that?" The English accent had a cultured ring to it.

"Fine, it's good," I heard myself say. As I reached out to pull the door closed, the faces at the windows were still there to watch the lift off. I couldn't resist a royal wave.

"Where to?" He obviously hadn't been briefed. I was suddenly a little apprehensive. A few months ago, the same day as the La Mon bombing, a Gazelle had been downed in South Armagh after being shot at from the ground.

"Are you OK to fly over west Belfast?" I ventured with a little hesitation. "Can you circle over Twinbrook and the green fields adjacent to it? Poleglass?"

"It will be a pleasure, we'll be there in a jiffy. And..." The engine note changed and dials on the instrument panel gyrated as he opened the throttle: "...and...off we jolly well go." The helicopter lifted off the ground and, nose lowered, swept round to head across the city.

The flight was uneventful. We flew over Beechmount, Andersonstown and Suffolk and followed the Stewartstown Road to Twinbrook, from where I got my bearings. We circled Poleglass a few times. I looked down on my project and saw the pattern of green fields and hedges I already knew were there. I took a few photographs. Pretty useless really.

We flew back across the city and touched down where we started. I opened the door, unbuckled the safety harness, and bade farewell with effusive thanks.

As I stepped down I could see that the noise of the helicopter touching down had once again drawn faces to the windows. I imagined they are thinking I must be someone important. I smiled and waved, making an effort to look the part as I strode confidently away from the helicopter. The faces were smiling back. In fact I can see some were pointing and smiling. They all look very pleased to see me.

Suddenly my head jerked back and I fell awkwardly to the ground.

I lay there for a moment, unsure at first as to what had happened. The wrench of the headset, still connected and at full stretch, was as painful as it was unexpected. Indeed it came as something of a shock. I gathered myself together, picked up the device and stumbled my way back to the smiling pilot. He mouthed what I imagine were comforting words like "People do that all the time."

For weeks afterwards, however, civil servants working in Parliament Buildings would come up to me and say: "So then you must be the guy who..."

Planning in a divided community proved to be both interesting and intensely challenging. I quickly learnt that the mass movements of population in the early seventies had produced an overcrowded and youthful Catholic inner city, interwoven with a sparsely-populated and elderly Protestant inner city. The aim of the geographical extension into the green belt at Poleglass was to ease overcrowding in Catholic West Belfast.

Poleglass was a bold political decision. It amounted to the relocation of Catholic families from inner Belfast into the green fields of a Protestant-controlled and elected council at Lisburn.

In the 1980s, planning faced new challenges. In 1981, the Government specifically identified housing in the city as its prime social priority. As a result, at a time when every other local authority in the UK was being denied money for council housing, a billion pounds would be spent on housing in Belfast over the next ten years.

The Housing Executive had inherited the unenviable task of rebuilding broken communities, devastated in the late 50s and early 60s after swathes of inner city land had been cleared by Belfast Corporation, which had then hesitated and dithered over the more challenging follow-up phase – the building of new homes to replace those lost through clearance. People were faced with little option but to up sticks and move to peripheral estates; to double up and wait to be re-housed or to re-build their lives in the unfamiliar

New Town environment of Craigavon and Antrim. To cap it all, 1971 saw the greatest forced migration seen in Europe since the War, as 77,000 people were driven from their homes as a consequence of sectarian hatred that led to monstrous overcrowding in west Belfast in the very year the Housing Executive was brought into being.

The Housing Executive rose to the challenge of redevelopment and rehabilitation in the inner city, promising that internal space standards would not be compromised and that no new high rise blocks would be built. Working closely with local communities, the Executive placed emphasis on providing properties built with traditional materials and with generous living space.

While living conditions were undoubtedly improved, critics of the community approach argued that it reinforced the polarisation of communities and territorial interface lines that would for many years into the future will be marked by what euphemistically became known as peace walls. However the reality which the planners faced was that people felt safe only if they were rehoused within their own enclaves. Peace walls were never planned or imposed by authority. They were erected and remain in place at the express wish of the communities affected.

In the 1980s, 10,000 new homes were provided in the inner city of Belfast at the hands of NIHE – including existing, run-down dwellings which acquired from the private sector and restored. Virtually all would be two-storey terrace or semi-detached homes.

The programme brought distinction and international recognition to the achievements of the Housing Executive by insisting on the highest standards of layout design, in doing so often standing firm in the face of pressure brought by financial stringency and inflexible highway regulations.

I am proud to have played a small part in support of the work of the Housing Executive in particular. The achievement in the 70s and into the 80s, in the face of adversity, is a credit to the work of Chairman Charles Brett and my friend and ally, architect-planner Bob Strang, whose work provided inspiration for future generations of town planners.

I pulled over and parked my car where I had done so on previous occasions to catch a glimpse from the Glen Road of construction in progress on the slopes of Poleglass below. I was delighted to see a panoramic view had now opened up. I knew just about everything there was to know about the programme for implementation, but something was happening here – something I had not been informed about.

An excavator was in action filling tipping trucks in removal of the roadside fly tipping eyesore that obstructed the view and marred the amenity of Colin Glen. I took a note to record that Lisburn Council had taken an unplanned initiative that would need to be fed into the co-ordinated action plan.

I raised the matter at the monthly Poleglass progress meeting at Stormont and was not altogether surprised to learn that the Council was not in fact involved. I was, however, more than a little surprised to learn that it was the work of a recently established voluntary organisation called the West Belfast Environmental Action Group. It was a group about which I knew nothing and, as it happened, a group that would never be heard of again.

I had no idea the men supervising the welcome clearance of the fly tipping at the side of the Colinglen Road overlooking Poleglass were carrying 9mm Walther PPK pistols under their waterproof jackets and that one man in every two-man team held a concealed Sterling sub-machine gun.

Shortly after 2pm on Tuesday 11 March 1980 they found what they were looking for.

It was the body of Thomas Niedermayer – the 45-year-old general manager of the giant west Belfast Grundig electronics plant where my Grundig tape recorder had been manufactured in the early 1960s.

Niedermayer had disappeared after been taken from his home in nearby Glengoland more than six years before.

The West Belfast Environmental Action Group turned out to be a fictitious environmental organisation that had been set up as a cover for a ground search by the security forces who had been tipped off as to where his body might be found.

Niedermayer's disappearance in 1973 had all the hallmarks of a kidnapping, an action which the IRA had threatened in response to the life sentences imposed on six men and two women convicted of planting two bombs in central London earlier that year. But nothing further was heard from the IRA. No demands were made. If it was a kidnapping, the police had not been able to find his kidnappers; they couldn't find Niedermayer and, as the months passed and it became increasingly likely he was dead, they couldn't find his body.

The fact that Niedermayer was also the West German consul in Northern Ireland heightened the pressure on the investigation team, but it would be a full five years before there would be any hint of a breakthrough.

The breakthrough came following a series of arrest and interview operations in response to an upsurge in IRA activity in west Belfast – concerted activity that led to convictions and the gathering of considerable intelligence on both the Provisional IRA and the Irish National Liberation Army. One promising tip-off indicated that Niedermayer had been killed in a botched kidnapping and that his body lay buried in a shallow grave at the side of the Colinglen Road, now deep beneath a mountain of rubbish that would take weeks to clear.

The undercover operation was conceived and given high level backing. It was dangerous, but the deception paid off. The first the IRA knew about it was when the announcement was made that the body of Thomas Niedermayer had been found, more than six years after he disappeared.

It was news to me, too.

On Tuesday 5 January 1988 I found myself yet another visiting planner on a strife ride round the city. His name was Mike Gibson. Easy to remember: same name as my rugby star school mate. It was twilight as we headed towards Poleglass on the last leg of the tour.

The term 'strife ride' has been coined by my colleagues at the office. It has become something of a must-do for members of the planning profession visiting Northern Ireland. Despite the many distressing things about Belfast, there are planning achievements of which we can be justly proud. Mike Gibson, nationally elected member of the Council of the Royal Town Planning Institute, had been told there is something different going on here. Besides, the idea of a conducted tour of the inner city and sectarian interfaces in a war zone carries a frisson of excitement.

As we drove by the Woodbourne RUC/British Army barracks on the Stewartstown Road, I pointed out the well-protected building that was once a hotel, and mentioned casually the fact that a soldier had been shot by an IRA sniper in an attack on the barracks the night before.

Gibson looked alarmed.

We drove on up the hill and into Poleglass where I gave a running commentary of the layout design. He was silent and I suspect was no longer listening to anything I had to say. The culs-de-sac looked a bit spooky bathed in the monochrome yellow of the cost-saving sodium streetlights. He breathed a sigh as we turned back down the hill in the direction of Andersonstown.

The engine suddenly chugged to a halt and my car, a Renault 12 Estate, freewheeled to a standstill directly outside the Woodbourne. "Oh, God – I think I just ran out of petrol."

Gibson was speechless.

I stepped out of the car and wandered over to the fortified sanger by the gated entrance where I was greeted by a smiling policeman. I explained the situation. He seemed to think it was funny.

"Well I can't help you – you'll have to walk to the nearest filling station which is about a mile up the road, near Finaghy Road. Your passenger will have to stay in the car."

I returned to the vehicle and explained the situation to Gibson. He was now shaking with fear. I set forth and came across a large woman stepping into a Black Taxi.

On the spur of the moment I followed her into the taxi which already contained an equally large woman who took up much of the back seat. I struggled with the rear-facing drop-down seat, but the two ladies would have none of it. They shuffled apart in what was clearly a familiar separation routine. "Over here, love," said one warmly, patting the six inches of exposed upholstery. "Plenty of room," said the other.

I wriggled comfortably in between the friendly women, smiling and apologising for the inconvenience. I explained to the driver that I just need to be dropped off at the filling station at Finaghy junction. I heard myself explaining why. They all found it hilarious.

As he pulled up he reached over and pushed down the passenger window. As I rose from my comfortable seat, I banged my head on the roof. At that moment I suddenly remembered something important. Bent over, poised to open the door, I realised my pockets were empty. No cash.

"Ouch!" I exclaimed as my head hit the roof. "Oh God..." It was a combination of pain and resignation. Patting my pockets pointlessly, I could only announce: "I've just realised...it seems I...look, fact is I find I have come out without any..." I tailed off as one of the large ladies, now in convulsions and gasping for air, felt compelled to complete the sentence for me. "Cash. Never carry cash, right? Ha, ha, ha. I'm sure yer man here will accept a Diners Club Card, won't you love?"

Hysterics.

The driver waves me away with a smile and a friendly "On you go..." This buck eejit had made his day.

As he drove off he left the window down so I wouldn't miss his last remark to the grinning women in the back seat:

"Probably works for the BBC. Wonder how he thinks he gonna pay for his petrol..."

I turned my mind to that not insignificant point as I waited to cross the road. Filled with apprehension, I explained the situation to the filling station attendant who happened to be the owner. He produced for me without hesitation a can which he filled with petrol on a promise that I would pull in on the way past and that my friend would pay.

It took me 20 minutes to walk back in the dark. On the way I remember thinking of how we had driven by the Glengoland bungalows from which Thomas Niedermayer had been kidnapped in 1973. I thought about the clandestine operation that led to his body being recovered from a rubbish tip in nearby Colin Glen eight years later. I thought of the jobs lost when the Grundig factory closed.

Mike Gibson was still there in the car. He had his fists on the dash. I could see his white knuckles from 20 yards.

To lighten the conversation on the way back to the city centre, I talked about my other life as a band boy, and about my treasured Grundig tape recorder that had been manufactured here in West Belfast. I left out the part about the botched kidnapping of Thomas Niedermayer and how the factory had closed following the discovery of his body on my patch.

Chapter 26

A Taste of Honey

Down the years, the Dominoes on many occasions had to look for guys to step into the breach when one of us couldn't make it. Barry McCrudden stood in on several occasions on keyboards, as did that true head and living legend, Ivan Black. Music shop-owner Harry Baird stood in a few times on bass – and we even had jazz bassist Willie McAlpine (the Pine) play a rock and roll gig with us despite his aversion to any form of pop music. He loved every minute of it.

Stand-in drummers I can readily bring to mind include Johnny Bassett, Tony Martin and Michael Murray from the early years, and latterly Davy McKnight; Harry Burns; Roy Kane and Colm Fitzpatrick. And John 'Junior' Wilson, of course, who stood in for 8 years.

I remember once we had a guest drummer who told us at the outset he had a huge memory bank of country classics that he could sing if called upon to do so. We thought we would pass on that one, but found ourselves swept along when he responded instantly to a request from the floor for a song none of us had ever heard before.

"I know it!" shouted the stand-in, launching full belt into the number; his drumkit bouncing as if it had a life of its own.

He pulled his boom mic tight to his lips and bellowed his way through the song from start to finish while the rest of us stood there with fixed smiles, pretending to play. Nobody noticed anything unusual.

Stand-in drummer P J McGirr, distinguished sound engineer with the BBC outside broadcast team, sat back satisfied not realising he had performed the entire song accompanied only by his own drums. He was applauded warmly.

I would never claim to have the musical talent to stand-in for anyone in another band, although I feel compelled to mention that on two occasions I was asked to gig with the Rodney Foster Jazz Band standing in for David Smith on double bass. "Of course you can play it," said Rodney when I explained I had never played an upright bass. "Sure it's just a big guitar." I fell for it, played two gigs and spent a week nursing my aching fingers.

I also remember being enormously chuffed to be asked by Malcolm Gooding to play my Philicorda in a jazz band he had put together for a short series of gigs in the Bayardo Pub on the Shankill Road. He was clearly exploring something different. He may not have got what he bargained for, but for me it was fun.

The Bayardo was later blown to pieces by the IRA, with the loss of five lives. The bomb was planted in retaliation, some say, for the alleged involvement of the Ulster Volunteer Force (UVF) in the shocking Miami Showband massacre two weeks before.

I met Rory Gallagher for the first time on Saturday 17 December 1966, the night he played his first gig in Belfast. It was at Sammy Houston's Jazz Club. The Group had a residency on the top floor of SHJC, where Maggie Gilchrist and Martin Everard had just opened a late night club they would call The Penthouse. Ricky, Fred and I were setting up the gear when Sez appeared at the top of the stairs.

"Come here quick – you gotta hear this!"

On the stage was a really good play-loud three-piece blues/rock group. We were pleased that after their gig the three scruffy looking, leather-clad, fast-talking guys came upstairs to The Penthouse. We got talking and asked the young guitarist/singer to go get his guitar. He needed no persuasion to get up and play.

A few weeks later we came upon the same guys sitting in The Coffee House in College Street talking to Blair Whyte and Marshall McMonagle. It was a Saturday morning and The Group was due to play in The Pound that afternoon. Blair got Arnie to pay them 10 quid for a guest appearance. It was the only occasion on which The Group shared the afternoon gig with another band.

Bass-player Eric Kitteringham and drummer Norman Damery arrived first with their belongings in suitcases. The pair of them looked like they could do with a good night's sleep. They were lean and hungry looking. In fact they looked like they had been living rough for a week, which would not have been altogether surprising.

Rory arrived late, humping his Vox AC30 onto the stage. He looked different from the other two – younger, hairier and more cheerful. He was modest and spoke with a softer brogue than the others. It was hard to follow Eric and Norman who spoke rapid-fire Cork. We teased them about coming all the way to Belfast to find fame and fortune. You won't find it here, mate.

We chatted for a while before Rory opened his battered guitar case. Sez, always interested in these things, peered in and was quick to recognise a 1961 Sunburst Fender Stratocaster. It had seen better days. In fact it looked like it had been used as a shovel. It was to become a much-coveted axe.

We opened the gig as normal and then announced we were handing over to the trio from Cork. We had never thought to ask if they had a name. We stepped off the stage to take up their vacated seats. Once they started up, no-one in the room could take their eyes off Rory and his low-slung Strat. He had them spellbound. His voice was compelling, and he sure could play that guitar. No pedals, no echo – just a mic'd-up Vox with a primitive treble-boosting device. But what a sound. What a performance. The crowd roared for more and wanted to know where they could hear him again.

'The Trio from Cork,' as they were billed for weeks afterwards, very quickly found gigs in beat clubs of Belfast. They accepted every offer and were soon playing five nights a week. Rory spent most days in Dougie Knight's record shop in Great Victoria Street, where he found inspiration from the expanding specialist blues collection.

I remember some time later meeting up with Rory Gallagher in an empty bar in the old International Hotel at the back of the City Hall. He was relaxing ahead of the biggest gig he had performed in Belfast up to then. Taste was booked to play the Ulster Hall. I tagged along as his back stage support – which was good because there was already a long queue of fans wanting to be sure to get into the Ulster Hall to hear Taste. Well, let's face it – to see Rory.

He told me about how he had moved to Cork as a youngster having been born in Donegal; how he started out as a school boy in a local showband; how he had been playing in Hamburg before coming back to Ireland.

But despite this experience, this Ulster Hall gig was the big one for him. He told me he was apprehensive about performing on a big stage before a sell-out audience with nothing more than his trusty treble-boosted Vox AC30 amplifier. Right enough, I thought. It was over a year since we had opened for Cream in the same venue, with Clapton's awesome ten foot high stack of Marshall speaker cabinets towering behind us.

In the event there was no problem. Rory proved that all you need is a mic'd-up AC30. The tiny amp on the floor behind him was part of what distinguished Rory from the rest. He was a great player.

Taste moved from strength to strength, earning international acclaim after performing at the Isle of Wight Festival in 1970, with John Wilson on drums. The Festival is probably best remembered for the performance of the Jimi Hendrix Experience. After it was all over Jimi Hendrix was asked what it was feels like to be the greatest guitarist in the world.

"I don't know," he said. "You'd have to ask Rory Gallagher."

....

Maybe prayer is the only answer. Of their own volition, my eyes seem to be closing.

"Now tap your fingers." I tap away happily. As with every other movement exercise I have been asked to undertake today, I cannot detect anything odd.

"Now make your left hand fingers do the tapping."

"See that?" The consultant is now addressing Miss Wong.

Hold on a minute. Only my right hand fingers want to do the tapping. Even when I concentrate on my left hand, I can't keep up with my right hand.

What does this prove? I am right-handed, for God's sake.

Now he wants me to walk down the corridor. The consultant and Miss Wong are deep in conversation about what they observe.

We return to the consulting room. Miss Wong takes her seat at the back of the room, opens her notebook and writes energetically.

The specialist consultant pulls his chair so he is seated directly in front of me. He is looking me straight in the eye. The expression on his face prepares me for what he is about to say. It is a kind, sincere and genuinely compassionate look – as you would expect of a vet delivering his conclusion that your family pet has to be put down.

"I think you might have early Parkinsonian symptoms."

I have been living with this for nearly two years and all there is to back up such a finding is a finger on my left hand not quite keeping up with my right. Come on.

He's Wong, I'm thinking. Definitely Wong.

Chapter 27

Surfin' Safari

It was in a bar near Roselawn cemetery. He was sitting on his own at a table with an empty glass in his hand. I had spotted him at the funeral. Although it was years since our paths last crossed, memory for once served me well. Gerry Shaw waved an invitation to come over and join him.

Michael was with me. "Here," I said, tugging his sleeve. "I want to introduce you to someone."

Gerry clasped my hand warmly and wasted no time diving head first into the cloudy waters of his lost youth. He addressed Michael, who hadn't been born the last time we met.

"I'll never forget that night," he began, his eyes moistening as he looked through Michael while still gripping my hand.

"I was there the night that your Dad opened the show in the ABC Cinema and The Group blew The Beach Boys off the stage..."

As it happens, I also have fond memories of that night. It was Wednesday 3 May 1967, and it was indeed the ABC Cinema. I know because I was in the audience. I was also mighty impressed with the band that performed the first half of the show that night. It was The Freshmen.

In fairness it must be said that the Beach Boys were not having a good tour – Brian Wilson had opted out of the tour at the last minute, and they struggled to put on a good performance. The Freshmen on the other hand were terrific – despite being prevented by contract from playing any of their acclaimed covers of Beach Boy numbers.

I have long endeavoured to kill this myth, but still people persist in the belief that it was The Group on stage that night. Some assert that it is my memory that is at fault. It is an embarrassment. But for some reason – maybe it was because we had been to a funeral – I decided on this occasion I would let it go. Gerry had clearly dined out on this story and I was not going to be the one to burst his bubble.

"Ah yes, indeed..." I heard myself say.

Michael, who was about to interject with what he knew to be the truth, was stunned into silence. From that day forth he has never believed anything I said about my rock and roll years.

So for his sake, if no-one else's, it is time to set the record straight.

I never appeared on stage with The Kinks. I never opened for The Troggs. I never played in Liverpool's Cavern Club under the pseudonym of King Size Taylor and the Dominos. I never sang 'Layla' with Eric Clapton in Derek and the Dominos.

Do I remember when Dunno opened for Led Zeppelin in the Ulster Hall on Friday 5 March 1971 when the Blimp performed 'Stairway to Heaven' for the first time ever? Eh, no.

I am not Van Morrison's uncle. And the guy with the same surname from The Doors who is buried in Pere Lachaise Cemetery in Paris is definitely not me.

But from the roar of the greasepaint, no one has immunity.

I did eventually meet Gene Vincent. It was Saturday 29 November 1969. He was in Belfast for a gig in the Floral Hall and the promoters arranged for him to make unannounced appearance with his band The Wild Angels in the Starlite.

He was dressed in his leathers and stood legs apart with the mic stand at an angle leaning towards him. He had no choice but to stand that way because of a steel sheath permanently around his left leg which was shattered in a

1955 motor bike accident, and further damaged in the accident in 1960 that killed Eddie Cochran.

Gerry Giffen introduced me to Gene Vincent. He had a reputation for being a hard man – after all, his greasy-haired leather clad appearance was a role model for the lawless rockers of the nineteen-fifties. According to those who toured with him in 1960 he carried a freshly sharpened Bowie knife which cut through a silk tie in a wink of an eye – and a gun with live ammo that he would casually point at others to keep them on their toes.

But I saw no sign of that. I was impressed with his soft Virginian accent and the way the word "sir" appeared somewhere in every sentence. He was extraordinarily polite in conversation and coped well with an indifferent teenage audience who were barely out of nappies when he was carving his way into rock and roll history.

The progressive sixties were not kind to Gene Vincent. The teenage audience had no time for him. It must have been humiliating to face an empty dance floor and he looked to be genuinely in pain as he struggled through his set. He died two years later of a perforated ulcer: destitute, confused, overweight and alcohol dependent. He was buried in black leather in Newhall, California. He was just 36.

I shook hands with Chuck Berry, whose 1958 hit 'Sweet Little Sixteen' was a game changer for me as I emerged from the skiffle era. It was Saturday 11 March 1995. I had been out to dinner with Jim Dornan and we had missed Berry's show in the Maysfield Leisure Centre. We reckoned he would end up in the bar of the Europa and that it would be worthwhile nipping down to see if he was there. We were right. There he was.

I walked over and said something that makes me cringe when I think about it now. Something like: "Would you mind if I shake the hand of the greatest rock and roll star of all time?" He said "Sure," and reached out the biggest hand I have ever seen: a hand that totally engulfed mine. My hand disappeared like it had slipped into a huge boxing glove. I was fixated on my swallowed hand and just a little alarmed that he seemed reluctant to let go.

I had to wait until Thursday 18 January 2007 to hear Chuck Berry play guitar and sing – in the Waterfront Hall. Michael came with me.

He was eighty years and counting. It is hard to believe that there wasn't an empty seat in the house – all age groups prepared to stump up £32 a time. But then he is a rock and roll legend, and this was his only UK gig. He told his audience that he was 29 years of age when he recorded 'Sweet Little Sixteen.' I was 14.

He came on stage in his dress suit trousers, a big sparking red shirt, a yachting cap and a big smile – with his famous red Gibson guitar. The initial thought that he can't possibly be 80 was quickly dispelled as he looked for help to plug a lead in his guitar. He then played a loud muffed chord, found his way to the microphone and muttered a few well known lines of 'Hail, Hail Rock and Roll' while his giant hands searched out a chord that he knew must be there somewhere.

He then signalled with a cutthroat gesture for the band to stop – which they did. He started again and soon gave up the search for a chord and happily hit an occasional clonk. Then he would crash out a big noise that would put you in mind of Marty McFly at the Back to the Future "Enchantment Under the Sea" dance – the scene when, standing in for 'Chuck' in time-shift back to 1955 playing 'Johnny B Goode,' he cranks up the amplified sound of his guitar into 1985 Van Halen-style screaming cacophony.

The octogenarian carried on like that for an hour. The stuff of amateurs – and the crowd yelled for more.

Awful though it was (and it really was awful) every now and then he would hit the right fret and a chord would fight its way out through his big fingers and "sound so sweet."

And, yes, he could still do the duck walk. I couldn't do that after the age of 20. His voice was as strong and distinctive as ever, although he sped through and shortened every line. He never sang more than a couple of verses. But they were all there – 'Memphis Tennessee,' 'Johnny B Goode,' 'Reelin' and a Rockin',' 'Little Queenie,' 'No Particular Place to Go.' Or did he? Maybe he forgot to play that one.

The Belfast audience was very forgiving – even when he confessed to not being sure where he was but noticed that people spoke English. He played it up of course. He gave a big smile for local photographer Chris Hill, saying "Was that a better one, Chris?" Most songs he started on his own, and he usually converted to a twelve bar blues with the occasional power chord coming in late – several times a semitone away from where it should be. But only musos notice this sort of thing – punters lap it up regardless.

'Oh Carol' drifted into such a twelve-bar. When he returned to the mic, he had to ask his son Charlie what song it was that he had started singing.

For Michael, it was sad to see what happens to rock and roll survivors as they near the end of the line. For me, well I now have no interest in growing old gracefully.

I got an email from Michael today. He knew I would be amused to hear about a conversation he had had with a female colleague at work. They were talking about live music and the subject came round to the fact that Michael had played drums in a group. He was telling her that there were lots of part-time musicians in the civil service.

"Right enough," she said. "I worked in the same office once with a guy who used to be in THEM."

"THEM? Really?" Michael was interested. "Who was that, then?"

"Och, I can't remember," she said. "But he went on to become the head of the city planning office."

The seed of yet another urban myth.

Chapter 28

Back on the Road Again

I have already mentioned the person who in 1981 was to blame for putting The Dominoes back on the road for thirty years. Jim Dornan is a close friend I have known since we moved in to a house opposite his in 1972. Chips played at his engagement party. We brought up our families together, enjoying wonderful holidays in France and in west Cork. He is one of UK's most respected gynaecologists and obstetricians with over forty years of experience in his field. He was Director of Fetal Medicine at the Royal Maternity hospital in Belfast for twenty years. He holds chairs at both Queen's University Belfast and the University of Ulster, and is a past Senior Vice President of The Royal College in London.

When The Dominoes come to town, there is nothing this extraordinary character likes more than to be called to the stage to sing 'One Night With You' with the band. On a big night, he will encore with 'The Great Pretender.' It goes down well.

Another claim to fame for Jim, of course, is that he is the father of actor, musician and film star, Jamie Dornan. Jamie, the hottest man on the planet according to a 2015 poll by Glamour Magazine, was just 16 when his Mum died. Lorna would have been so proud of him.

Jim Dornan's big gig was at Shane Park on Friday 20 November 1981, six months before Jamie was born.

Putting a band together was a bold venture and we had no idea what we were doing. We knew why we were doing it, of course. It was because Dornan gave us no option. The almost original Dominoes, he announced, were coming together for a can't-miss one-off gig in their old stomping ground of Shane Park to raise money for his Royal Victoria

Hospital Perinatal Fund. He would put us up for a weekend in a family cottage in Portaferry so we could rehearse.

Mike and I borrowed two battered AC30s from Baird Sound Systems in York Street. A bemused Harry Baird was persuaded to lend them out on the promise that we would purchase two Hohner 'copy' Stratocasters. Fred still had his old bass and Chris had never taken down his kit of drums.

We played non-stop for almost six hours that night. We even covered the intermission with skiffle music. It nearly killed us.

We were persuaded to do a follow-up gig in Shane Park. It was not so memorable, but then we got a call from Candy Devine to ask if we would do an interview with her on Downtown Radio. It involved recording a series of songs with Rastus, the popular local recording engineer, at the desk. Robin Lavery, now back in the country and at a loose end, joined us in these recording sessions. When we emerged, we had found the formula that allowed Chris to play the piano and Robin to play drums. We were a five-piece band again, with Robin carrying much of the lead vocals.

It was a privilege to have been in a recording studio with Rastus. He was a well-respected recording engineer who in the nineteen-seventies produced for local radio memorable recordings of bands such as the Undertones, Rudi and Stiff Little Fingers.

Like all who knew him, I was shocked to learn in 2004 that Rastus had been brutally attacked by a gang of eight or ten thugs who burst into the Chimney Corner as he was packing up after running a disco. They left him for dead after battering his head repeatedly with a metal bin and an ashtray as he lay helpless in the foyer.

Belfast coroner Brian Sherrard was told that earlier that evening Rastus had thrown someone out of the disco for drug-peddling, making it clear that such behaviour would not be tolerated. The inquest, held six years later, was told that the attack had been sanctioned by senior members of the UDA (Ulster Defence Association), and that the drug-dealer had made chilling threats as he was thrown out of the disco.

Rastus, born Stephen Nelson, was murdered in a horrible crime for which no-one has ever been convicted. He was in a vegetative state when he died in hospital six months later, aged 55.

And then there was Eric Cairns.

I first met Eric in 1980 after Lyn and I made up our minds to move from Winston Gardens. I was summoned to his office at the back of Brian Morton's estate agency in Arthur Street. He was seated behind a rather grand desk, the epitome of sartorial elegance, complete with a silk handkerchief stylishly stuffed into the breast pocket of his dark suit. As I entered, Eric leapt to his feet; reached out and grasped my hand firmly. His well-chosen words boomed round the room. Lyn had told me to explain to this man Cairns that things were all very tentative, and to be sure he understood my request to see him was nothing more than an exploratory enquiry.

By the time we parted company that afternoon we had confessed secrets; shared each other's life stories and found common purpose in life. He had accepted my invitation to be the keynote speaker at a conference aimed at doing something to revitalise the ailing central city; I had bought tickets to see him perform as the dame in a Groomsport pantomime; I was buying a house we could barely afford and he had bought a pair of shoes, seemingly influenced by my nod of approval. The shoes cost a staggering fifty pounds.

A few months later we invited Eric and his wife Gail to a dinner party to meet Jim Dornan – an encounter that would result in Eric Cairns becoming a Founder Chairman of the

Northern Ireland Mother and Baby Appeal (now called Tiny Life).

If Jim Dornan was to blame for bringing The Dominoes back together again, Eric must shoulder a greater responsibility.

He instructed The Dominoes to play at what was billed as "The Last Night at Caproni's." Caps was a Ballroom of Romance on the shores of Ballyholme Bay; a mecca for generations of teen and twenty-somethings who lived for the moment each week when they would be admitted to the Saturday night dance. Entry for young males in particular was strictly controlled; not everyone was prepared to suffer the indignity of having a stand up haircut in the foyer – often by Mr Caproni himself. But for most it was a price worth paying.

Friday 14 January 1983 was the date those famous doors were opened for one last hurrah before the bulldozers cleared the building to make way for a block of flats.

"The Donaghadee District Round Table will organise and The Dominoes will play," he announced as he showed us round the immaculately preserved dance hall.

"But Eric, none of us ever actually played Caproni's." For me, this was not strictly true. My very last gig with Chips was a cameo appearance in Caps.

"You need a showband...and they'll be expecting a whole lot of stuff we don't know. And they will want brass."

"Well, become a showband, then." Eric was not taking no for an answer. "You have two weeks, and by the way, you're on the radio tomorrow morning."

It was a hard one to pass up. The prospect of one last waltz at Caproni's had already grabbed the attention of the media and there was a clamour for tickets.

This was a lean time in the music scene locally. I phoned George Jones.

"You mean play for nothing? All night? Gimme a break. Learn all that stuff for a one-off gig? You gotta be kidding..." He paused. "Of course, I'll do it – and so will Kelly."

"Trevor Kelly?" Now there was a blast from the past. "What about Dave Glover? Would he put in an appearance?"

"He's packed it in, but he might do a walk-on. He'd expect to be paid, but I'll see what we can do."

The rehearsals with Geordie and Trevor were a lot of fun. The stage performance was as you would expect from a bunch of buskers, but the event was a sensation. People flew in from abroad to be part of the 1000-strong crowd. Mums, daughters and grannies were there shaking hands, remembering faces and forgetting names; there were people shedding tears in the street because they couldn't get in.

All they wanted was for just one last time was to saunter into the ballroom through that door – the one above which a sign conveyed the message that everyone wanted to believe:

Through these portals pass the most beautiful girls in the world

Suddenly the original Dominoes were back in business. So too were George and Trevor – and with Gerry Rice and Harry Adair on horns the Dave Glover Showband was on the road again.

The re-formed Dominoes were busy during the 1980s and we had a lot of fun. For a time the band had a Saturday night residency in Crawfordsburn Country Club, re-branded as Blueberry Hill. It was reminiscent of the Boat Club twenty-five years earlier. Robin Lavery quickly earned his stripes and became a Domino. He sang most of the songs, and kept the band buoyant with a regular injection of new material. Well, not new exactly. Let's just say new to us.

I am especially fond of Robin Lavery. We first played together in 1969 and shared the experience of breaking new ground with Chips. We joined forces again after I returned from St Lucia and he was instrumental in getting the show back on the road in 1981. He carried most of the singing with the band from then on.

Robin would smile and happily introduce songs we had never played before, keeping the band on its toes. He extended his talents by playing guitar and learning the words of hundreds of songs. He was popular at house parties with an expanding repertoire that would keep people entertained all night. In the early 1990s we formed a spin-off acoustic group called The Dots with Chris Doran playing whatever upright honky-tonk was available. The Dots needed no drums. Robin stood at the front and sang with his guitar. I sat on a stool, strumming along with acoustic twelve string guitar, and Fred played bass. We had a lot of laughs, rocking away in intimate club venues with Chris, introduced always as Jerry Lee Heartthrob, using a paint roller to help with the sweeps and chops.

Robin Lavery left the band for a time in 1996. He was difficult to replace as he carried most of the singing. John Wilson agreed to be our guest drummer until, as he put it, either he got fed up with us or we found someone better. Wilson was guest drummer with The Dominoes for almost eight years.

In an astonishing revelation years later, it emerged that Wilson had also auditioned for Peter West's Top Town back in March 1960. The 13-year-old was a member of the uniformed Templemore Avenue Silver Band, who politely applauded the fledgling Dominoes electrifying performance of Marty Wilde's 'Bad Boy.' I would like to report that the

Dominoes left a lasting impression, but John only remembers being there. It was clearly not a life-changing experience.

I have fond memories of working with John, Linley Hamilton and Nicky Scott in 2002 as they struggled to get the concept of Making Music Workshops into the mainstream of community arts. Now firmly established and widely acclaimed, the Workshop travels the country providing opportunity for teenagers to come together, create and perform under the guidance of Northern Ireland's foremost session musicians. The concept of the Making Music Workshop has proved hugely successful. For school kids, some of would be venturing into the world of music for the first time, the result of a few days collaborative working under professional guidance is mind-blowing.

John Wilson was a professional drummer whose mission in life was to lift the game of the rest of the band. That he did. But he was replacing a drummer who carried much of the vocals, and he made it clear we would never get him to sing. The answer was staring us in the face.

 Clare Doran, Chris's 25-year-old daughter, was invited to join the Dominoes. Clare had been singing in bands since schooldays, and had five years with Jackie Flavelle and Ronnie Greer in The Blues Experience. She was a sensation: stage presence; great voice; stunningly attractive, and of course the added bonus was that she reduced significantly the average age of the band.

Clare and Wilsie were on top form the night we played at a recorded open air gig in the docklands at Laganside on 21 June 2000. We played way above our game that night. It was the last gig for Mike Shanks, who felt the time had come to hang up the Stratocaster and retire gracefully.

His place was filled by my son Michael on guitar. He stayed for the duration.

In 2003 Robin Lavery was back in the band. John Wilson decided to devote his energies to a new Taste with Sam Davidson on guitar and Albert Mills on bass.

Gigs were getting fewer now and at several points we thought it was time to bring down the curtain. Fred's death in December 2003 was devastating and none of us wanted the Dominoes to perform ever again. There were a few dates in the diary we agreed to fulfil with the thought that we could leave the name Dominoes to rest in peace alongside Fred. I found it difficult to refuse to play again because I basically enjoyed playing in a band with my son.

There was no question of having to hunt around for someone to the play bass guitar. Keith Baker had always been the one we turned to if for whatever reason Fred was unable to do a gig. The hollow-bodied Epiphone bass guitar he used way back with Dunno had been gathering dust while he pursued a successful career as a journalist and novelist.

Keith had come a long way since Dunno – a career in which he worked in newspapers, PR, radio and television. He was a columnist and production executive with the Belfast Telegraph before joining BBC Northern Ireland where he became Head of News and Current Affairs and Chief Editorial Adviser. He wrote four acclaimed thrillers. But playing the odd gig with us inspired Keith to eventually return to his first love – playing bass guitar.

But the name of the band was a lingering issue for us after Fred died. We thought if we were not ready to pack it in, we should at least perform under a different name. In deference to Fred, we never spoke of ourselves as The Dominoes again. The trouble was we never came up with alternative name and consequently The Dominoes lived on in the minds of others.

Then eighteen months after that, on 23 May 2005, the wonderfully talented Chris Doran, Clare's beloved dad, passed away at the age of 62. That was enough for Clare. I passed on responsibility for managing the bookings to Robin and agreed to do one last gig.

It was at Malone House. It was here Robin introduced me to Ray Donnan who was to play keyboards. "He sings, too," said Robin. Did he ever.

Ray was great to play with. He gave the band with no name a lease of life lasting a further five years. We had a lot of good time together as I took to playing a Rickenbacker 12-string, which chimed well with Ray's keyboards. He has a great voice which currently finds expression in a Male Voice Choir. I looked forward every night to Ray singing oldies like 'Sherry' and 'Be My Baby.'

Ray had been in the Freshmen in the early seventies and had played regularly in the Pound from 1975 to 1981 as a member of Bronco, with Kenny McDowell, Jim Armstrong, John Wilson and Alan Hunter.

I'm sitting in Horatio Todd's having a pint with Michael mulling over old times when I spot a bloke shuffling past my field of vision, heading for the exit. He is obviously not in the best of health. He catches my eye. Instantly I know what is coming.

"Hey, big lad." He speaks with a little difficulty, pointing at me. "You won't know me, but I remember you. From The Pound – aw Gawd, but them were great days. Do you remember?"

How could I forget.

"You played the..." He holds out his hands and dangles his fingers.

"And you had Smicker on drums. And Seth? What a guy. And what about your man with the quips?"

I help him out. "Yes indeed – Fred. Sadly..." He carries on.

"And you played in the Jazz Club – and the Queen's Court. But Jeez Saturday afternoons in The Pound , they were the best – just brilliant..."

I'm eager to make some contribution to the conversation. "You know, I played there every Saturday afternoon for two and a half years..." He interrupts. He is not to be deflected.

"And the Marquee Club...great days; great days. I just can't have the music they play now, can you?" He looks at my 39-year old son. Michael opens his mouth to speak, but the moment has passed.

He reaches for my hand. I stand up, clasp his hand firmly and then relax my grip. He continues to clutch my hand tightly and doesn't let go for five minutes. His wife joins us and waits patiently for her man to release my hand. She has seen it before. She has to sit down.

Truth to tell I am quite chuffed when this happens – and it happens more often than you would ever believe.

Chapter 29

Shrug

I was delighted when, at an early age, Michael displayed a talent for playing drums. He was 12 when he played his first gig with me at North Rugby Club. There was always band gear lying about our house, and it wasn't long before he was teaching himself to play guitar. We tried to get him into proper music classes at school where he might learn to read and write music. The problem was he was born with impaired vision, leaving him with something like ten percent of normal sight. He simply couldn't see a manuscript on a music stand – let alone learn to read the birds on the telegraph wires. It wasn't just a problem with music. He couldn't play ball, cross the street safely or see where a bus was heading. It was remarkable that he got to university without being able to see anything written on a blackboard.

But Michael has the music in him. He can play by ear, which is all you need really. Sure is as much as I can do. Good enough for rock and roll.

Michael took drumming lessons from Robin Lavery in Crymbles Music Shop in Dublin Road. Later I would take Michael on Saturday mornings for lessons from John Wilson at his Comber Drum Studio. He couldn't have got better instruction than from these guys.

On his thirteenth birthday, Michael got his first invitation to join a band doing U2 covers. He was five years younger than the others but had been recommended by John Wilson as the best "kit drummer" under his instruction at the time. Sadly the band, called Exzt, was short lived, as the older guys soon had to head for separate universities.

Michael played with November Skies and Purple Leaf during his time at Campbell College before he left to be taught at Sullivan Upper in his A-level year.

He got occasional stand-in gigs with the Dominoes and the Dots at this time. He was called up as a stand-in drummer when, on 5 February 1994, the Dominoes played at an engagement bash for Belfast-born guitarist, Peter Bullick, and his fiancée Deborah Bonham. Bonham was a distinguished rock and blues performer who lived in America with her band. Michael was quick to pick up that she had a connection with Led Zeppelin. Deborah Bonham was a sister of the late John Bonham – widely regarded as the greatest rock drummer of his time.

Showing no fear, John Bonham's sister stepped up and sang with the Dominoes. She mentioned her brother and dedicated her song to the teenager on the drums. Endorsement from a Bonham – now that was cool.

Michael, after a spell in a Kibbutz, commenced a course of study at Dundee University. Within a few days of arriving in Dundee, he was jamming with a young poet called Gary Lightbody and a brainbox called Mark McClelland. The reason I know Mark is smart is because his A-Level maths teacher told me he was the best pupil she ever had.

On Sunday 1 June 2008, I was quaffing wine at a reception in the nave of Liverpool Cathedral. It struck me at the time as an odd place for a party. It was in fact a warm-up for a conference run by my chums in the Town and Country Planning Association that was due to take place the following day. I decided to sneak out early and head for Anfield to see Paul McCartney who, as it happened, was that very night performing to a sell-out audience – a home crowd comprising the good people of Liverpool. I had to be there. It would have been rude not to. Of course if I had planned this better I would have acquired a ticket in advance. But of course planning was never my strong suit.

The concert was well under way when I reached the towering walls of Anfield football ground. The doors were firmly shut, but I knew I would be able to get in for nothing to see the second half. I had done this sort of thing before. The trick is to hover outside and sooner or later the doors will open to let someone leave early. Someone will say: "Oh all right then, come on ahead...the show is nearly over." It certainly worked for me when I was dragged along to Avoniel Leisure Centre by my teenage daughter Sara to see Howard Jones.

But it didn't work this time.

I stood outside listening to the roar of the crowd and the hopelessly muffled sound of the performance until dusk, at which point I knew I was licked. I set off back to my hotel in need of a drink.

The town centre was deserted. Was every scouser at Anfield for this concert performance by their favourite son? The streets were silent except for the sound of my own footsteps. Shops, restaurants and pubs were closed. There were no buses; there were no moving cars. The empty pedestrian precincts were like a stage set, bathed in moonlight tinged with the orange glow of street lights.

Suddenly I heard the sound of a guitar. A plaintive voice began to sing.

No, it wasn't a young Mexican girl calling for Speedy Gonzales – although I was indeed walking alone along a moonlit street. I could see no adobe haciendas. I checked to make sure.

This was for real. It was impossible to tell where the sound was coming from but the tune that reverberated around the entire city centre was instantly recognisable. I stopped in my tracks. Somewhere a bloke was singing, all alone. The song was Gary Lightbody's magical composition 'Run.'

"Light up, light up..."

The hairs on the back of my neck rose as I took this in. I kept on walking towards where I expected to find a busker standing with his guitar in a darkened doorway. I really wanted to find where the rich sound was coming from.

Whoever was singing this deserved a few bob from me. He certainly had no hope of getting a contribution from anyone else.

I never found him.

It was the afternoon of Tuesday 27 December 1994 when I first met the young Gary Lightbody. I was keen to meet the members of Michael's new band, who were all from Northern Ireland and had met one another in their first term at the University of Dundee.

Michael hadn't told me much about who plays what, but had said most of their material was written by the guy in the living room. I looked into the room which was littered with Dominoes gear and drum kit items Michael had brought in from the garage. Michael was in the kitchen making coffee.

The guy in the living room was examining my recently purchased Vester semi-acoustic guitar that was lying on the sofa. "Yours?" he asked. I nodded and waved consent for him to sling it round his neck. He launched into an unfamiliar tune with an interesting chord progression.

With no inhibition he began to sing. It registered with me immediately that there was something distinctive about what I was hearing – a simple chord driven melody with words that flowed out in an anguished whisper from a voice that was both soft and powerful.

"You must be Mark," I said reaching out my hand.

He corrected me politely. "Gary, actually" he said.

Soon the house was filled with sound. It was really good. It was different.

The three-piece decided to call themselves Shrug. They made quite an impact when they gave their first performance in Dundee a couple of weeks before. Ten of the fifteen numbers in that set were based around Lightbody poems.

In 1995 they recorded their first demo: 'The Yogurt vs Yogurt Debate.' The odd title emerged following a heated discussion over pronunciation of the word in the different regional dialects. The inside sleeve intentionally confused matters further by highlighting that there could also be a debate about how the word is spelt. Here the title of the compilation is 'The Yogurt vs Yoghurt Debate.' Spot the difference.

The cassette is now a collectors' item. There were 250 copies put into circulation. Serious collectors know that 50 per cent of the inserts carry the words THE BEGINNING in the bottom left hand corner. In the other 50 per cent it reads THE END.

I'm letting you into a secret. The most valuable collectors' item is the matched set. You need to have the end as well as the beginning.

I think the first 'home' gig for Shrug was at The Bear in Holywood in January 1995. I was the taxi driver. I was also the one who loaned them gear, humped it up the stairs and helped them set up. They were good – and I was impressed by huge crowd they pulled. It was a bit of an eye-opener for me and for all the friends and relatives who were present that night. This band could be big.

Band dates in Belfast were plentiful in the academic holiday breaks in 1995. Shrug played in the Duke of York; Thompson's Garage; Robinson's 'Rock Bottom' Bar; the Crescent Arts Centre; The Front Page and the Empire.

Gary, Mark and Michael signed a 5-year management contract with Jeepster Records in London, with whom they recorded two further demo takes including an early version of Snow Patrol's first single release, 'Starfighter Pilot,' on which Michael played guitar. As record company interest was continuing to grow, in November 1996 the band changed their name to avoid potential legal complications with an American band that had claimed the name Shrug.

Shortly after that, Michael took ill and returned to Belfast where he was hospitalised with what turned out to be manic depression – or bipolar disorder as it is now more commonly known. It fell to me to be the one to break the news that it had been decided by the record company that the band had to find a new drummer. It was heart-breaking.

A fresh recording of 'Starfighter Pilot' was released by the band, by now calling itself Polar Bear, on 15 June 1997. A few months later the band became Snow Patrol.

Mark McClelland parted company in 2005 just as Snow Patrol was heading for international stardom. He now has his own band.

Mark McClelland's family continue to live a few hundred yards from my home. Mark's dad Peter is another rock relic from the sixties. In his heyday he was Storm Winterly. Great name. Larry Parnes would have been proud of that one.

Mark's dad was considered to have very good stage presence. According to irishrock.org, Peter McClelland drove the girls wild. Check it out.

Peter McClelland certainly has credentials. In 1965 he was the lead vocalist in a band called the Barons with a line-up that for a time included Gary Moore, the Ashfield school kid that Fred and I bumped into at The Who concert in Lisburn.

Michael's first drum teacher, Dominoes drummer Robin Lavery, also played with Gary Moore in The Beat Boys in 1964 while still at Ashfield School. Small world.

I recently had the pleasure of being present when the mature Storm Winterley appeared on stage with the very respectable Knock Golf Club House Band led by Gerry McWhinney – alongside Rick Slater and a number of other axe-wielding golfers. Colm Fitzpatrick and blues head Ronnie Greer were on stage as guests. Blues music is alive and well and living in east Belfast.

I have also met Gary Lightbody's dad, Jack. I never asked him, but as far as I know Jack Lightbody lays no claim to being a source of musical inspiration, or to having driven girls wild as a young man.

But as I found myself wandering through the deserted streets of Liverpool that night, listening to a disembodied voice projecting Gary's composition around the empty streets, I was thinking to myself – where does this come from?

It is the lyrics that make Gary Lightbody a song-writing legend. 'Run,' composed in 2000 and a hit several times over, would have got my vote as the song of the decade. Ironically it was another Lightbody song, 'Chasing Cars,' which topped that particular poll when it was announced in New Year 2011.

Make no mistake about it, Gary is not just a singer and a musician, he is a gifted poet. He displayed a natural talent for contemporary verse in his early teens. He won the prestigious John Bartley Verse Prize at Campbell College two years running – in 1993 and 1994.

As I reached my hotel, with 'Run' a muffled echo in the distant streets, I was thinking – as I do and always will – about how proud I am of my son Michael and the way he came to terms with his destiny.

In September 2014, Q Magazine ran a feature around the fact that Pete Best wasn't the only original member of a subsequently world famous ensemble to be left behind at the starting gate. It took guts on Michael's part to offer the following candid response to the question posed by the columnist "How did you feel about leaving the band?"

"Bear in mind that at the time I was facing a diagnosis, it wasn't only the band I left at the time, my entire university career had gone down the tubes. Three years of university, plus that band, plus all my friends gone. And the realisation that I'd kinda gone mad. Nowadays there's a bit more awareness...you hear statistics that one in four people have mental health problems, but back then it was just: "Mike has gone mad." Nobody knew what to do or what to say...it was just really weird, awful..."

Three years after the initial event that caused Michael's exit from Shrug – the band that became Snow Patrol – he was formally diagnosed with the Bipolar mood disorder with which he would have to live for the rest of his life.

But Michael has fond memories of a golden period of his life, just as I do when I reflect on my time playing with The Group. For each of us, it amounted to little more than two years in the public gaze.

Maybe for some of us, that's enough.

Chapter 30

Whole Lotta Shakin' Going On

Patrick Pentland is my Godson. He is a fine guitar player, singer/songwriter and member of the highly acclaimed Canadian rock band, Sloan.

This great four-piece band from Nova Scotia, has been together for more than 20 years. They are huge in Canada. Their 1994 Indie Rock studio album, Twice Removed, was in 1996, and again in 2005, voted by readers of Chart! Magazine as the best Canadian album ever recorded.

On Friday 13 January 2006, Lyn and I were seated amongst the capacity crowd in the TD Banknorth Garden Stadium in Boston listening to Sloan open for The Rolling Stones. I got up from my seat and took a bow when they played a number for the Godfather. Not often you get a chance to wave back to 19,000 punters.

Patrick's father is of course Dick Pentland. Dick went professional with Chips after I left and Paul Lyttle joined the band. Yes, my replacement was a real musician who could sing and play both keyboards and guitar. DP stuck it for about a year travelling the length and breadth of Ireland while trying to hold down a day job.

It is Saturday 27 February 2010, and I am working off the effects of swine flu. Those pigs have a lot to answer for.

Where I am now is not a bad place for a bit of recuperation. We are on holiday in southern Goa in the company of an old friend and colleague, architect-planner Ian Davison. Ian and Judy have opted to spend the winter months here in Luisa By The Sea – an unspoilt beach environment that has to be one of the nicest places on earth. It is our last night and we are at Joe's River Cove restaurant – a popular eating place. Also at the table is Ian's business partner Richard Silson – another wannabe rock star who long ago played bass guitar in a blues band. There's a lot of us about.

I'm having a good time, until...

My ears prick up. Did I just hear my name in an announcement from the stage? I look up and see Joe is standing at the microphone, pointing at me. I'll spare you the Indian accent.

"We have a big star here tonight. What an honour. Let's have a big hand for leader of the Dominos. He used to be Kingsize Taylor when his band played in Liverpool's Cavern Club before the band changed its name to Derek and the Dominos." I recognise the misinformation from boozy banter at a beach bar the previous night. I will play along. I smile; rise to my feet and prepare to take a bow.

Joe's voice is in crescendo. "He is a top guitarist and tonight he is going to play with the band. Give great Goan welcome for the one and only big Bill Morrison."

I promptly sit down again. This is not just a matter of taking a bow. It is time to leave the building.

The excellent Goan lead guitar player has already unslung his Fender Telecaster and is thrusting it out in my direction. Joe is smiling broadly. I am unsure how to handle this.

"Layla," he calls out.

WHAT!?

Whoever wrote his script, the man knows his anthems. The diners take up the chant. I feel everyone's eyes upon me. Davison, sitting at the top of the table, sets down his cutlery and dabs his lips with his napkin. Right now he looks like the Godfather. His smile tells me for sure this is all of his making. The musicians in the band are good, by the way – very good.

They are having a laugh. They know what is going on.

Everyone in the open air venue, having responded enthusiastically to the presence tonight of somebody famous, is now silent. The diners are looking at me expectantly. I plead with Silson to join me, but he is having none of it.

"You're on your own, mate," he says helpfully.

I can see no way out of this. There is nothing for it. I push back my chair and stand up. To enthusiastic and sustained applause, I walk hesitantly to the stage.

Now there are a few problems here apart from the obvious. The vocalist has raised the height of the microphone stand as far as it can go, and I can see right away it doesn't reach high enough.

The lead guitar player is small and wears his guitar high on his chest, strapped around his neck as if it were a ukulele. It won't be long before he realises I am just a duffer who can't play the thing very well anyway, but at this point he is eager to help. I explain I must have it slung low. He looks sad and shakes his head. The strap has been cut short – meaning there is nothing I can do about it. I stare at a bewildering bank of foot pedals.

They didn't have this sort of thing in my day.

I pull the strap around my head and yes, I am choking. The band is clearly looking forward to this. They seem a little disappointed when I suggest 'Mustang Sally' in the Key of C – they have probably sussed me out at this point on the basis that there is nothing too challenging about the guitar riff.

The guys start immediately with an impressively tight sound. I get in the groove as best I can. I walk to the microphone and stoop down.

Despite the fact that I know full well I haven't made any attempt to sing since the flu pigs visited me two months ago, it comes as something of a shock to wake up to the fact that I can't sing at all.

The best I can do is speak the lines.

We are talking flat-line here. I literally can't sing a note. There is no point in carrying on. It's a one-note Samba. Wilson Pickett has left the building.

I wave my left arm in a downward movement that signals to the guys to drop the volume and play quietly. I am going to have to call for someone – anybody – from the audience to come up and sing this number.

I suddenly have a brain wave. I thrust my arm forward, finger pointing to Richard Silson. In the mono pitch voice from which I cannot escape, I speak to the mic: "We need a singer, don't we? Who would you like to sing 'Mustang Sally'?"

My breathy whisper commands attention.

"So here he is. Ladies and gentlemen, give it up for the man himself. The front man with the band – heeeere's Derek."

Silson rises to it. The beat gets louder. Silson grabs the mic and without any prompt from me, calls out:

"And let's have three girls for the vocal backing – who remembers the Commitments? Who wants to sing 'Ride, Sally, Ride...?'"

Every female in the room seems to be of a mind to apply for the job. There is a rush for the stage. The Goan band prepares to repel boarders. Their set list will never be the same again.

Why should I be surprised? I mean, hey, is this not what you want when you are on holiday abroad and you have a few drinks on board – a bit of active participation. Silson is in his element. This is way beyond Karaoke. The chance to be once again part of a live band – this is where you get the real buzz.

I know. I've been doing it for years.

····

"So that confirms it?"

Dr McConnell gives a barely discernible nod of his head. He is telling me that the nuclear imagery confirms his diagnosis. I have Parkinson's disease.

I hear him tell me about the part of the brain that is responsible for controlling muscles and movement. I am looking out the window. I've read all about it. I don't need to be reminded of the big words I struggle to bring to mind and string together in speech: progressive neurological degeneration. I don't need to hear him tell me that what he saw in that scan was clear evidence of the death of brain cells that make dopamine. I don't need him to tell me that dopamine acts like sunshine on your mood – the reason 40 per cent of people with Parkinson's get depressed. Ain't no sunshine when you're gone.

"How long have I got, then?"

He's clearly not going to answer that question. I hear comforting words about medication, stem-cell research; how one in 500 people have it. Basically he is telling me that it won't kill me. I will carry on living but I can expect that living will get pretty tough as the years wear on.

I'm still looking out the window. Suddenly just getting to my feet seems to call for mental effort. I hear the shuffle of papers as he closes my file to signal the consultation is over.

I'm thinking of Mohammed Ali – frail, quivering and barely able to raise his hand. I'm thinking of people in wheelchairs; shaking uncontrollably; unable to make a cup of tea or make their mouths form the words they want to say. Of course it is not just Muhammed Ali. Parkinson's sufferers include Michael J Fox, Billy Connolly, Roger Bannister, Shay Healy, Linda Ronstadt, Johnny Cash, Bob Hoskins, Robin Williams, John Betjeman, Enoch Powell, Adolf Hitler…

Adolf Hitler?

There is no denying Parkinson's triggers bleak reflections. It is a chronic neurological disorder and you can't get away from that. It is a one-way ticket. Apart from the shake most people associate with the disease, there is an inclination to stoop and walk about with your mouth open; your face becomes expressionless; sleep patterns disturbed. I fumble with loose change and my handwriting has become tiny. Every internal department is on go-slow. My speed of thought has slowed down. Some days I feel fine; other days I feel totally shattered and have to take cat-naps four or five times a day. I struggle with speech – both in terms of voice projection and in marshalling thoughts. I have to opt out of conversation when there is background noise. Multi-tasking, never easy at the best of times, is a challenge – even trying to converse during a meal.

But many of these manifestations are not obvious to others. People with Parkinson's don't lose friends; they stay young at heart and tend to have a wrinkle-free fresh-faced look about them. And I am not going to give up without a fight. When I'm feeling down, I shall vamp chords on the piano or pick up my guitar and play. When my hands are shaking and my knees are weak I will remember Elvis. I shall fight it on the beaches. I shall fight it in the fields and the streets…

Chapter 31

Them and Us

The original Dominoes came together again in 1981 and stayed on the road until I threw the head up after that gig in Fermanagh in 2011.

Robin Lavery was the drummer for most of that time, but for the eight year period from 1996 to 2004 when John Wilson played all the Dominoes gigs. John was a professional. We would tease him about the fact that when quizzed about being one of the Dominoes he would carefully distance himself from the rest of us duffers by describing himself as 'the guest drummer.'

John Wilson kept us entertained with showbiz stories. He has been around. For example, he had a lot of time for Brian Rossi, whose group Wheels was first out of the block after THEM, and who shared with Dino Martin the deejay role in the Plaza. He described Rossi as a man who believed that if he behaved like a celebrity, he would become a celebrity. Consequently he would do things like climb into a taxi at the front of the City Hall; wink at the cab driver who would know to drop him off where the queue was gathering outside the Plaza, which of course was only 150 yards away. Much better than arriving on foot or stepping down from a bus.

Even a cool dude like John Wilson could be star struck on occasion. He told us how when on a tour of the States with Taste he opened up a conversation with a stranger in a bus that was taking the touring musicians to the next gig. It turned out that he, too, played drums. "Jerry Allison," he said reaching across for a handshake.

For once in his life Wilson was speechless. Jerry Allison is a legend. Every rock drummer in the world has studied video of the Crickets play "Peggy Sue" on the Ed Sullivan show, puzzled at the way Allison appears to be playing in slow motion a right, left, right right, left, right, left left technique. Paradiddles. Why paradiddles? It was Wilson's opportunity to ask the question that has been puzzling rock drummers for years.

The modest Mr Allison explained this was just the way he warmed up. It fitted the metre and tempo of the song they were about to record, and Buddy Holly felt he should stick with it.

Wilson had stories to add to the many urban myths attendant upon Van Morrison – best known as Van the Man; the man of whom everyone who comes from East Belfast is most proud; the man recently made a Knight of the Realm.

The more recent tales can possibly be sourced to John Rogers: aka Harpo. Harpo was a roadie with Chips in the late seventies, and has had a role as Morrison's tour manager on and off for years.

Like the one about Barry Manilow. The story goes that Manilow had sought out an introduction to Morrison, and when the encounter finally took place, choreographed by the Manilow publicity machine, the cabaret crooner spoke earnestly and at length about how the Ulsterman's music and song-writing had had such a profound influence on his career. Not one for small talk, Morrison maintained a polite silence throughout the one-sided conversation. As he turned and walked away, still within earshot of the Manilow entourage, he was overheard questioning Harpo: "Your man there. What does he do?"

Or the time when travelling with his band in a tour bus through a small town in middle America, Morrison spotted a crowd outside a club where a sign indicated a tribute band was on that night playing – The Van the Man Band.

"Stop!" he says, as the story goes. "Get me in there – I'd like to see that." Morrison gets out, dons his hat and stands by the vehicle while Harpo goes to the ticket desk and explains how he would wish to arrive incognito: "...and so could we get in by a back door, maybe?"

"Nope," says the man behind the glass panel, glancing over at Van who is leaning against the car with his arms folded. "He'll get in if he cares to stand in line over there with those other cowboys in shades and black Stetsons..."

I never met Van the Man, although I have seen him perform many times. We have a mutual friend in Peter Lloyd, whose early recording set Morrison on his path to the top. I have had the pleasure of sharing the stage with guys who were there with him in the early days – John Wilson of course, and George Jones. Other contemporaries of Van the Man who made memorable guest appearances with the Dominoes and The Group from time to time were Geordie Sproule, Roy Kane and Eric Wrixon.

And on one memorable occasion, Billy Harrison.

"Well, look who it is..." Wilson is first to spot the unsung hero of the original THEM line-up. Harrison was the man who came together with Van Morrison to record Belfast's first R&B hit back in 1964.

He starts pounding the kit to a beat we recognise as 'Gloria.' Harrison, a familiar figure at the Yacht Club where he helps yachtsmen with electronic gadgetry, gets a cheer as he steps up and grabs the mic, which is stuck firmly in its holder. The mic resists his first attempt to remove it, but on the second attempt, leaves the stand at unexpected speed, smacking him firmly and painfully in the mouth. He utters an oath and spits. A tooth falls to the floor. Groaning, he turns away from the audience and, with his hand to his mouth, sinks almost to his knees. He signals to stop but we were in full swing. He wasn't going to get away that easily. This is show business. Besides, you don't often get the chance to back the legendary Billy Harrison.

Wilson picks up steam, embellishing the intro with rhythmic drum play. The temperature rises. The crowd is drawn to the stage to see what's happening. They clap on the on-beat (why do people do that?), unclear as to why our guest star is bent over holding his mouth. They cheer loudly as he rises to his feet and turns to face his fans. He has a fat upper lip and a trickle of blood runs from the corner of his mouth. The first verse is interspersed with words that are unprintable, but as he gets into his stride he knows he has the crowd in the palm of his hand.

Wilson's spectacular drum crash ending, ridiculously extended and reminiscent of Ginger Baker closing Cream's farewell concert at the Albert Hall in 1969, finally comes to an unexpected stop. A momentary silence precedes a spontaneous burst of applause. Wilson starts up again. He loves these over-the-top endings. When he eventually grinds to a halt, the crowd falls silent. Seizing the moment I extend an arm in his direction and speak softly into the microphone like Jools Holland live on a Saturday night:

"Billy Harrison, ladies and gentlemen..."

Timing is everything. Harrison justifiably got the biggest cheer of the night. He smiled. The gap in his teeth added visual interest.

Gerry Giffen was the man promoters would engage to look after visiting pop stars. He could be relied upon to keep them out of trouble and to get them to the gigs on time. Gerry lived in Earlswood Road, a stone's throw from Roderick's bedroom in Kincora Avenue where it all started for me.

He encountered people in show business from an early age. He was in the right place at the right time when in 1959 Don Arden asked Phil Solomon to find someone personable and reliable to look after the rockabilly Virginian, Gene Vincent – 19-year-old Gerry Giffen got the job.

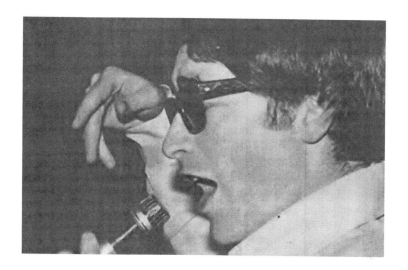

I was a Teddy Boy in 1959 even though I didn't look like one. I was really more of a make-believe Teddy Boy. I had a make-believe knee-length long jacket with felt lapels, make-believe skin tight jeans and a make-believe duck's ass haircut. I saw myself as Gene Vincent as I plonked my guitar and warbled 'Be-Bop-A-Lula.'

When I heard later Gerry had the leather-clad rocker sitting in his home in Ballyhackamore I was impressed. Actually, I was really peeved. At first I simply didn't believe it, but it turned out to be true.

In the mid-60s, if there was a pop star in town, odds on Gerry would be at his side. He worked with the big promoters – Jim Aiken, Trevor Kane, Dermot O'Donnell and Don McLeod. His job was to 'look after' visiting pop stars. In 1969 he opened his very own night club in Victoria Square – Just Jerry's. He wore shades that looked the part and never missed an opportunity to get up and sing Little Richard's 'Lucille.'

On 16 March 1967, about three months before the Small Faces night, we played in Sammy Houston's Jazz Club with a band called Next in Line, fronted by Peter Adler. Adler was studying at Trinity, and his dad was Larry Adler, the great harmonica player, who was then living in Dublin. Gerry Giffen was hired to shepherd Peter and his band on a tour of Irish dancehalls, and Ricky McCutcheon and I decided to tag along for the Dublin gig. Well, I tagged along – Ricky had a girl to meet.

We noticed that everyone in the tour party, including Gerry, seemed to find it necessary to wear shades.

The gig was in Dublin and we hung about as Gerry and his entourage checked in to the Inter-Continental Hotel. We found a B & B across the street and went out for the night, promising Gerry we would weigh in afterwards.

We never found the girl Ricky hoped to meet, so we returned early and settled for a few pints in the hotel lounge. Suddenly I spotted a face I thought I recognised sitting at the bar on his own. I whispered to Ricky:

"The fat guy in a suit and tie over there – isn't that Orson what's-his- name?"

"Orson Cart?" ventured Ricky helpfully.

"Very funny. But what's his name, really? You know who I mean. Movie actor. It's Orson... eh...yes I know: Orson Welles!"

At that moment Gerry and Peter Adler arrived. Wearing a matched set of dark shades. I pointed to the fat man. "Look who's here, Gerry. It's your man. Orson Welles."

Gerry and Adler picked off their shades simultaneously, blinking as they adjust to the light.

"That's not Orson Welles, you pillock. That's Burl Ives." "Little Bitty Tear?" asks Ricky.

"That's the one. In films as well."

Gerry and Adler were up in a flash and over talking to the distinguished troubadour. In about twenty minutes Gerry came back, thrusting his car keys in our direction. "Guys – do me a favour and go get that guitar out of the boot of my car."

When we returned, Ives was sitting on a stool by our table. His tie was already bound around his head and he looked like he meant business. He had the guitar in tune in seconds and launches into songs that bring the conversations in the room to a standstill. 'Little Bitty Tear;' 'Big Rock Candy Mountain;' 'Ghost Riders' etc.

Suddenly Larry Adler appeared and the impromptu concert that followed lasted well past closing time – you could have heard a pin drop as Ives drew the night to a close by folding his arms across his guitar and inviting the great Larry Adler to conclude proceedings with unaccompanied rendition of Gershwin's 'Rhapsody in Blue.'

Roy Orbison was one of the all-time greats of rock 'n' roll. In 2001, I visited Sun Studios in Memphis, Tennessee where I first learned that Roy Orbison was one of the 'Million Dollar Quartet,' comprising Elvis Presley, Jerry Lee Lewis, Carl Perkins and Johnny Cash. But there was something else on that seminal recording, made on 4 December 1956 – the unmistakable voice of Roy Orbison. When no photograph could be found of all five together, it Memphis press built the story around the four stars that were featured in the only available – the now famous image of Lewis at the piano with Presley, Perkins and Cash looking over his shoulder.

It was thanks to Gerry Giffen, that in September 1968 The Group ended its two-year existence touring the main theatre/cinemas in Ireland, on the bill in support of first the great Roy Orbison and then, a month later, with Tom Jones.

When Orbison's popularity had waned. It was four years since his last hit 'Pretty Woman.' In that period, Roy had witnessed first-hand the instantaneous death of his wife Claudette when the motor cycle she was riding, with Roy on board, hit a pick-up truck which pulled out in front of them. But nothing prepared any of us for the news – news that Gerry Giffen had to impart on the Monday afternoon – that there had been a dreadful blaze in the Orbison family home in Tennessee, in which two of his three sons had tragically lost their lives. Orbison fulfilled what I think was the last concert on the tour, but retired to his room immediately afterwards . We left him to his own thoughts in the hope that somehow he would find a way to come to terms with this further tragedy.

Tom Jones told us the story of what happened when he met Elvis Presley. I sat spellbound with Sez and Ricky on his bed in the Intercontinental Hotel in Dublin as he gave us a first-hand account of what happened when Elvis travelled four hundred miles from Los Angeles to see and hear him perform in the Flamingo Hotel, Las Vegas. By coincidence, the encounter took place on Saturday 6 April 1968 – the very same date The Group was recording in The Pound and heading for a memorable night in The Marquee.

The world's media was focused on the event where the voice from Pontypridd, the 'Not Unusual' Mr Jones, was expected to topple the King. Elvis at this stage had not played live for some years and was now regarded more as a movie star. Despite the fact that he was still producing hit records – his most recent release being 'Guitar Man' – the press reckoned the Crown was now up for grabs. And this could be the moment because Jones, the leading contender, was to perform live in Las Vegas.

Jones told us how Elvis had phoned ahead to tell him he intended to be there to hear the show and that he would arrive unannounced. He would not wish his presence to in any way deflect attention from the Welsh singer whom he admired enormously and desperately wanted to hear live. He would sneak into a seat at the back of the hall when the lights were down and slip away unnoticed at the end of the performance. He would be seated before the show began.

But that was not quite the way it turned out. Perhaps that was the plan before Colonel Parker got his hands on it.

Jones, who was in good humour, described how he was later told the Colonel had choreographed exactly how this encounter would be handled. Jones downed his customary glass of port in the wings, took a deep breath and ran onto the stage on cue. He was jolted at the sight of the King sitting with Priscilla and his entourage right at the front of the stage. There was a spotlight trained on Elvis from start to finish, highlighting his enthusiastic reaction to every number. The crowd cheered as much for Elvis as they did for Jones. The press hastily phoned their respective networks with instruction to re-write the breaking news. Elvis was back and the world got the first inkling of his comeback tour.

Elvis, Jones told us ruefully, was still the King.

While there is always a good story to be told around a brief encounter with a famous person, there is nothing to compare with the ad lib and banter shared between members of the band – and how fortunate we were to have someone like Fred Isdell to keep the audience entertained with his rapport.

To this day people still talk about 'Fred's quips.' The week before the event we recorded in The Pound, on Saturday 30 March 1968, Fred announced earnestly to a hushed audience that for those interested in the result of the

Grand National, the winner by five lengths was Dobbin, a 200/1 outsider.

There was a brief pause as people looked quizzically at one another. "Who? What did he say?" One by one people began to laugh until the whole place was heaving. Only a handful of people present knew for a racing certainty that there was no horse called Dobbin at the starting gate. The punters who would know were, of course, out watching the race at the bookies. No mobile phones in those days.

Spontaneous wit does not travel easily into the written word, but Fred's jests really were very funny at the time – I guess you'll just have to take my word for it.

The bar staff at Culloden Hotel still talk about the night when he announced a prize of a meal for two in the prestigious hotel would be awarded to the first to come up with the correct answer to a simple question. It sounded like a good prize. There was a stampede to the front. The winning couple were brought on stage and took a bow as Fred interviewed them earnestly. The reaction when he presented the prize-winners with a plate containing two sandwiches was priceless.

There was another occasion when Fred really did have a gift voucher to give away as a prize. It doesn't bear thinking about, but the vouchers were in an envelope that somehow got mixed up with an exactly similar envelope containing the band's wages for the night. Negotiating the very public exchange left the band a bit aghast, but it brightened up the proceedings for everybody else that night. That, too, has gone down in barman folk lore.

Fred knew a lot of people, and most knew to expect to be teased by him from the stage. He would pounce on anyone he spotted on the dance floor and come up with something new every time. Former schoolmate and senior medic Mike Crooks told me the other day that people have never let him forget the time Fred brought proceedings to a halt announcing from the stage that he, Mike Crooks, had agreed to give a tap-dancing demonstration. The crowd instantly formed an expectant circle around the focus of Fred's attention. Wilsie and Chris, on cue, launched into a foot-tapping 'Puttin' On The Ritz.' There was no escape for a man who had never tap-danced in his life. The band was well entertained.

On Thursday 20 July 2000 we were playing at a wedding reception in the Europa Hotel. In town that night appearing in a local talk show, was TV presenter Mark Lamarr – then at the height of his career hosting the extraordinarily popular TV show Never Mind the Buzzcocks – and the then equally famous socialite, Tara Palmer-Tomkinson. The pair had gate-crashed the gig.

All attention shifted to the two instantly recognisable A-list celebrities as they entered the room. I heard afterwards they had been courteous enough to ask the bride if it would be okay to join in. They said they liked the music that the band was playing.

From the stage, we spotted the diversion immediately. Our star singer Clare, daughter of keyboard player Chris Doran, felt the need to identify the young celebrities so we can dedicate a song to them. Good thing, I'm thinking. Here we are, trying to look cool. We wouldn't want the punters to think we didn't know who these trendy people are.

"He's going to sing with the band!" exclaimed the wide-eyed 'It-Girl' who, glass in hand, was pointing to her co-celebrity. The wedding guests picked up the chant as Lamarr, eager to perform, worked his way through the crowd to the stage.

"Sing with the band!" "Sing with the band!" "Sing with the band!"

"'Gloria,'" Lamarr called out when he reached the stage. Well, I thought, you couldn't have picked a better one, mate. This is an anthem that we knew would go down really well with the Belfast crowd – as it did when Harrison sang it the year before.

We fired straight in and I'm impressed. He sings it really well, clearly loving every minute of it. The wedding crowd crush together at the front of the stage. They joyfully chant the words and spelt out the name.

Wilsie, as I knew he would, indulged in a long drum solo which kept it lit right to the end. Lamarr was chuffed; Palmer-Tomkinson was blotto. The crowd called out for more. Clare was excited, and the five dads in the band were flushed with success, feeling thirty years younger.

Lamarr blew a kiss to the audience and turned to applaud the band. Good man, I thought. He's not going to do an encore. It would be hard to follow that.

Wilsie picked this up too, and started up the Gloria beat again. We followed and were back in for a reprise. Another final chorus for Lamarr: another breath-taking drum solo ending in a thumping bass-drum and a cymbal crash that lasts a full 20 seconds.

When the roars of appreciation died down, Fred walked over to the mic, put his arm round Lamarr's shoulders, and gave him a playful Eric Morecambe slap on the cheek.

"That was really good. Just great." He turned to the audience: "Let's one more time give a big hand to..." There is a pause. He looked back at Lamarr and we cringed at what we all somehow knew was coming next.

"Er...what's your name again?"

In fairness it must be said Lamarr took it well.

When he retired, Fred fulfilled his long-held ambition to visit New Orleans. Like Solly Lipsitz, he regarded New Orleans as the birthplace of traditional jazz. But Fred felt New Orleans symbolised more than that. It was the fountainhead from which flowed many musical streams including blues, be-bop, modern jazz and Rock 'n' Roll. It was the mecca for all who, like Fred, possess catholic taste in contemporary music.

This must have been in his mind when, coming up to retirement, we went to see Fats Domino and his band play in the Ulster Hall. There was a pause in the proceedings, to facilitate a sound check, and Fred walked over to have a word with the bass player who was standing on stage patiently waiting for the show to continue.

"You from New Orleans too?" Fred called out. "Sure am," came the reply: "we all from Nawleens, man."

A conversation ensued that led to an exchange of contact details, and ultimately to Fred and his wife Christine being introduced to the heads in Preservation Hall and shown round other historic music venues of New Orleans. This was no open-top bus ride. This was a one-off person-to-person guided tour by a man who knew a thing or two about the place. Fred talked about it for weeks afterwards.

Fred saw playing in a pop group as enriching his life. He loved every minute he was on a stage with his mates. He laughed at his own jokes. It was infectious. Often as he approached the mic, the very thought of what he was about to say would reduce him to convulsions causing the priceless gem to be lost in his own snorts of mirth.

Off-stage too, if there was a light-hearted way of expanding on a point or defusing a point of difference, Fred would find it. Don't get me wrong, he was not carefree. He thought deeply about things. His one- liners were often insightful but never barbed or hurtful. His quips would never offend. They would always leave you smiling. Fred was a popular character all his life. He had a successful career in marketing, retiring as a partner in PricewaterhouseCoopers on his sixtieth birthday.

He kept himself in good physical shape by pushing himself hard in daily jogs – cutting a familiar figure as he pounded the streets. I remember climbing Cave Hill with him at his insistence just a few days after he had undergone major surgery. He drove through the pain barrier in a determined effort to reach the top. I was left far behind.

Somewhere along the narrow coastal path between Craigavad to Helen's Bay you might spot beneath your feet "The Dominoes" etched in drying concrete by Fred, who knew at that point what lay in store. I don't know exactly where this little memorial is but I know it is there.

At a Service of Thanksgiving in celebration of Fred's life, the surviving members of the band walked to the front of the packed church. We said a very few words and, with the aid of a piano, led the congregation in singing 'Blueberry Hill.' We thought it was a fitting tribute. He died on 10 December 2003 at the age of 61.

The loss of Chris Doran, just 18 months after Fred died, was devastating.

I well remember the house party at which I first heard Chris play piano like I had never heard it played before. I had to fight through the crowd around the piano to see who was playing this rock and roll music. Strangely the music he played was, even then, regarded as old fashioned. The Beatles had put it into history.

We poked fun at Chris. He would introduce him as Jerry Lee Heartthrob. While his use of a paint-roller as a painless way to sweep up the ivories was a great idea; his habit of carrying all his keyboard effects and attachments in a black bin bag was not so smart. Yes, you guessed it – the bin bag was left behind one night and despatched to the dump. To his enormous relief the black bag was retrieved the following day from the Council skip. The bond between us all grew stronger as we just kept on – and on – playing. It was really good fun.

Music meant a lot to Chris, but it was by no means his only talent. He was acknowledged to be a very good architect – the one with the ideas. He designed and implemented a complete redevelopment of the Belfast Zoological Gardens, and went on to design and develop Exploris, the Northern Ireland Aquarium at Portaferry.

His special design skills came to be acknowledged across Ireland, and he was responsible for several award-winning projects. He was particularly proud of his design for the spectacular Oceanworld Aquarium, Mara Beo, overlooking Dingle Harbour in County Kerry.

His devoted wife Maureen passed away just 18 months after he died, compounding the tragedy for daughter Clare and her equally talented sister Emma. Parties at the Doran home were unique. While I will remember Chris for the way he played the piano, I will remember him also for his gentle nature. I really miss them both.

Chapter 32

The Pound
Saturday 6 April 1968 – 16:50
Morning Dew

I suggest to Fred that we play 'Morning Dew' next as I know it is one Smicker plays well. It will give him a chance to shine in the presence here this afternoon of several local drum heads - including Ali Stewart and Dougie McIlwaine. John Wilson from Cheese is here, too.

Gerry Giffen spots us looking his way and gestures for us to come over. It is time for a short break, anyway. I have a wee gem that's bound to get a laugh. I tuck my elbows to my sides and let my hands and fingers dangle in front of my chest. I breathe down the mic: "Short paws..." Nobody laughs. I might need to practice that one.

I put the reel to reel on hold and we shuffle off the stage. Smick wanders across to talk to the heads from Bangor who play with High Wall and the Carpetbaggers. There are a lot of heads in the place this afternoon. Fred and I rise to Gerry's invitation.

"I want you to meet Andy Fairweather Low," says Gerry. We forego the handshakes. I find myself giving a limp hand wave. These pop stars are all so young. He looks about 15. "First time here?"

"No, we played Belfast last year." Jeez, I'm thinking – when he was fourteen?

We chat for a while. I know what's coming, and, sure enough Gerry says: "I tell you what. Why don't you get up there and give them a few verses of 'Bend Me?'" The Welsh chart-topper wisely does not commit himself.

"You know it, Bill, don't you?" asks Gerry. "Err, yes," I hear myself say.

We return to the stage, Fred and I prepare the other two guys for the possibility that we may be called upon to back your man.

"It's easy enough," says Fred. Easy for you, mate, I'm thinking. "What key is it in?" says Sez, the practical one.

"Dunno. We'll ask him when he gets up. Let's do it now and get it over with."

I reach for the microphone and inform the gathering that once again we have a visiting pop star here in The Pound this afternoon. People crane their necks to see who it is.

I build up to the introduction, and swing the palm of my right hand in a wide arc:

 "It's Amen Corner – it's Andy...Andy..." I hesitate as I my eyes fall on a vacant chair. Where the hell is he? Fred intervenes: "I think he has gone for a pee." Roars of mirth.

Have to think fast here. If it turns out the Welshman is going to welsh on us, one option might be to get Wrixon up instead. Like Trevor Kelly, Wrixon never needs much persuading.

Eric Wrixon's claim to fame is that he was a founder member of THEM. He lost out on stardom because he was too young when the breaks came for THEM. His folks wouldn't allow him to sign the record contract that propelled the blues group into the stratosphere. Fair enough; he was only 16 at the time.

He is a keyboard player and is always keen to pound the keys with any band in preference to sitting around watching them. He has been known to get up on stage with us here in The Pound. In fact, he doesn't need to be asked. I have known Wrixon to rise to his feet at the back of the room and scramble across tables in order to get to the stage and nudge me off my stool.

If I call him he will come. Eric would enjoy playing 'Morning Dew.' But it would have to be performed his way and, well, to be honest it is hard to get him to go and sit down again.

I consult Fred.

"We'd best leave it," says Fred wisely. "And we'd better be quick – I see Wrixon is on his feet."

"OK, guys – quick now. Morning Dew."

We are in the last chorus of "Morning Dew" when the kid singer with Amen Corner returns to his seat. He gives us the thumbs up as he walks past the front of the stage. What does that mean? I'm thinking. Is he going to get up? I think maybe he is. Gerry Giffen looks animated. Now he is signalling to get me to repeat the announcement to get the kid up to sing.

"It looks like we're on, guys," I say to the boys. "Anyone any idea of the key?"

Sez is on the case. "I think it is in C. It starts with saxophones." "Saxophones?" Fred and I in unison. I'm beginning to realise I know bugger all about how this goes – this could be a total cock-up.

"Who's going to do the saxophone bit? Can you handle it, Sez?" Sez looks nonplussed. I guess that's a yes.

Smick says "I'll start, you follow." He waves his sticks over the top of his hi-hat and gives a vocal impression of what he intends to play: *'Dit- da-dit-da-dit-da-dit...'*

As Fairweather Low gets up from his seat and comes to the stage with Gerry Giffen in tow, I grab the attention of the crowd for the second time: "You're in for a treat, folks. Here he is." I learnt how to give a crescendo announcement by being at the wrestling in the Ulster Hall years ago.

"Here he is. From Amen Corner. The man himself – the one and only – from Top of the Pops. Let's give a big Pound welcome for…"

Heckle from Gerry Hall "Get on with it."

"Yes indeedy. Ladies and gentlemen, we present *ANDY...FAIRWEATHER...LOW!*"

He climbs on to the stage to the biggest round of applause of the afternoon, and tips the upright mic stand forward.

"Hello, Belfast!" Why do they always say that? And why does it always get a cheer? I guess that answers the first question. "Do you want to hear 'Bend Me, Shape Me'?" More cheers fill the room.

"I can't hear you," said Fairweather Low. Clearly he too learnt something from wrestling announcements. "Do you want to hear 'Bend Me, Shape Me'?" Frenzied affirmation.

"Well..." he said.

I wasn't expecting this.

"I will be singing it with Amen Corner in the Starlite tonight and I look forward to seeing you there."

I look at Smick, poised to launch into his drum intro. Smick looks at me, his drumsticks frozen in mid-air. The frenzy is dying down.

"But right now..." The Welshman is not finished yet. "...right now it is my pleasure to bring on a man I know needs no introduction – give a big Pound welcome to Gerry Giffen, ladies and gentlemen." He steps down and with a wave to his fans returns to his seat. Giffen, ready and waiting, steps up. He nods to the band as he removes the mic from its holder.

"'Lucille' in E. Okay?"

The crowd doesn't know what is happening – but we do. And we are straight in there. It's Gerry's signature tune and we know how to play it.

As Gerry is warmly applauded off the stage, he turns to me and says: "I can't wait to hear the recording of that." I give him the thumbs-up.

But he'll have a long wait, I'm thinking. I forgot to fire up the Grundig.

Chapter 33

The Pound
Saturday 6 April 1968 – 17:05
Sgt Pepper's Lonely Hearts Club Band

We're on a roll now. The punters are well-oiled and appreciative. They know we will play on well past closing time – as of course we always do. They know there will be one encore. They also know we have another gig to play tonight.

I leave the Grundig running.

Smick is kicking out a pounding on-beat on the bass drum – Ba-Boom, Boom, Boom, Boom...

Fred joins in with what we know to be the key note. He has turned up the volume and the thump of his bass guitar in sync with the bass drum resonates throughout The Pound. I reinforce it on the organ. Sez is facing Smick, adding to the sound by muffing his open bass string, with distortion pedal giving it added cut. A fair number are on their feet; hands in the air – clapping in time with the pounding build-up. They, too, know what is coming.

I am shouting down the mic: "This is the last song we'll be playing in The Pound for quite some time – so we'll let you all join in..."

Smick:: "Three, Four..."

Sez swings round to face the audience, kicks off the distortion boost and opens up the familiar intro to Sgt Pepper before stepping up to the mic.

The punters are right with us. They even give us a cheer as we cover the three-part brass band instrumental link between the first verse and chorus the only way we can – by singing the trumpet parts, unaccompanied. It's not great but it gets us through. We can hear Gerry Hall commenting on our approach to this little interlude. "Fawkin' eejits." Never lost for words.

I just love this.

"Morr'son! Enough already. Enough of this pop crap"

It's the familiar voice from the back of the room. Funny how we can hear him clearly. His voice seems to transcend the cheers of the crowd.

"Blooos!" "Blooooos!" He starts a chant. People join in.

Sez cranks up a notch, and after a glance at me, swings round to face the audience as he launched into psychedelic hard rock blues. It is what everybody wants and we know we are good at it.

Encores are spontaneous – never announced.

The Pound
Saturday 6 April 1968 – 17:15

It's all over.

I am looking forward to listening to the recording we made of this afternoon in The Pound. We thought we were sounding pretty good and it all went down well. The rowdies have all left the building, encouraged to leave by the bouncers: "Have youse no homes?"

Time to get out of here.

I have given the keys of the Bedford to Blair Whyte. Blair and Marshall McMonagle are helping load the gear and getting it across to the Astor for tonight. With any luck that will leave us time to walk round to the Marquee offices, grab a Wimpy on the way – and get signing those bloody voting slips.

Ah, yes – the voting slips. The CityWeek Pop Poll.

It was Smick who persuaded us the CityWeek Poll could be important. He told us that in 1965 he was voted the top drummer in the country.

He produced his mother's carefully preserved scrapbook to prove his point. It is true. It is there in black and white. The masses rate him Ireland's best. Not just Belfast's top drummer; not just the best in Northern Ireland: the proclamation, in print and therefore a true bill, is that in 1965 there was no better drummer in the island of Ireland.

Supporting articles explain that John Smyth, Ireland's best drummer 1965, is the man behind the driving beat of the Exiles, featuring fellow student of Stranmillis Teacher Training College, Teddie Palmer. Palmer and the Exiles also featured high in other categories. The consequence was that fan clubs were established and more people came to their gigs. Promoters took note. The Exiles increased in popularity and fees went up a notch.

How did that happen? Well, you guessed it.

As Smicker explained, it was a matter of buying up every copy of CityWeek the guys could get their hands on, cutting out the voting slips, filling them in and posting them off. The Exiles were acclaimed to be the top beat group in the country, elbowing their way past THEM; Moses K and the Prophets; the Alleykatz and the Interns.

So now The Group is determined to score well in the CityWeek Pop Poll for 1968.

We now know, of course, that the process has become fiercely competitive. All the groups and showbands are at it. We knew we had to get a head start, so we were out on the streets first thing on the day the polling forms were published. It has cost us a fortune but we have managed to empty the shelves in the shops in central Belfast. We have left heaps of CityWeeks in the back room at the Marquee office, and we have been spending hours this week filling out hundreds of voting slips.

Marquee Office
Saturday 6 April 1968 – 18:00

When we reach the Marquee offices in Donegall Street, we head straight for the room at the back. We nod to Ashtar. Still here.

"Tiger and the boys are here doing the votes," he says. Well, fair enough, I'm thinking. We're all part of the Marquee family and we'd want the Tigers to be placed. There is no way, however, they would have been able to buy up as many copies as we did. We cleared the shelves.

Sure enough here we have Tiger Taylor and his band sitting round the table in a fog of curiously sweet-smelling cigarette smoke, working their way systematically through a pile of neatly folded newspapers. But hold on a minute. That's not their pile: that's our pile.

"Real nice of you," says Fred, seemingly oblivious to the possibility that the growing pile of completed forms might be votes for the opposition.

For his part, Tiger seems equally relaxed and welcoming.

"Come on in guys; look at this – look! Hundreds of CityWeek poll papers. Ashtar got them for us, but we've done enough – we are just heading out now for an early gig in Carrickfergus. You guys can make use of what's left. We'll see you later back at the Astor."

I am speechless. We have just lost about 500 votes for which we paid good money. We sit in silence until they have all gone.

"Ashtar. What the fuck...?"

Before Ashtar can compose what would undoubtedly have been enlightening mystical explanation, in walks Arnie Knowles and Colin McClelland. Arnie quickly takes control of the situation.

"Relax, guys," says Arnie. "Tell them how it works, Colin."

Colin hesitates. He writes for CityWeek and clearly believes the less said about this process, the better. He opens his mouth to speak. Arnie continues:

"We're working with CityWeek on this. The paper makes a killing out of bands buying up copies. They love it. They double their print run – right Colin?"

Colin winces. He knows what is coming.

"And, of course they don't bother to count the votes."

Smick looks horrified. "They don't count the votes?"

"Believe me, Smick, when you topped the poll..." Colin is trying to salvage some journalistic integrity from the conversation.

Ashtar puts his head round the door. "Hey, man – there's some head on the phone."

Colin seizes the opportunity to leave the room. Arnie lowers his voice conspiratorially:

"The Marquee groups will do alright. We've made sure of that. The best group of 1968 will be Taste – because they are the best and we all know it; Tigers will be second because with Teddie leaving him in the lurch, Tiger needs a break."

"What about us?" asks Fred.

"The Group will come third because soon you will be off the road to prepare for your exams." Silence. Nice to think Arnie cares about our exams.

"Sam will be top group vocalist of course and, as you would expect, Rory will take the top guitar slot."

Smick starts to snigger. It evolves into a guffaw. Soon we are all splitting our sides. Silence returns when the laughter dies down. Fred speaks:

"But Arnie, if you knew all this, why didn't you tell us we would be wasting our money buying up all those copies?"

"Figure it out," says Arnie.

'Sgt Pepper's Lonely Hearts Club Band' was a Lennon McCartney classic – the opening track on their acclaimed and massively influential studio album of the same name.

Released on 1 June 1967, it was destined to become one of the best-selling albums in history. As of 2014, more than 30 million copies of what became the definitive psychedelic rock album have been bought around the world.

Chapter 34

Astor Marquee
Saturday 6 April 1968 – 19:00
Dust My Blues

We are in the Astor checking the gear is all set up and ready to go.

Even empty as it is at this time, the place has an extraordinary atmosphere. There are now two stages side by side running much of the length of the far wall. The grand piano is there to the right of the stage beside where I am when we are doing our bit. Hendi's DJ Box is in the far left hand corner. The stage area is designed to look like a Marquee tent with a covering of broad strips of alternatively blue and white material draped over concealed wires.

Opposite the stage, in the centre of the near wall to our right as we enter, is a pre-fabricated scaffolding structure, devised initially by Colin McClelland and Blair Whyte. Ashtar is perched on the top with several slide projectors, his shirt stained with many colours from messing with glass slides containing pigments, oils and soap. Every slide is an experiment with different combinations, creating a constantly changing light show with explosions of colour as the slide expands and contracts under the heat of the projector bulb. The effect is simply wonderful.

We chat with Hendi who reckons that with payday last week and Easter coming up next, this promises to be a big night. We noticed on the way in that a queue was already forming outside. Hendi gives us a handwritten note of the programme for the night. Cahir O'Doherty's band, Gentry, is the guest group that we have on tonight and their gear is already set up on the new stage to our right as we face the audience. Gentry had changed their name to Nobility, but for some reason have changed back to Gentry. I must ask Cahir about that.

"Where's Cahir?" asks Smick.

"Over in the Herc." The Hercules Bar.

"Well, I'll head on over," says Smick. "I'll see you there. We're on at 8:30 right?"

Hendi says Arnie wants us to factor in a slot for Platform 3. "That's them over there by the piano. They'll want to know if it's okay to use your gear."

We step up onto the stage and have a word. One of them looks about fourteen.

"No problem, guys," I say. "What do you need?"

"Guitar, bass, drums." says the teenager. "We met at The Who concert in Lisburn."

Right enough. Can't remember his name.

The Hercules Bar
Saturday 6 April 1968 – 20:00

We're in the upstairs lounge of the Hercules Bar in Castle Street, a short walk from the Astor.

Smick is entertaining Cahir and Frankie Connolly in the far corner of the lounge. Sez is in the opposite corner with a blonde girl he has been seeing. Fred and I are at a table with Eric Wrixon, who looks pretty good considering he is likely to have spent all afternoon in The Pound. He has been in a lot of bands since THEM – most recently in England with Brian Rossi and Wheels. But since those guys have split he is doing mostly session work. He obviously has a night off.

He never shuts up but is always good for an update on who is doing what.

"Why did Nobility change their name back to Gentry then, Eric?"

"Dunno."

Not in a talkative mood tonight, then. I'll try another one. "What about Rory? How is Taste making out in London?"

"All right."

This is not like him at all. He seems depressed. I'll get him talking about himself. "What about..."

He interrupts me, leaning forward and whispering: "I can't say much but the Cork boys have been dumped." "Eric and Norman are out?"

Now this is news.

"Yea. John Wilson and Charlie McCracken are leaving Cheese and heading to London to take their place."

This is bigger news. I expect Eric was hoping they would be looking for a keyboard player.

The Marquee
Saturday 6 April 1968 – 20:30

We have to fight our way through the crowd to get in. It is a warm evening for early April. The crowd, comprising those who can't or won't spend the early part of the night in the pub, is rowdy but happy. Some are fashionably dressed. The fashion for many includes clutching a brown paper bag concealing a bottle of Buckfast or Scrumpy. The bottles never come out of the bags. At regular intervals, mystifyingly synchronised, brown bags collectively arc heavenward. Every drop has to be consumed and the brown bag and its contents disposed of before the consumer will be allowed in.

Tonight the Marquee guys have thought up a great wheeze to keep people happy. They have installed speakers from the disco pointing out into College Court. The crowd waiting to be let in make the most of the pounding beat which reverberates in the confined space. Hendi has got feedback that the waiting crowd is appreciative. He milks it. He is re-cycling 'Dancing in The Street' by Martha and the

Vandellas followed in repeated succession by the Mamas and Papas version.

People are dancing in the street.

The Marquee
Saturday 6 April 1968 – 21:30

We have been playing for an hour and it is time to hand over to Hendi. Gentry are setting up on the stage beside us. We hang about for the first couple on numbers and then elect to go back to the Hercules. Sez stays behind with his girl, while Smick goes back to join Frankie who is keeping everyone entertained.

The Marquee
Saturday 6 April 1968 – 22:30

Last orders at 10 pm. We collect Smick and a woosy Frankie Connolly follows. He wants to sing Otis Redding. 'Mr Pitiful.' The place is bunged and the atmosphere is incredible. Platform 3 are playing what we assume to be their last number – using our gear as planned. Luckily Sez was on hand to help them set up. They are going down well.

Sez comes over to us: "These guys are very good. Listen to that guitar."

"We know him actually; he lives off the Upper Newtownards Road opposite Stormont. What's his name – do you know?"

"Gary Moore."

The Gentry come back on. Frankie pleads for Cahir to let him sing. Cahir will have none of it.

The Marquee
Saturday 6 April 1968 – 23:30

We are back on stage. Frankie Connolly is standing centre stage holding the mic stand. He is loved by the crowd who want him to sing a song. And hey, why not? We decide to put Frankie on right at the beginning. He is itching to go.

"What'll it be, Frankie?"

"Otis. Mr Pitiful."

Smick knows the beat and starts drumming; Sez knows the key. I tag along. Frankie struts imperiously, poised to give it his all. He is a great soul singer and the crowd is captivated. This is going to be good, I'm thinking.

Half way in and Frankie is way out there. He is grunting like no soul singer I have ever heard before. The crowd is cheering him on. I am not altogether clear whether he is extemporising on the soulful lyric or has merely forgotten the words, but this is powerful stuff. His face is contorted as he delivers, with feeling, a succession of random phrases containing the word pitiful. He certainly hasn't forgotten the title of the song and he is right there, giving it his all. Frankie is Mr Pitiful.

By the time we approach the end, he is on his knees blurting single syllables into the microphone, which he has dragged, still on its stand, right down to the floor. Suddenly he gets to his feet, swings round to Sez and projects a high velocity vomit over Sez and his cherished Gibson guitar. Sez stops playing instantly, staring down at the readily recognisable yellow slime of beer-laden chinese takeaway topped with pieces of carrot that was now clinging to his shirt and dripping through the f-holes. The crowd roars.

We think we may have to ask Gentry to come back on while Sez composes himself and cleans the guitar.

The Marquee
Sunday 7 April 1968 – 00:30

We are due to end at midnight, but this is going well and nobody has called upon us to stop. Sez's guitar is now a different colour and Frankie is nowhere to be seen.

"Here's one you can all jive to," says Fred. Typical Fred humour. People are packed together shoulder to shoulder. Even a smooch could prove difficult.

He spots Sam Mahood at the back of the hall.

"No wait a minute." He pulls back from the mic. "Let's see if we can get Sam up for the last number."

Sam is with Tiger Taylor and Nean Irwin. We know Tiger and the guys would be dropping by, but it looks as if Sam and the Soul Foundation have also decided to look in. Sam is dressed in a frilly white shirt. This could be good.

"Big hand for Sam Mahood, ladies and gentlemen." Sam is clearly up for it and he works his way through the crowd. He leaps up on the stage and grabs a microphone. He growls into the mic "Dust my Blooos." Loud cheering as Sez immediately crashes out the intro. Sam pulls a harpoon out of his pocket and he is socking it to them.

It's great – rough, coarse and never ending. Ashtar pans a spotlight across the dance floor. A thousand synchronised heads can be seen nodding up and down to the pounding beat. Eventually Sam indicates he would like a bit of cool. He talks to the crowd and calls for the Soul Foundation to make their way onto the stage. Up comes Mervyn Crawford and the girls, Rusty Crooks and Karen Byrne. He calls out for new member John Cox to play guitar. The front stage is crowded.

Meanwhile young Gary has plugged in to the Gentry's amp on the adjoining stage and Nean Irwin has taken over their drum kit. Smick sees it as competition and hits harder. Sam pulls Cahir O'Doherty on to our stage to share the vocals. He grabs another mic and is trading lines with Sam.

Over on the right hand stage Tiger is looking for somewhere to plug in. The two stages are now awash with heads.

Sam pushes past me and climbs up onto the lid of the grand piano that had stood at the side of the stage in the Astor since the dance orchestra days of the 1930s and 40s. He struts his stuff and the crowd eggs him on. His mic lead, at full stretch, catches round my chin.

With Sam Mahood you must expect the unexpected, but I feel a sense of foreboding. This is not going to end well.

Sam is about to step off the grand piano. He sees two steps to get down onto the stage. Step one has to be – can only be – the keyboard of my Philicorda organ.

I reel back to avoid my fingers getting in the way. My foot catches the lead of the swell pedal and wrenches it out of its jack socket. Sam strides off the grand piano. I gasp as his foot plants itself firmly on the keyboard. Miraculously it doesn't crumble to the floor under his weight. Another stride and he is down on the stage where he catches the cable of the swell pedal, ripping it clean apart from its jack plug. Sixteen keys, defined by the outline of his footprint, remain permanently depressed, producing an awful cacophony. The jarring racket is amplified by the absence of the hitherto restraining swell pedal, and compounded by the persistent hum of an amplifier that is no longer safely earthed. Furthermore my organ was connected directly into the PA system so what we are talking about here is not just a cacophony; it is a cacophony at high volume. Pete Lloyd's PA system is on a test to destruction.

I take a bow. As far as I am concerned this is thank you and goodnight. I yank the plug out of the amp with a flourish at what I decide is the end of the night. But Sam is not of a mind to end his performance just yet. He starts into yet another verse of 'Dust My Blues.'

Whether in self-defence or in the vain hope the keyboard would have fixed itself, I plug it in again when it comes to what surely now has to be the final crescendo.

Out comes the cacophony again. Sam is drowned out. Sez is inspired to hit a never-ending succession of power chords with the fuzzbox at maximum gain. The beat is lost with Nean speeding up and Smick slowing down. It looks as if Smick was seriously contemplating kicking the drums off the stage but hasn't the energy left to do so. Fred is thumping random chords on his bass oblivious of the danger of blowing his speaker.

But my organ is determined to have the last word. Now everyone on stage, including Sam, is staring at me. I hear Cahir shout: "Pull the plug for Chrissakes."

I smile and with one hand on the lead, I raise the other hand and slowly finger a countdown: "One; two; three…" in preparation for a cutthroat gesture. All stop precisely on cue. The silence is merciful. I grab a mic. Through the ringing in my ears I hear myself thank Sam graciously for putting my organ permanently out of commission.

Not that anyone is listening. Every punter in the hall is heading for the door.

A few weeks later Smick was fired.

Booze was to blame. Sez, a man of few words at the best of times, laid it on the line. He gave a speech making it clear he would leave the band if we didn't do something about it. Smick felt this was directed at him and took the hump. So it was over to Fred to sort it out. Fred was always ready to step up to the plate.

Smick knew that Ricky was back in town and could see where this was heading. Whether he had inkling of what was on the cards I don't know – but after a late night confrontation on a sofa in the Astor Ballroom, Smick was out and Ricky was back in the band.

In no time at all Smick had persuaded top musos to join a new group – The John Smith Band. Amongst them was a particularly talented keyboard-player, Alastair "Haggi" McKenzie. Haggi turned out to have an even greater enthusiasm for booze – on one occasion having to be carried into the gig and propped in an upright position behind the keyboards. Everything is relative, I suppose.

Smick, now feeling the burden of being group leader, laid it on the line. Haggi, a gentle soul, hung his head in shame. He left the band and headed for London where he was hired to play with the chart-topping Suzi Quatro. In a probing press interview, Smick was quizzed about this:

"Do you see any irony in the fact that getting pie-eyed is rumoured to have been the reason you lost your last job drumming with The Group?"

›News

so parched of
e rumours must
big oaks from
d I'm the man
n.
ve come in for
ination in these
and who were
be breaking up

'I SACKED
THE GROUP'
–SMICK

Smick put the record straight with a quote that was elevated to an eye-catching headline.

Chapter 35

Reflections

Back in the early 50s a young man was setting up his kit in a Chicago nightclub, where he was due to appear as a substitute drummer with the Stan Kenton Band later that evening.

This was an important gig for him and he got there early. He was a good player, and his drums were made by Ludwig - perhaps the most famous drum company of all time. He practised a little in the quiet of the afternoon, accompanied only by the clink of glasses and bottles as the bar staff prepared for the evening onslaught. There was only one customer in the room that afternoon, sitting by the bar, casually observing the technician at work.

The musician became clearly frustrated with the functioning of his bass drum pedal, which was unable to match the demands placed upon it by his pounding right foot. After a few moments, the man at the bar came over and asked if he could help.

"I doubt it," said the drummer, "This pedal just isn't up to it."

"Well, we will just have to get that seen to - what's your name, kid?" asked the customer.

The kid was Joe Morello - and he was set to become the best in the business. This was many years before he reached fame for his mastery of unusual time signatures used during his long career with Dave Brubeck. The five beats to the bar 'Take Five' was one of very few jazz classics which ever made it to the top the pop charts - back in 1961. Morello was cited as the greatest influence of all time on modern drumming techniques by that guru of heavy rock, Led Zeppelin's John Bonham.

The customer left the building and returned with a brand new pedal of a kind Morello had never seen before. It made all the difference. "Here's my card," said the man, as he turned and walked away: "I'll be back tonight with my staff and I'll want you to tell us all how you got on with it."

Morello struggled with words to thank the man, and stared at the door as it swung closed. Only then did he glance at the card to learn the name of his mysterious benefactor.

The name on the card was William F Ludwig, Jr Vice President of the Ludwig Drum Company.

Michael started playing drums at the age of 12, and when he had mastered percussion, he picked up a guitar and learnt to busk the way I did. He has an appetite for knowledge about the instruments that I never had. He would read from cover to cover every book he could find on drums and guitars. He has ended up with a house full of such books and magazines (never thrown out) – and ultimately a collection of valuable and authentic drums and guitars.

The story about Joe Morello is typical of what musicians search for in music books and magazines. Watch them seek out the pages that feature a particular product and examine the provenance of instrument manufacture.

A musician is not in the least interested in exploring his or her own personal genealogy – but will have an insatiable appetite to know as much as there is to know about the names Ludwig, Rickenbacker, Gibson, and Gretsch. These names mean little to the man in the street, but to anyone in the music business, they carry a special magic.

It is extraordinary how few alterations there have been in the design of musical instruments over the last 100 years. Even the evolution of electric rock music, the sound of which is seen to have moved light years from more traditional forms of music, has not seen any matching evolution in the appearance of the instruments. A keyboard is a keyboard. The Fender Stratocaster guitars played by Buddy Holly and the Crickets are virtually indistinguishable in appearance from those used by the rock and pop bands of today.

Perhaps this explains why there are so few names in the musical instrument manufacturing business, and why enthusiasts place such value on authenticity. We have Japanese and Korean imitations at half the price – and Chinese copies at a quarter – but a musician will only value quality in an instrument if it carries one of the big names and he can trace its origins.

The internet is now the means by which anyone obsessed with a particular musical instrument, or anything else for that matter, can make contact with others across the world, and indeed how people discover just how many other like-minded individuals there are. Michael plays drums and guitar and his obsession revolves around the equipment used by his heroes.

On Friday 1 April 2005, the Dominoes were poised to provide the music at a wedding in Newcastle, County Down. It was just another gig, but we met somebody interesting on the way in.

We hung around outside the room with our gear, waiting for the tables to be cleared. There were six of us in the band at this time; four ageing rockers and two younger ones - Michael and Clare - all dressed in black.

I became aware of a man standing beside me. He was about my age, dressed in what I could perhaps best describe as Scottish golfer garb. He had the healthy glow of a man who had just come into the warmth after spending about five hours chasing a little white ball through the wind and rain.

His accent was Scottish but with a slower drawl that he later explained was the result of spending most of his working life in America.

He clearly wanted to engage with the band. What kind of stuff do you play? What instruments? What equipment?

He talked to me to begin with. "Is that a Rickenbacker 12-string in the case? What picks do you use?"

"Jim Dunlop mostly," I replied. "Ernie Ball strings?" I nodded. "What effects-pedals?" I told him I used a Marshall fuzz box from the 70s and a Jim Dunlop Compressor. "To make the Rick chime?" I was impressed. "You seem to know about these things."

At this stage the golfer said something about himself, along the lines of being interested in this sort of thing because he made bits and pieces for the music industry. Could he have a look at the gear? We had time to kill, so I opened my guitar case, revealing my 12-string and an elderly soap box containing about 20 picks.

The golfer looked through the soap box, lifting the picks out one at a time. I got curious and began to pay a bit more attention when he announced, "I made that – and that one – oh and look. That's been around a long time. It was one of the early ones." He turned to Michael who was listening attentively. "You play the guitar too, son?" he asked. "Try some of these."

As Michael pored over a fistful of what was described as a selection of experimental picks, the golfer reached out his business card. "Write to me and tell me what you think of them." "My name is Jim Dunlop." Not William F Ludwig or Adolph Rickenbacker - but a name to conjure with all the same.

Chapter 36

Where Are They Now?

John Smyth and I meet up regularly these days. We enjoy each other's company and get a lot of laughs despite the fact that he has had to endure protracted treatment for mouth cancer - which I am happy to report is in full remission.

Smick had been part of The Group for about a year – nearly half the total lifespan of the band. The band was rejuvenated by the return of Ricky, but within four months Fred had left to study in Edinburgh and The Group broke up. In 1971 Smick and I were playing together again, with Sez, in Dunno.

Sez Adamson lives in Johannesburg. He is much in demand as a session musician and has won international acclaim for his creative melodic style of chord play on the Pedal Steel Guitar.

Dick Pentland is still living in Nova Scotia, near Halifax, where he was Port Engineer before travelling the world as a consultant on port development. He is as witty, contrary and creative as ever, and a master of the keyboard, which he plays every day, developing ever more complicated and obscure chord sequences.

In 2015, the record released by Dunno 44 years ago on the M and M label suddenly surfaced on the internet. But it was not 'Sunday Girl,' the A-side track for which Keith Baker and I proudly trousered £4.22 in composition royalties. It was B-Side that earned the unexpected acclaim. 'Magic Beat,' Dick Pentland's weird rap about rhythmic pulses reviving corpses, was selected for a compilation album published worldwide by the Electric Asylum described as 'Rare British Freakrock.' Fame at last.

Tiger Taylor lives in Dublin and is still performing.

Rory Gallagher died on 14 June 1995 from complications that arose following a liver transplant. He played the same distressed Stratocaster right through to his last gig in January that year.

Sam Mahood died on December 23 2006. His stage presence and sensational soul singing was never compromised by any of his excesses. Despite the way he left his footprint on my keyboard that night in the Marquee, I loved him.

The Philicorda was never played again after that event. I like to imagine that this incident must somehow have been the inspiration for Terry Gilliam's naked organist animation where a giant foot crushes the Monty Python title at the end of the opening credits. The little keyboard served me well from the early rhythm and blues of the Dominoes at the Boat Club right through to the west coast harmony sound of The Group in The Marquee.

Cahir O'Doherty lives in St Cloud, Florida. He is still performing.

Carol McCutcheon (née Clapham), **Gerry Hall** and **Marshall McMonagle** died ahead of their time. In the course of writing this book, we lost **Eric Wrixon** and **Haggi McKenzie**.

John Wilson has also come through protracted treatment for throat cancer, which in his case also involved major surgery. On Monday 29 May 2013 I found myself at the Empire in Botanic Avenue at a 'benefit night' event organised by his many friends in the music industry. While his cancer surgery was successful, his professional career has come to an end. The room was packed with musicians who had been inspired by John 'Junior' Wilson to perform to the top of their game.

A surprising number of Belfast's jazz heads, who were there before this whole thing started, are still standing. For them jazz is more than a passion: it is a way of life to which they became devoted. Relatively recently Trevor Foster nodded at me as he eased his clarinet away from his lips: "I have been playing that one for 50 years," he said. "And you know what? I've never played it better."

David Smith, leaning against the double bass he has hugged fondly for all that time, summed it up with a quote from local jazz aficionado and doyen of Irish jazz critics and writers, the late Solly Lipsitz. "The jazzmen of Belfast," wrote Lipsitz, "should be proud to have manned for a while an outpost of the New Orleans tradition." They are still manning that outpost and long may they continue to do so.

Roy Bradford's funeral in 1998 was well attended. Afterwards I spoke to David Bleakley, the defeated candidate in the 1965 Election, about whom I have long felt a little guilt. I asked him straight up if he felt the pounding beat music associated with the Bradford campaign played a part in him being ousted from Victoria Ward. I was somewhat taken aback when he responded "Not at all," he replied. "I lost it fair and square." But at least I was relieved of the burden of offering some form of apology.

As the years passed, I met Roy Bradford on a number of occasions and in different guises. In conversation he would always return whimsically to the 1965 General Election and to the significance of that jingle to his political career. He clearly thought the studio time was money well spent. I became good friends with his son Toby, a singer-songwriter and younger brother of BBC Radio Ulster presenter, Conor Bradford.

Thomas Niedermayer, whose body was searched for and found by the security forces in that clandestine operation in 1980, turned out to be the victim of an IRA hostage venture that went badly wrong. The intention had been to force the release of eight Provisional IRA conspirators who had been jailed for life for their part in the planting of two car bombs in central London on Thursday 8 March 1973. 216 people were injured.

The 45-year-old German diplomat and boss of the Grundig electronics plant in Belfast, was unintentionally killed the day after he was kidnapped. Apparently he was trying to escape. Thomas Niedermayer's wife Ingeborg and two teenage daughters, Gabrielle and Renata, had to wait seven years before his body was found lying face down at the bottom of that illegal rubbish dump in Colin Glen.

The West German company immediately closed down the west Belfast plant with a loss of 1000 jobs. My Grundig TK14 tape recorder, in perfect working order after 50 years in a cupboard, bears testimony to the quality of workmanship.

After her husband's body was found, a devastated Ingebord moved back to Germany. Mother and daughters were haunted by the murder and distanced themselves from one another after Gabrielle married and Renate moved to South Africa. In 1990 Ingebord resolved to return to Ireland. She booked into a hotel in Wicklow, requesting a room with a sea view and a double bed. Her body was found on the shoreline the following morning. She had walked into the sea and drowned.

It didn't end there for the tragic Niedermayer family. Within 10 years, they were all gone. Ingebord's two daughters Gabrielle and Renata had also been driven to take their own lives.

John McGuffin died in 2002. Writing in the Belfast Telegraph after his death, Eamonn McCann described how his friend for 40 years – 'a gifted, utterly undisciplined writer, eschewing the pedantries of structure and all strictures of taste' – had practised as a lawyer in San Francisco for 15 years, advertising his services under the slogan:

Sean McGuffin
Attorney at Law - Irish-friendly
No crime too big, no crime too small

McCann went on to explain that McGuffin only did defences, and preferred getting people off who were guilty because that way it was more fun.

He moved to Derry in 1998. In 2012, to mark the tenth anniversary of his death, his former friends and colleagues unveiled a striking red and black-coloured anarchism-inspired paint job on Free Derry Corner – elected to give the now historic landmark Free Derry Corner a makeover as a mark of respect. A large billboard to the rear carried a quote from John McGuffin:

No Gods, No Masters!

That must be what he had tried to explain to me on the day I left Campbell College.

Major Ronald Bunting, who led the placard waving protesters that advanced down Pansy Street on election night was the same "buffoonish" Major Bunting who, by then professing to be a follower of Ian Paisley, led the ambush of the students at Burntollet Bridge. But his son Ronnie Bunting, interned alongside McGuffin, followed a path to something much more sinister. Within a few years, Bunting Junior would become Northern Ireland's most wanted republican terrorist.

In his autobiography, *The Beginning of the End: The Crippling Disadvantage of a Happy Irish Childhood*, the US-based writer

Walter Ellis describes graphically the uneasy relationship he had with his cousin Ronnie Bunting – with whom he had grown up in Ballyhackamore in east Belfast.

Ellis tells how Bunting crossed the sectarian divide, making enemies in both camps as he worked his way to the top ranks of republican para-military organisations. He became Chief of Staff of the fringe terror group, the Irish National Liberation Army (INLA). In that role, he masterminded the murder in the car park of the House of Commons of Airey Neave, the Shadow Secretary of State for Northern Ireland. Neave, a decorated war hero who was the first British officer to escape from Colditz, was a close confidante of Conservative leader, Margaret Thatcher, who was deeply affected by the callousness and audacity of this assassination.

Ronnie Bunting, son of high profile ex-army officer and staunch loyalist, Major Ronald Bunting, was shot dead on 15 October 1980 by a group of masked men who burst into his adopted west Belfast home in Turf Lodge. No-one ever claimed responsibility for his murder.

Was there some explanation for Bloody Friday? It transpired that around three weeks before, the IRA had announced a truce in advance of secret talks in London between the IRA and Government Ministers, the outcome of which was regarded by both sides as constructive. The secrecy was impossible to maintain; tensions heightened as diplomats scratched their heads to give effect to the practicalities. In this vacuum, volunteers were lined up; hoax callers briefed; 22 explosive devices were commissioned, primed and ready to go. Clearly such a well-orchestrated event had to have been planned well in advance.

On 21 July 2002, 30 years after 'Bloody Friday,' the IRA issued an apology for what it admitted was a mistake, asserting that the aim of the IRA that day was merely to cause disruption. The statement added that the IRA had overestimated the capacity of the security forces to deal with the situation with which they were confronted. Most analysts, however, think it more likely that the hoax warnings were deliberately used to reduce the effectiveness of the security forces in dealing with the real bombs.

In the event, the killings and maiming had a profound effect on most people in Northern Ireland. 'Bloody Friday' also led to the decision to gate the city centre, effectively killing off any residue of night life. It also led directly to the implementation of Operation Motorman (31 July 1972) when, in the biggest British military operation since the 1956 Suez crisis, the British Army entered and ended the 'no-go' areas of Belfast and Derry. The two tribes were no longer interested in accommodating differences.

It is often said that after Bloody Friday the middle classes left for the golf course and haven't been back since. Could that metaphor be said to apply to me?

If so, I'm not proud of it.

The Pound exists no more. Townhall Street was swallowed up in the 1980s by the muscle-flexing Musgrave Street Police Station. The Laganside Court building, opened in 2002, now sits across the land that was once occupied by Roddy's Bar and The Pound. The Maritime has gone - as has Sammy Houston's. Of the dance studios upon which Belfast's beat groups depended, probably only Clarke's dance studio is still in business. Instruction in the art of pole dancing is prominently featured in the notice on the door today.

As we entered the Astor Ballroom that cold, sharp Friday morning in February 2001, dozens of pigeons, the only living creatures to have been in the building for nigh on thirty years, noisily flew en masse out through holes in the roof. The shafts of sunlight that leaked in were sufficient to fuel and ultimately seal our fond memories of the **Marquee Club.**

There was no hint of the cheap perfume, nor did we detect any recognisable whiff of wee Gerry's plimsolls, but I was able to tell Colin McClelland that the cash desk was there; the wood panelled cloakroom that had been unchanged since the thirties was still there; the bar, the mirrored powder room, and the little back stairway were all there – exactly as he would remember it.

Collapsed roofing timbers and pink coloured ceiling tiles lay where they fell on the ballroom floor that had been the pride of the McMahon family. It was covered in pigeon shit. The soft seating on the raised area around the oval dance floor was curiously untouched by the pigeons or the detritus from the collapsing ceiling. The grand piano was gone, but otherwise the stage was just as we fondly remembered it. Still in place was the distinctive frame of the Marquee canopy that we installed purposefully all those years ago – and there, suspended from the frame, was a handful of the original drapes, quivering gently in the cold air as if to say: "We waited for you. We knew one day you would come back looking for us."

The Astor ballroom, home for the Saturday night Marquee Club, was demolished two weeks later to make way for an eight-storey block of apartments.

The Saturday night Marquee Club existed for just 12 months. It was a hit with punters from Day One - a commercial success far beyond expectations. After a year the opportunity arose to review the situation and the McMahon family naturally started thinking about running the Marquee themselves. The arrangement with Knowles was terminated. Pat McMahon promptly engaged the influential CityWeek columnist Donal Corvin on a hefty retainer to advise on a re-branding of the 'club' under the new name 'Birdland.' But the novelty had gone; The Group had gone; Fanny Flickers had gone, and the drive simply wasn't there anymore. If the name 'Birdland' had any currency at all, it was many years later when the pigeons found their way into the derelict building.

Arnie moved the Marquee Club to Hill Street where the Black Box is today. He brought to the new venue the drapes, the lighting effects, Ashtar, the top groups, and the newspaper advertising – but the punters didn't follow. The team members went their separate ways.

He never became a tycoon. We thought he had the Midas touch, but not everything turned to gold.

Ashtar was last spotted in Paris in October 1980. Arnie had followed up a tenuous line of communication. Ashtar apologised for rushing away, explaining as climbed into the back seat of a black French government vehicle that he was on his way to a meeting with some senior members of the Air Force. It was something to do with flying saucers. Arnie doesn't know what happened to Jake.

The Golden Irish Showband Annual carried an article suggesting that in 1966 there were around 800 showbands operating in the 32 counties. It went on to comment on the extraordinary upsurge in the number of beat groups in the greater Belfast area aspiring to follow in the footsteps of THEM. The survey indicated that there could as many as 400 groups had sprung up in the previous 12 months - all looking to Pete Lloyd to make them sound good on a recording that would bring fame and fortune. The Solomon empire offered recording contracts to Wheels and the Mad Lads, but for the rest it was back to playing the odd date to help pay off the instalments on the gear. Of all the bands throughout the island of Ireland with contact details were listed in an annex, fifteen per cent were based in east Belfast.

The legacy of 1967-69 could be said to have encouraged the punk explosion in Belfast that followed 10 years later, led by the Undertones and Stiff Little Fingers. There was now knowledge, and indeed a history, showing it was possible to overturn the status quo and create venues where a new type of music could be played and where people who dressed in peculiar clothes and with strange hairstyles could congregate freely.

Looking back forty-five years to that particular day around which this book is written, Saturday 6 April 1968, I can see how life was good for the young dude in Belfast. I can see how fortunate I was to have been associated with The Pound and The Marquee. I have lasting friendships with the people who created and sustained these hubs of activity. It was a privilege to have been there and to have walked the talk - for in that fleeting moment, a moment that preceded thirty long years of discontent, Belfast was thriving.

The rock 'n' roll years from 1966 to 1969 should be celebrated. I like to think of this as a time when the young people of Belfast, of whatever religious background, found common purpose in music and socialising. I like to think sectarian differences were taken out of the equation. In some ways it was an age of innocence. We lived a carefree existence that is often paraphrased as drugs, sex and rock 'n' roll. The rock 'n' roll was real. It was earthy and it was innovative. The sex was real if you were lucky. Amphetamines and cannabis were real, to be sure, but popping pills and smoking dope was a minority sport at this time. The drug of choice was alcohol.

Did those who frequented The Pound and The Marquee transcend the sectarian divide during this little interlude? I can offer no hard evidence to back this up, but I have always believed micks and prods were equally at home and comfortable at these venues. Gerry Adams writes in his autobiography how as a 19-year-old he would look forward all week long to Saturday night at the Marquee Club. From the other side of the tracks another 19-year-old called Terri Hooley felt exactly the same. Certainly if you had any talent as a musician, you would be invited to join a band without anyone asking where you lived or what school you attended.

So did we all mix together at this time in a way that was outside the norm? Did the younger fans that were drawn to the Marquee Club break new ground in that respect? Was it the music? Was it simply a time when sectarian differences were eclipsed by the feel-good factor of the Summer of Love; the thought of California Girls; the prospect of man walking on the moon or the Beatles telling us that All You Need is Love?

For a few hours every week, the young people of Belfast would come together in The Pound and The Marquee. We were not naïve. We were a generation that believed in peaceful protest and we knew change was necessary to ensure that issues of unfairness and inequality would become a thing of the past. We believed the attitude of mind of our generation held promise of a better life for all. Not for one minute did anyone expect it would give rise to violence and conflict. The future should have been very different.

Around 137,000 people in the British Isles are believed to have Parkinson's, which causes tremors, slow movements and muscle rigidity. There is currently no cure and no way of halting the disease. But the progressive nerve cell damage produced by Parkinson's is thought to begin long before any symptoms appear.

One person every hour is diagnosed with the condition. Currently Parkinson's patients only discover they have the debilitating neurological problem when the symptoms have already taken hold.

We still await the promised breakthrough which will slow down the progression of Parkinson's.

But there are reasons to be cheerful. Parkinson's UK offers great support. After I made contact with the Charity through a call to England, I had a visit from the sky-diving Johanne Meredith. Her hobby wasn't the only thing that impressed me. She arranged for me to attend group discussions and be visited at home by a Health Service occupational therapist and a speech therapist.

The medication makes a difference. I take exercise; I go for walks and spend an hour in the local gym three times a week. I see a physiotherapist for help dealing with arthritic joints and emerging back pain. I fill my diary with appointments for lunch or coffee with former work colleagues and my muso chums.

But the last word on this subject has to be for Lyn, my long-suffering wife who married me for better or for worse in 1970. I still chuckle when I think of her ice-breaking reaction to the news that I had Parkinson's – "Well, I just hope you're not thinking you can blame Parkinson's for all your failings."

I can escape from it all by short bursts of singing and playing the piano or my Rickenbacker 12-string guitar – turned up loud. I am on a mission: to complete this book – after which I'll set myself another challenge. I may have Parkinson's but it doesn't have me.

Colin McClelland took on the job of managing of Chips, and moved to Dublin where he rose to the position of Editor of Sunday World. His main interests in life are horse trials (he is press officer for Horse Sport Ireland), and listening to classical music.

As he sits in his armchair, headphones clasped to his ears and absorbed in the New World Symphony, he must reflect from time to time on that little interlude, and the memories that are evoked by a very different sound of music. I imagine that, like his mother, he gropes for the words that aptly sum up The Pound and The Marquee. Maybe, like me, he ponders why in the general excitement of what we were doing, no-one ever thought the moment in time would come to be regarded as anything out of the ordinary. Maybe in the innocence of our youth we thought it would last forever.

On Wednesday 1 April 2015 I invited a number of other friends from the bands and groups of the 1960s to take a 'bus pass' train ride to Dublin to spend a few hours with colleagues they had not seen for years. The emotional reunion of John Wilson and Brush Shiels was a very special moment that will remain with me always. The event gave rise to the title of this book "Big Hand for the Band" and to the website:

www.bighandfortheband.com

We were there. Let's hear it one more time:

Big Hand
for the Band

Epilogue

The songs were not performed in the order indicated in the book. Easy listening warm-ups were required on a Saturday afternoon gig at The Pound. It was a relaxed gig and the punters needed time to settle down, drink and converse before giving any attention to what was on stage. We would never have allowed ourselves to squander a good number like I Can See for Miles against a background where gathering punters would be scraping furniture in the scramble for seats while their mates would be shouting to attract the attention of a barman for that urgent first pint of the afternoon.

The appearance of Andy Fairweather Low in The Pound in fact occurred three weeks earlier.

Platform 3 was on stage in the Marquee that night, but 16-year-old Gary Moore had in fact moved to Dublin to join Skid Row a couple of months previously. His jaw-dropping performance in the Marquee was when Platform 3 took the stage after The Group on Saturday 27 January 1968.

Frankie Connolly, that splendid and ever popular soul singer, was often invited on to the stage in the Marquee to sing with The Group. I apologise to Frankie for the story that he threw up on stage that night singing Otis Redding's Mr Pitiful. I know that not to be true. I know because it didn't happen that night. It in fact happened the week before.

If you want to check out what The Group actually sounded like that day in April 1968, you can now listen to it on a CD. The only digital modification has been to compress the mono sound to a consistent output volume; a modest adjustment I was able to make on my PC using free software.

This book is the third re-print. It is supplied with a dust jacket and incorporates a CD published under license from MCPS (Mechanical Copyright Protection Society) containing the original recordings of The Group playing in The Pound on 6 April 1968.

This 'warts and all' CD is an amateur recording, with the sound recorded through a single mic suspended in front of a PA speaker. It might be of interest to any reader wanting to hear the sound of The Group, or simply wanting to get an aural impression of what it was like in these legendary venues in 1968. There will be some readers with fond memories of The Pound who will want to clamp headphones firmly to their ears in the hope of hearing their own voices transcend rising above the clink of beer mugs. For a handful of anoraks it will be of interest purely and simply because it is the genuine article.

The CD opens with a medley of four songs played that afternoon. The remaining tracks for the most part were also recorded at the time. The exceptions are 'Good Vibrations' and 'Hey Jude' which were recorded in The Queen's Court, Bangor with Ricky McCutcheon back on drums. The final track 'Dust My Blues' is from the Saturday evening of 6 April 1967 when Sam Mahood was called to the stage, took the mic and worked his way onto the grand piano. Listen for the moment Sam steps down via my keyboard leaving a footprint of permanently depressed keys.

Yes, this is the way it was.

Cheese Exiles
Sh'Boo Wheels Orpheus Astor
Starlite People KingBees Interns Aztecs
Telstars
Dominoes Deltones **BigHandForTheBand**
JustFive Gamblers Marquee
Maritime SkidRow CollegeBoys Trixons Tigers
BrianRossi Clubsound RoryGallagher AndwellasDream BoomBoomRoom
HerculesBar JustJerrys TheGroup GeordieSproule Chips Carpetbaggers Spectres
Spike FrankieConnolly Tech MosesKandtheProphets VeniceCafé SpanishRooms Alleykatz
SoulFoundation MintImperial Inst EireApparent GlenmachanStables FivebyFive BettyStaffs MadLads
JohnSmithBand Misfits Midnighters BillyHarrison GoldenEagles Pennyfeather SharePark
Clarkes Heart'n'Soul SamMahood TigerTaylor Platform3 SquareOne Plaza
Bronco Freshmen ThinLizzy HighWall TeddiePalmer PennyLane Penthouse
Pedros Abercorn ClubRado JohnWilson VanMorrison Fugitives Dunno SHJC
Taste Gentry ThePound Romanos
Method

The Magnificent  MARQUEE

Now in its 7th scintillating week

PRESENTS ON 8th DECEMBER

THE GROUP &
THE GENTRY

What the Critics said:—

"An absolute triumph," Joe Freeshomil;

"Fantastic." President Onuga of Masataba;

"Daring, delightful," Hymie Fieldman;

"Has to be seen to be believed," Eric 'Smiler' Beansprout;

"A disgrace," Maotsetung;

"Sensational, marvellous, out of this world, brilliant, fabulous—definitely the best in town. Magnificant, unbelievable," Arnie Knowles.

COMING ATTRACTIONS:—

A welcome return of Stuttering Sinn's
MOURNE VALLEY STOMPERS

And first appearance in Ireland of
Nick McClelland MAGNOLIA MASHERS

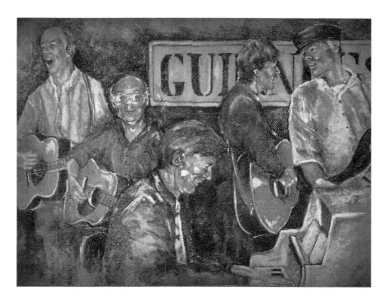

MARQUEE

SATURDAY, 11th May, 1968.

MR. MOON'S MASKED BALL

with THE TIGERS
SAM MAHOOD and the SOUL FOUNDATION
THE HIGH WALL, D. J. HENDI.

And now, thanks to thousands of our supporters the Marquee
Ad. continues with :

THE INCREDIBLE STORY OF BLINK. Part One—

December, nineteen twenty-two
In Paris, as the snow falls through
The bare trees on the boulevards
And settles in the cobbled yards
A figure through the darkness looms
Shivering as the fog horn booms.
It turns along the riverside,
The Seine flows deep and dark and wide,
Then underneath the lamplight's glare
We see the face that few will dare
To look upon—pinched, cold and pink
His eyes glint gold, his name is Blink,
A person who in weeks to come
Will haunt your dreams and scare you dumb.
He turned—the night broke with a slam,
A bell tolled once in Notre Dame.

WHO IS BLINK? WILL HE VISIT YOU TO-NIGHT?

READ NEXT WEEK'S EPISODE

If YOU Dare !

Big Hand for the Band – The Way It Was

Mechanical Copyright Protection Society
CD Catalogue Number: BH4B0001 1 December 2016

**ALL RIGHTS OF THE PRODUCER AND OF THE OWNER
OF THE WORKS REPRODUCED RESERVED**

**UNAUTHORISED COPYING, HIRING, LENDING, PUBLIC
PERFORMANCE AND BROADCASTING OF THIS RECORD
PROHIBITED**

I Can See For Miles	Townshend
Heroes and Villains	Wilson/Parks
Hey Jude	Lennon/McCartney
Walk Away Renee	Calilli/Sansone/Brown
Sgt Pepper's Lonely Hearts Club Band	Lennon/McCartney
Good Vibrations	Love/Wilson
Even The Bad Times Are Good	Callander/Murray
Sac O' Woe	Adderley
I'll Go Crazy	Brown
God Only Knows	Asher/Wilson
Reach Out I'll Be There	Dozier/Holland/Holland
Show Me	Tex
I Can't Make It Without You	Lane/Marriott
Shake	Cooke
Surfin' USA	Berry/Wilson
Everybody Knows	Reed/Mason
Girls On The Beach	Love/Wilson
Midnight Hour	Cropper/Pickett
You're So Good To Me	Love/Wilson
I Feel Free	Brown/Bruce
Morning Dew	Rose/Dobson
Something You Got	Kenner
Baby Now That I've Found You	MacAuley/MacLeod
The Letter	Carson
The House That Jack Built	Price
Knock On Wood	Cropper/Floyd
If I Were A Carpenter	Hardin
Land of 1000 Dances	Kenner
Dust My Blues	Johnson (Protected D Shares)/ Josea/James

Acknowledgements

Brian Bird (1958), *Skiffle – the Story of Folk-Song with a Jazz Beat,* Robert Hale Ltd

John McGuffin, (1973), *Internment,* Anvil Books

John McGuffin, (1974), *The Guineapigs,* Penguin Books Ltd

Jo and Tim Rice, Paul Gambaccini and Mike Reid (1979), *The Guinness Book of British Hit Singles,* Guinness Superlatives Ltd

Graeme Wright (1986), *Brown Sauce – The Life and Times of Joe Brown,* Joe Brown Productions Ltd

Vincent Power (1990), *Send 'em Home Sweatin' – The Showbands' Story,* The Kildanore Press

Tony Parker (1994), *May the Lord in His Mercy be Kind to Belfast,* Harper Collins, London

Gerry Adams (2001), *Before the Dawn – an autobiography,* Brandon

Colin Harper (2003), *Seaside Rock,* North Down Borough Council

Clinton Haylin (2003), *Can You Feel the Silence – Van Morrison a New Biography,* A Cappella Books, Chicago Review Press

Colin Harper and Trevor Hodgett (2004), *Irish folk, Trad and Blues – a Secret History,* The Collins Press

Johnny Rogan (2005), *Van Morrison: No Surrender,* Secker and Warburg

Walter Ellis (2006), *The Beginning of the End: The Crippling Disadvantage of a Happy Irish Childhood,* Mainstream Publishing Company Ltd

Patricia Craig (2007), *Asking for Trouble – the Story of an Escapade with Disproportionate Consequences,* Blackstaff Press

Derek Dean (2007), *The Freshmen Unzipped,* Merlin Publishing

Andy Neill and Matt Kent (2007), *Anyway, Anyhow, Anywhere: the Complete Chronicle of The Who 1958-1978,* Virgin Books

Robert Ramsay (2009), *Ringside Seats – an Insider's view of the Crisis in Northern Ireland,* Irish Academic Press

Alan Simpson (2010), *Duplicity and Deception,* Brandon, O'Brien Press, Dublin

Brian Dempster (2012), *Tracking Jazz – the Ulster Way,* Shanway Press

Professor Jim Dornan (2013), *An Everyday Miracle,* Blackstaff Press

Eimear O'Callaghan (2014), *Belfast Days – a 1972 Teenage Diary,* Merrion Press

British Library, London – CityWeek newspaper archive

Golden Irish Showband Annual 1965

www.historyvshollywood.com

www.irishrock.org

www.songfacts.com

www.songmeanings.com

www.ardsbangor.com

www.irish-showbands.com

www.irishshowbands.net

Photo Credits

325

Index

Motelands Publishing
1 Motelands
Belfast
BT4 2JH

Printed and bound by
CPI Group (UK) Ltd, Croydon, CR0 4YY